Work, Family, and Community

Exploring Interconnections

SERIES IN APPLIED PSYCHOLOGY

Edwin A. Fleishman, George Mason University,
Jeanette N. Cleveland, Pennsylvania State University
Series Editors

Gregory Bedny and David Meister
The Russian Theory of Activity: Current Applications to Design and Learning

Winston Bennett, David Woehr, and Charles Lance
Performance Measurement: Current Perspectives and Future Challenges

Michael T. Brannick, Eduardo Salas, and Carolyn Prince
Team Performance Assessment and Measurement: Theory, Research, and Applications

Jeanette N. Cleveland, Margaret Stockdale, and Kevin R. Murphy
Women and Men in Organizations: Sex and Gender Issues at Work

Aaron Cohen
Multiple Commitments in the Workplace: An Integrative Approach

Russell Cropanzano
Justice in the Workplace: Approaching Fairness in Human Resource Management, Volume 1

Russell Cropanzano
Justice in the Workplace: From Theory to Practice, Volume 2

David V. Day, Stephen Zaccaro, Stanley M. Halpin
Leader Development for Transforming Organizations: Growing Leaders for Tomorrow's Teams and Organizations.

James E. Driskell and Eduardo Salas
Stress and Human Performance

Sidney A. Fine and Steven F. Cronshaw
Functional Job Analysis: A Foundation for Human Resources Management

Sidney A. Fine and Maury Getkate
Benchmark Tasks for Job Analysis: A Guide for Functional Job Analysis (FJA) Scales

J. Kevin Ford, Steve W. J. Kozlowski, Kurt Kraiger, Eduardo Salas, and Mark S. Teachout
Improving Training Effectiveness in Work Organizations

Jerald Greenberg
Organizational Behavior: The State of the Science, Second Edition

Uwe E. Kleinbeck, Hans-Henning Quast, Henk Thierry, and Hartmut Häcker
Work Motivation

Laura L. Koppes
Historical Perspectives in Industrial and Organizational Psychology

Ellen Kossek and Susan Lambert
Work and Life Integration: Organizational, Cultural, and Individual Perspectives.

Martin I. Kurke and Ellen M. Scrivner
Police Psychology Into the 21st Century

Joel Lefkowitz
Ethics and Values in Industrial and Organizational Psychology

Manuel London
Job Feedback: Giving, Seeking, and Using Feedback for Performance Improvement, Second Edition

Manuel London
How People Evaluate Others in Organizations

Manuel London
Leadership Development: Paths to Self-Insight and Professional Growth

Robert F. Morrison and Jerome Adams
Contemporary Career Development Issues

Michael D. Mumford, Garnett Stokes, and William A. Owens
Patterns of Life History: The Ecology of Human Individuality

Michael D. Mumford
Pathways to Outstanding Leadership: A Comparative Analysis of Charismatic, Ideological, and Pragmatic Leaders

Kevin R. Murphy
Validity Generalization: A Critical Review

Kevin R. Murphy and Frank E. Saal
Psychology in Organizations: Integrating Science and Practice

Kevin Murphy
A Critique of Emotional Intelligence: What are the Problems and How Can They Be Fixed?

Susan E. Murphy and Ronald E. Riggio
The Future of Leadership Development

Margaret A. Neal and Leslie Brett Hammer
Working Couples Caring for Children and Aging Parents: Effects on Work and Well-Being

Steven A.Y. Poelmans
Work and Family: An International Research Perspective

Robert E. Ployhart, Benjamin Schneider, and Neal Schmitt
Staffing Organizations: Contemporary Practice and Theory, Third Edition

---

For more information on LEA titles, please contact Lawrence Erlbaum Associates, Publishers, at www.erlbaum.com

Work, Family, and Community
Exploring Interconnections

Patricia Voydanoff
University of Dayton

2007

LAWRENCE ERLBAUM ASSOCIATES, PUBLISHERS
Mahwah, New Jersey   London

Lawrence Erlbaum Associates, Inc., Publishers
10 Industrial Avenue
Mahwah, New Jersey 07430
www.erlbaum.com

Cover design by Kathryn Houghtaling

Library of Congress Cataloging-in-Publication Data

Voydanoff, Patricia.
Work, family, and community : exploring interconnections / Patricia Voydanoff.
    p. cm. — (Series in applied psychology)

Includes bibliographical references and index.
ISBN 0-8058-5620-X (cloth : alk. paper)
ISBN 0-8058-5621-8 (pbk. : alk. paper)
ISBN 1-4106-1535-9 (e book)
1. Work and family. 2. Community. I. Title. II. Series.
HD4904.25.V6942006
306.3'61—dc22   2006010550
                                                          CIP

Books published by Lawrence Erlbaum Associates are printed on acid-free paper, and their bindings are chosen for strength and durability.

Printed in the United States of America
10 9 8 7 6 5 4 3 2 1

To
Dan

Contents

Series Foreword

Jeanette N. Cleveland
Pennsylvania State University

Edwin A. Fleishman
George Mason University

Series Editors

There is a compelling need for innovative approaches to the solution of many pressing problems involving human relationships in today's society. Such approaches are more likely to be successful when they are based on sound research and applications. This Series in Applied Psychology offers publications that emphasize state-of-the-art research and its applications to important issues of human behavior in a variety of social settings. The objective is to bridge both academic and applied interests.

Family and work continue to be among the most important domains of our lives. As the field of work and family expands so does the need for greater inter- and multidisciplinary research approaches to address both the challenges and health of workers, families, and their organizations. The need for interdisciplinary approaches to complex work and family issues has become critical. Work in the 21st century is increasingly 24-7, family structures are more diverse, and there are more working families (both adults work outside of the home with a nonblood-related adult caring for children) than ever before.

Patricia Voydanoff's book *Work, Family, and Community: Exploring Interconnections* joins three other books on work and family in our Series in Applied Psychology: Poelman's, *Work and Family: An International Research Persepective* (2005); Kossek and Lambert's, *Work and Life Integration: Organizational, Cultural and Individual Perspectives* (2005); and Neal and Hammer's *Working Couples Caring for Children and Aging Parents: Effects on Work and Well-Being* (2007).

During the last few decades, scholars have investigated the linkages between work and family domains, but little research explicitly considers the larger context within which both work and family are embedded—specifically, the community. Voydanoff's book fills this gap and skillfully identifies how our work and family relationships are intertwined with members, resources, and limitations of the larger community. The boundaries among work, family, and community domains are increasingly permeable. For example, the atypical and growing number of work hours may adversely affect families unless there are sufficient after-school or after-traditional-hour childcare resources within a community.

Building off her previous book, *Work and Family Life* (1987), Voydanoff provides a review and analysis of the employee research connections among work, family and community life. Her conceptual model uses ecological systems theory to guide us through these linkages and how they influence our performance at work, at home, and our individual health and well-being. Successive chapters extend the conceptual model. Facets of individual and family stress theory are incorporated to more fully understand both the direct and indirect effects of two important work factors on individual and family well-being; namely, economic instability and economic deprivation.

Voydanoff elaborates on the ecological systems theory by examining the demands and resources within a given domain (e.g., family, work, and community) and across domains. Often a within-domain approach (e.g., focus on either work or family) is used to investigate work–family conflict (demands) and work–family facilitation (resources). A significant contribution of this book is the inclusion of boundary-spanning demands and resources depicting the interface among domains. Few work and family experts have examined across-domain relationships as the units of analysis.

Work–family fit and work–family balance are two linking mechanisms introduced within the framework of demands and resources both within domains and as boundary-spanning strategies. For example, individual well-being and family functioning each is influenced by (a) the extent to which family resources are sufficient to meet work demands and (b) the extent to which work resources are adequate to meet family demands (work–family fit). Strategies are described that may reduce conflict or misfit by modifying factors in either the work, family, or community domains.

The book concludes with an agenda for future research based on the conceptual model developed through the book. Voydanoff identifies areas where there is empirical support for the model and areas where more research is needed. These include methodological and measurement issues associated with viewing family–work–community interfaces within a temporal process.

The book fills two significant gaps in current work and family research. First, it includes a theoretical discussion of the role of community in work and family research. Second, the book represents a first step in the identification and development of components and processes that comprise and shape the work–family–community interface.

The book is appropriate for students in several disciplines including industrial and organizational psychology, management, community psychology, sociology, human development and family studies, gender studies, and social work. Both work and family researchers and policy makers will find this book essential to understanding the larger societal context of their research and the implementation of work–family interventions.

Preface

It has become evident over the past few decades that work and family are interrelated domains. Based on this realization, scholars began investigating the nature and extent of linkages between the two domains. Extensive research has documented that work characteristics (e.g., the number and scheduling of work hours, job demands and control, workplace support, and work–family policies) influence the organization and quality of family life. In addition, family characteristics, such as the amount of time spent caring for family members and support from spouses and relatives, affect the extent to which family members are able to perform their jobs effectively. This research has revealed some of the changes that are needed to bring the organization of work and family life more in line with each other, for example, increased workplace flexibility and changes in the household division of labor. Such changes are important for the productivity of work organizations, the quality of family life, and individual well-being.

Until recently, researchers have focused exclusively on interrelationships among the work and family domains. However, scholars and practitioners have begun to recognize that workplaces and families are embedded in the communities in which they are located. Relationships between work and family are intertwined with relationships among members of various communities. Community life always has influenced the work–family interface, for example, by the lack of fit between school hours and work hours and assistance provided by community-based child care services. In addition, recent changes occurring in the work, family, and community domains are blurring the boundaries that differentiate one from another; for example, there is a lack of geographic separation between paid work, home, and community and overlapping networks and obligations associated with work, family, and community life. Other structural changes have increased the difficulties experienced by working families such as the lengthening of work hours for some at the same time that communities are becoming more limited in the services they are able to provide to working families. Other changes may be more positive, such as efforts to increase after-school programs. Therefore, communities may both help and hinder the efforts of work organizations, families, and individuals to enhance work–family integration. Understanding how

work, family, and community demands and resources combine to influence work, family, and community role performance and quality
and individual well-being provides a necessary foundation for designing work, family, and community policies and programs that increase
the ability of workplaces, families, and communities to meet the
needs of their members.

This book provides the first comprehensive review and analysis of
the theoretical and empirical research and scholarship that has examined the complex interconnections between work, family, and community life. It builds on my earlier book, *Work and Family Life*,
published in 1987. The years since this book was published have seen
an explosion in empirical research in several disciplines; the development of more sophisticated theoretical and conceptual approaches;
important changes in the structure and operation of the economy, the
workplace, and families; and recognition of the importance of the role
of community. However, no books have incorporated these changes
into a comprehensive and integrated review and analysis. This book
does that.

The primary audience for the book is scholars, researchers, and
students who are addressing the theoretical, empirical, and pol-
icy-relevant issues associated with the work–family–community interface. The book incorporates and integrates literature from several
disciplines including sociology, industrial–organizational and occupational health psychology, human development and family studies,
management, gender studies, and social work. Although most of the
work–family literature originates in the United States, interest in
these issues is extensive and growing among scholars and students in
Europe, Australia, Canada, Asia, and India.

The book consists of eight chapters. The first chapter uses ecological systems theory as a basis for the development of a conceptual
model of linkages through which work, family, and community characteristics influence work, family, and community role performance
and quality and individual well-being. This model serves as a framework for summarizing and integrating the theoretical, empirical, and
policy-oriented literature on work, family, and community connections in the remaining chapters. The chapter also provides a broad
economic and social context for the model by documenting significant
patterns and trends in the economy, the workplace, families, and
communities.

Chapter 2 extends the general conceptual model by incorporating
aspects of individual and family stress theory to provide an understanding of the effects of problems with the worker-earner role on
family and community role performance and quality and individual
well-being. The model suggests that two objective worker-earner

problems, employment instability and economic deprivation, have both direct and indirect effects on family, community, and individual well-being. The indirect effects operate through the subjective perception of economic strain as well as coping resources and strategies. The chapter reviews and synthesizes the literature that addresses the relationships proposed in the model.

Chapters 3 and 4 use a demands and resources approach to conceptualize the processes through which within-domain work, family, and community demands and resources influence work, family, and community role performance and quality and individual well-being. Within-domain work, community, and family demands limit participation in other domains by reducing the time or involvement available for other domains or by creating negative psychological spillover across domains. Within-domain resources such as enabling resources and psychological rewards engender processes that enhance participation when they are applied across domains. Chapter 3 reviews the theoretical and empirical literature on how within-domain demands are related to work, family, and community role performance and quality and individual well-being and addresses the role of work–family conflict as a linking mechanism between within-domain demands and outcomes. Chapter 4 discusses the effects of within-domain resources on work, family, community, and individual outcomes and considers work–family facilitation as a linking mechanism.

In Chapters 5 and 6 the focus shifts from demands and resources associated with one domain to boundary-spanning demands and resources, which encompass the interface between domains. Boundary-spanning demands involve trade-offs deriving from the continuum of segmentation to integration across domains (i.e., work, family, and community-based transition problems, and role blurring), whereas boundary-spanning resources encompass several types of boundary-spanning supports (e.g., work, family, and community-based work support policies and programs, family support policies and programs, and normative support). Chapter 5 reviews relationships between boundary-spanning demands and work, family, and community role performance and quality and individual well-being and examines the role of work–family conflict and facilitation as linking mechanisms between boundary-spanning demands and outcomes. Chapter 6 does the same for boundary-spanning resources.

Chapter 7 introduces two other important linking mechanisms: work–family fit and work–family balance. Work–family fit is of two types: work demands–family resources fit (the extent to which family resources are sufficient to meet work demands) and family demands–work resources fit (the extent to which work resources are ad-

A Conceptual Model of Work, Family, and Community

Work, family, and community are major domains in which individuals live out their lives. The ways in which these domains are interrelated varies over time according to the structure and organization of the economy and society. For example, recent reviews of American history (Piotrkowski, Rapoport, & Rapoport, 1987; Skolnick, 2001; Wallen, 2002) reveal dramatic economic and societal changes from preindustrial times through the industrial revolution to the current transition to a postindustrial economy and society. During preindustrial times, the economy was mainly agrarian with no physical separation between work and family life. The division of labor was such that men worked mainly in the fields while women performed household chores such as cooking and weaving. Children also were active participants in economically based activities. Seasonal activities associated with farming such as planting and harvesting organized and integrated community life. The emergence of craftsmen and tradesmen maintained the home as the place of work but began the shift to industrialization.

The rise of industrial production in factories created a physical separation between the home and the workplace. This separation was accompanied by a greater distinction between the activities of married men and women, especially within the middle class. Husbands went to work in factories and offices while wives worked at home raising children and maintaining the household. This was accompanied by the "cult of domesticity," which considered work outside the home inappropriate for middle-class wives and mothers and imbued work in the home with moral value. This cultural norm was dominant despite the inability of most working-class and nonwhite families to attain it. Activities such as education and health care shifted from the home to institutions within the community. Many families moved from rural to urban communities.

Within this broad time frame referred to as the industrial era, several important events introduced deviations from the major themes associated with the period. The Depression of the 1930s created high levels of unemployment among men, who were expected to be major providers. The need for increased production and lack of available male workers during World War II led to increased employment among women who previously had stayed at home and the provision of day care programs for some of their children. The postwar period resulted in the return of many employed women to the home and economic prosperity that resulted in a growing middle class and the movement of families to the suburbs. These developments affected the nature and texture of communities by changing the physical and social environment associated with home and community life.

Recent decades again have revealed major economic and societal shifts that have important implications for the interrelationships among work, family, and community. Several important structural trends are evident in the realm of the economy and the workplace, for example, the shift from a manufacturing to a service and information economy, globalization, downsizing and restructuring, job loss and insecurity, changes in the psychological contract between workers and employers, and the development of information technologies, a contingent workforce, and a long-hours culture (Lewis & Cooper, 1999; Major & Germano, 2005). Increases in the employment of married women and mothers have created greater numbers of two-earner families. This has resulted in changes in gender norms and the division of labor among husbands and wives and a shift of some child care and food production out of the home. Increases in the divorce rate and childbirth outside of marriage have created higher numbers of single-parent families. The basis of community relationships has become broader and more diffuse and less focused on neighborhood and kinship. For example, workplace and virtual communities have become more important foci of community life.

Until the last few decades, behavioral scientists considered these three life domains as separate spheres that operate relatively independently of each other. However, recent widespread changes affecting families have challenged the myth of separate worlds (Kanter, 1977). Structural unemployment and job insecurity have taken a high toll on the quality and stability of family life. Strains and conflicts experienced by two-earner and single-parent families have become more apparent as these families increase in number. These changes have exposed weaknesses in the assumptions underlying the myth of separate worlds and have illuminated the connections between work and family. This recognition has led to an explosion of research on the multiple ways in which the work and family domains influence each other. This research has demonstrated that the demands and resources associated with one domain have important effects on the role performance and quality of life in the other, either directly or through mediating mechanisms.

More recently, it has become apparent that the analysis of work and family should be expanded to include community. Broad-based analyses have indicated that work and family life are embedded in the context of the communities in which they operate. Working families' participation in community organizations and informal neighborhood and friendship relationships provides important resources in their efforts to coordinate their work and family responsibilities and activities, whereas the lack of adequate community supports hinders participation in work and family activities (Bookman, 2004). Recent research is documenting that the characteristics and processes associated with one domain influence the ability of individuals to perform their responsibilities in other domains, the quality of life experienced in other domains, and individual well-being.

These relationships are becoming more pervasive as the boundaries among the three domains become less distinct. Several scholars have observed a blurring of boundaries among work, community, and family, as indicated by a lack of geographic separation between home and paid work and overlapping networks and obligations, for example, the development of social ties at work rather than in the neighborhood (Lewis & Cooper, 1999; Poarch, 1998). Social processes such as changing divisions of labor, trade-offs between time and money, patterns of reciprocity and obligation, and the quest for economic security in an unstable world cross the preconceived boundaries of work, family, and community (Thorne, 2001).

This book uses an ecological systems approach as a general framework to begin the conceptual integration of work, family, and community. This approach suggests that aspects of each domain occur at multiple ecological levels. The ecological model of human development articulated by Bronfenbrenner (1979, 1989) focuses on four ecological levels, each nested within the next according to their immediacy to the developing person. The most immediate level, the *microsystem*, consists of a pattern of activities, roles, and interpersonal relations experienced by a person in a network of face-to-face relationships, which occur in settings such as the family, the workplace, and the community. The *mesosystem* is the interlinked system of microsystems in which a person participates—for example, linkages between family and school. The external environments in which a person does not participate but which exert indirect influence on the person are referred to as *exosystems*. An example is the work setting of a family member. Finally, the *macrosystem* is the overarching pattern of the culture or subculture in which the micro-, meso-, and exosystems are nested. They consist of the institutional patterns and broad belief systems that provide the context for human development.

WORK, FAMILY, AND COMMUNITY AS MICROSYSTEMS

From the perspective of ecological systems theory, work, family, and community are microsystems consisting of networks of face-to-face relationships. The settings in which these relationships occur, that is, the workplace, the family, and the community, are characterized by factors such as place, time, physical features, activity, participants, and roles (Bronfenbrenner, 1979). Research on work, family, and community as microsystems incorporates a wide array of such structural and psychological aspects of the work, family, and community domains. This diversity has advantages and disadvantages. It may reflect a lack of theoretical focus that derives from the multiplicity of disciplines that conduct research on the work, family, and community microsystems. These include sociology, psychology, organizational behavior, family science, human development, social work, gerontology, family therapy, law, and occupational health. This lack of focus makes it difficult to develop comprehensive yet manageable theoretical frameworks for research. However, it is useful in documenting the complexity involved in understanding the work–family–community interface. Eventually, this complexity needs to be embraced to create meaningful theories.

Six broad categories of work, family, and community characteristics are used here as a framework for examining relationships among work, family, and community. These categories are derived from an analysis of the dimensions of work, family, and community used in previous empirical research. They include structure, social organization, norms and expectations, support, orientations, and quality. Structure, social organization, and norms and expectations operate at the structural, organizational, or group level, whereas support, orientations, and quality are individual-level categories (Voydanoff, 2001a, 2001b).

Characteristics of Paid Work

The most general definition of *work* refers to it as physical or mental activity that is intended to provide goods and services or to produce something of value for others. This definition encompasses both paid and unpaid work. More specifically, work has been considered as a set of prescribed tasks that an individual performs while occupying a position in an organization. This definition focuses on paid work or employment (Zedeck, 1992). This book views the work domain as the realm of paid work. Unpaid work performed within the family and the community is considered as part of the family and community domains.

Structure describes the basic organization and boundaries of a domain. Structure in paid work encompasses organizational characteristics, extrinsic characteristics, timing, and spatial location. Organizational characteristics delimit the basic structural characteristics of a work organization in terms of its size (e. g., the number of employees), composition (e. g., the types and diversity of job tasks being performed), and complexity (e. g., the number of organizational levels or extent of hierarchy). Extrinsic characteristics deal with the context in which work is performed, for example, pay, benefits, job security, and opportunities for advancement. Timing includes how much time is spent in paid work (i.e., number of work hours) and when the work is done (i.e., scheduling of work hours). Spatial location addresses where paid work is performed (e.g., in the workplace, on the road, or in the home) and incorporates work-based changes in spatial location (e.g., job-related moves and transfers).

The social organization of work encompasses the demands and content of a job. Job demands place limits on an individual's work behavior that must be accommodated such as heavy work loads, role ambiguity and conflict, health and safety hazards, tight deadlines, and responsibility for the safety and well-being of others. Job content includes intrinsic characteristics that tend to focus on the content and tasks involved in doing a job and opportunities provided on the job for self-expression and self-actualization. Intrinsic characteristics commonly include the kind of work done in terms of responsibility, self-direction, and decision making; variety, skill, challenge, and autonomy; opportunities for personal growth and development; and feelings of pride and accomplishment.

Norms and expectations include the explicit and implicit rules and guidelines that govern behavior in a domain. Norms and expectations associated with paid work are incorporated in formal job descriptions and duties (e.g., performance and productivity standards), employment policies (e.g., regulations and procedures regarding taking time off), and workplace culture (e.g., workplace climate, informal norms regarding interactions within the workplace, and the amount of flexibility associated with implementing employment policies).

Individual-level categories of workplace characteristics include support, orientations, and quality. Support encompasses the provision or receipt of instrumental and emotional social support. Workplace support generally consists of support received from supervisors and coworkers. Orientations include an individual's sense of involvement in a domain as well as the perception of cohesion associated with a given domain. Orientations to work consist of salience, involvement, commitment, attachment, and aspirations, as well as a sense of community in the workplace. Quality is an affective component that includes subjective evaluations of and satisfaction with multidimensional aspects of role domains. Work role quality includes overall job satisfaction and satisfaction with various job components such as aspects of the work itself, supervisors and coworkers, the work organization, and pay and benefits. Behavioral indicators such as absenteeism, turnover, job performance, and productivity are sometimes included.

Family Characteristics

Definitions of *family* are of two types. One is based on membership, that is, a family consists of persons who are related by biological, marital, or adoptive ties. In some cases the definition focuses on persons sharing a household, whereas others include persons not living in the household, such as extended kin and nonresidential children. In the second type of definition, a family is defined as those who share relationships based on affection, obligation, dependence, and cooperation. Thus, a family can be viewed in terms of its membership or as an emotional unit based on love and affection whose members provide and care for one another (Rothausen, 1999).

Family structure refers to the basic organization and boundaries associated with the family domain. It encompasses the size, age distribution, and gender composition of families. Usually, it consists of the number and marital status of adults and the number and ages of children in the household. However, sometimes extended kin, former spouses, and children living outside the household are included. Family social organization consists of the ways in which family members interact with one another in their daily activities, that is, the family division of labor. This division of labor incorporates the time spent in and the scope of activities involved with paid work and its associated earnings; household chores; personal, spousal, and parental activities; care for dependent members such as children and the ill and elderly; and community involvement. Family norms and expectations are the roles and expected behaviors assigned to each family member, the sanctions that guide the behavior of family members, and the power held by various family members. These norms generally are based on a gender ideology that incorporates beliefs regarding appropriate behavior for men and women.

Family support encompasses the instrumental and expressive social support provided to and received from family members. It includes the exchange of informal social support among relatives, for example, financial aid, advice, and services such as transportation or child care. More intensive support also is provided to ill and elderly family members. Family orientations consist of salience, involvement, commitment, attachment, and aspirations as well as family cohesion. The quality of family life involves overall marital and family satisfaction, satisfaction with various aspects of marital and family life, quality of the parent–child relationship, and child development outcomes such as psychological adjustment and academic achievement.

Community Characteristics

Definitions of *community* refer to two aspects: territory and social relationships. The territorial definition focuses on a community as a group of people living in a common territory who share a history, values, activities, and sense of solidarity. The relational definition emphasizes social relationships independent of territory that are characterized by consensus, shared norms, common goals, and sense of identity, belonging, and trust (Voydanoff, 2001a).

Structure in the context of community refers to overlapping social networks consisting of relatively enduring social ties, which form a patterned organization of network members and their relationships. The attributes of the networks making up territorial and relational communities include size, composition, heterogeneity, multiplexity, duration, density, forms of interaction, and accessibility. These networks occur within community service organizations, formal supports, churches, schools, neighborhoods, and informal networks. Social organization refers to structural connections and patterns of interaction among individuals and groups. Community social organization encompasses the different ways in which community participation is organized, that is, through formal and voluntary organizations, friendship networks, and social control. It often refers to the ability of neighborhoods to realize collective goals through the activities of an interlocking set of formal and informal networks and organizations. The rules and guidelines that make up norms and expectations within a community consist of cultural processes such as trust and norms of reciprocity. These norms facilitate community activities within social networks and define obligations among community members.

Community support includes formal volunteering and informal help exchanged among members of a network or provided to a community member in need. Formal volunteering is assistance provided through organizations such as professional or fraternal associations, whereas informal helping is assistance given to friends, neighbors, and extended kin. Community orientations include salience, involvement, commitment, attachment, and aspirations, as well as a sense of community. Quality of community life is represented by overall community satisfaction and the evaluation of various aspects of a community, for example, community services, safety, and attractiveness.

Work, Family, Community, and Individual Outcomes

The work, family, and community characteristics discussed above generally are considered as independent variables in relation to work, family, community, and individual outcomes. However, some are used as predictors in some studies and as outcomes in others, for example, time in activities and role quality. In general, outcomes focus on aspects of role performance and role quality. Role performance encompasses behaviors performed at work and in the home and community, whereas role quality refers to positive and negative affect, such as positive and negative moods and emotions derived from work, family, and community activities. Work outcomes include job performance and productivity, attendance-related issues, and job satisfaction and stress. Job performance and productivity refer to the extent to which individuals conduct their job duties so as to meet established standards. Attendance-related issues include absenteeism, tardiness, and leaving work early. Job satisfaction is an individual's cognitive or affective evaluation of the overall quality of the job or of specific aspects of the job. Job stress is the extent to which a job is perceived to have negative effects on an individual's physical and mental health.

Family outcomes encompass family role performance, family role quality, and child development outcomes. Family role performance reflects the extent to which family members fulfill their responsibilities by spending adequate time caring for family members and doing household chores. Family role quality incorporates marital and family satisfaction and marital risk and conflict. Marital and family satisfaction are an individual's affective appraisal of the overall quality of marital and family relationships or of specific aspects of such relationships, whereas marital risk reflects the perception that a marriage is in trouble and may end as well as high levels of marital conflict. Two important developmental outcomes for children are behavior problems and academic achievement. Internalizing and externalizing behavior problems tap two negative dimensions of children's adjustment. Internalizing problems refer to anxious and depressed behaviors, whereas externalizing problems encompass impulsive, aggressive, and antisocial behaviors. Grades and test scores are important components of academic achievement.

Community outcomes include the level of participation in various formal and informal community activities such as volunteer work, informal helping, and friendships as well as community satisfaction. Community satisfaction reflects the subjective evaluation of a community as a whole or the evaluation of specific aspects of a community. It can refer to satisfaction with community services, safety, the attractiveness and upkeep of the physical environment, and satisfaction with community participation, social relationships, and social support.

Individual outcomes incorporate several aspects of psychological and physical well-being, for example, depression, psychological distress, and physical health and illness. Because individual outcomes are interconnected with domain outcomes, some studies have examined relationships among outcomes; for example, individual psychological well-being has been considered as causally prior to and as a consequence of the quality of the work, family, and community domains.

A CONCEPTUAL MODEL OF THE WORK–FAMILY–COMMUNITY MESOSYSTEM

Mesosytems consist of the interrelationships among the microsystems in which an individual participates. Figure 1.1 shows the four mesosystems that can be formed through the connections among the work, family, and community microsystems. Three of these consist of relationships between two microsystems, that is, the work–family, work–community, and family–community mesosystems. The work–family–community mesosystem is created when an individual participates in all three microsystems.

Figure 1.1 implies direct relationships in which characteristics of one or more microsystems are related to characteristics of another microsystem. However, relationships among microsystems also may operate through linking mechanisms. This book proposes and elaborates a conceptual framework and model for examining these relationships and linking mechanisms. The most general form of the model is presented in Figure 1.2. The top of the model indicates that economic, workplace, family, and community contexts influence the demands, resources, and strategies that are expected to impact work, family, and community role performance and quality and individual well-being. These contextual factors are discussed in the next section. The remainder of the model proposes several ways in which characteristics associated with the work, family, and community microsys-

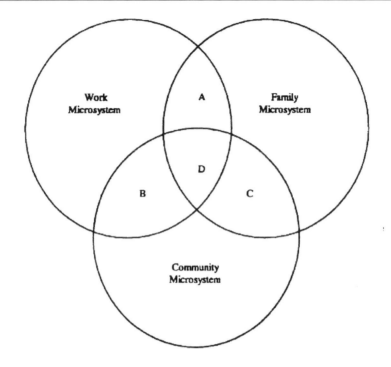

Note. A=work-family mesosystem; B=work-community mesosystem; C=community-family mesosystem; D=Work-community-family mesosystem

Figure 1.1   Relationships among the work, family, and community microsystems. From Voydanoff (2001a), with permission.

tems are related to work, family, and community role performance and quality and individual well-being.

The wide range of work, family, and community characteristics that have shown relationships to role performance and quality and individual well-being can be subsumed under two categories: demands and resources. Demands are structural or psychological claims associated with role requirements, expectations, and norms to which individuals must respond or adapt by exerting physical or mental effort. Resources are structural or psychological assets that may be used to facilitate performance, reduce demands, or generate additional resources (Voydanoff, 2004b).

The model in Figure 1.2 distinguishes between two types of demands and resources: within-domain and boundary-spanning. Within-domain demands and resources are associated with characteristics such as the structure and content of activities in one domain (e.g., job pressure and autonomy, time spent caring for family mem-

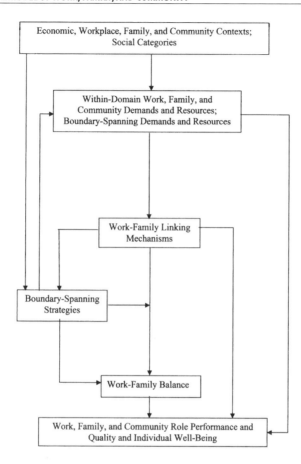

Figure 1.2   The conceptual model.

bers, or an unsafe neighborhood), whereas boundary-spanning demands and resources are inherently part of two domains (e.g.,
bringing work home and a supportive work–family culture). Although
boundary-spanning demands and resources originate in one domain,
they serve as demands and resources in other domains. For example,
when individuals work at home or perform family activities at work,
they are operating in both domains at the same time. When employers
acknowledge and address employee family needs through a supportive work–family culture and policies, the two domains are partially
integrated (Voydanoff, 2004b).

Work, community, and family demands and resources are derived
from the range of work, family, and community characteristics discussed earlier. For example, the structure of work, family, and com-

munity life encompasses the organization and timing of work life, the size and composition of family structures, and the social networks making up community life. The social organization of work incorporates the demands and content of jobs, family social organization consists of the division of labor among family members, and community social organization reflects formal and informal organizations. Norms and expectations associated with work include job descriptions, employment policies, and work culture. Families operate within the context of role expectations and gender ideology. Community norms are associated with the reciprocity and trust incorporated in social capital. In addition, the work, family, and community domains include various types of support from supervisors and coworkers at work, family members at home, and friends and neighbors in the community (Voydanoff, 2001a).

The model in Figure 1.2 proposes that within-domain and boundary-spanning demands and resources are directly related to work, family, and community role performance and quality and individual well-being. This general proposition is the basis for much of the extant research on relationships among work, family, and community life. The model also serves as a framework for proposing a chain of relationships through which these direct effects may operate. Demands and resources lead to linking mechanisms (e.g., economic strain and work–family conflict, facilitation, and fit). Linking mechanisms lead to outcomes and to boundary-spanning strategies, which are actions taken by individuals and families to reduce misfit between work, family, and community demands and resources. These strategies are proposed to have both mediating and moderating effects on relationships between work–family linking mechanisms and work–family balance. In addition, feedback effects are proposed from boundary-spanning strategies to work, family, and community demands and resources. Linking mechanisms also are expected to be related to work–family balance, which in turn is associated with work, family, and community role performance and quality and individual well-being. This model extends a previous model (Voydanoff, 2002) by specifying the types and operation of demands and resources and by incorporating community demands, resources, strategies, and outcomes into the model. The following chapters explore the model in greater detail and review the research relevant to its various propositions.

THE CONTRIBUTION OF EXOSYSTEMS

Both mesosystems and exosystems consist of interrelationships and linkages among two or more microsystems. In mesosystems, the individual member of a mesosystem participates in both microsystems, for example, a working parent. Exosystems are an extension of mesosystems that incorporate other microsystems in which the individual does not participate, for example, the work setting of a spouse. In exosystems, individuals are influenced indirectly by microsystems in which they do not participate.

The most commonly considered exosystem consists of the work–family exosystem in which the work demands and resources experienced by one member of the family influence the role performance and quality and well-being of other family members. Work resources of one family member (e.g., income and satisfying job experiences) can create positive effects on family relationships and other family members, whereas work demands (e.g., long work hours or a stressful job) can result in deleterious effects on the family and its members. This has been most clearly documented in the transmission of job stress and strain from one spouse to another, which is referred to as *crossover* (Westman, 2001), and in the effects of various aspects of parents' jobs on their children (Hynes, 2003; Repetti, 2005). However, the work–family exosystem also may incorporate the effects of a worker's family demands and resources on the work-role performance and quality and well-being of the individual's coworkers, for example, workers' family stress may be transmitted to their coworkers, thereby limiting the coworkers' job performance and quality and well-being. In addition, similar linkages may occur in the work–community and family–community exosystems.

The demands and resources embedded in exosystems and mesosystems are expected to operate similarly in the model presented in Figure 1.2. However, in exosystems they affect other members of the exosystem rather than the individual directly experiencing the demands or resources. Although little empirical research has examined exosystem relationships, the following chapters incorporate the research that is available. Most of this research addresses the effects of parents' work and community demands and resources on children's well-being.

THE MACROSYSTEM AS CONTEXT

According to ecological systems theory, microsystems, mesosystems, and exosystems are influenced by the larger macrosystem in which they are embedded. The macrosystem forms a "societal blueprint" for a given culture or subculture that consists of opportunity structures, resources and hazards, life course options, patterns of social interaction, shared belief systems, and life styles (Bronfenbrenner, 1989). Thus, the macrosystem forms the structural and cultural context in which the other systems are nested. The top part of the conceptual model presented in Figure 1.2 indicates that economic, workplace, family, and community contexts are expected to influence the relationships and processes that comprise the work–family–community mesosystem. The demands, resources, and strategies associated with the work–family–community mesosystem operate within these larger contexts.

The Structure of the Economy and the Workplace

The structure of the economy and the workplace set the stage in which individuals address work, family, and community issues. The economy determines the extent to which adequate employment and income are available. Economies differ significantly across cultures depending on the level of economic development in a given society. Two significant trends in the U.S. economy are having a great influence on patterns of income and employment. These are the shift from the dominance of goods-producing industries to a greater emphasis on service-producing industries, and increased globalization. Employment in goods-producing industries decreased from 34% in 1947 to 21% in 1996 while service-producing industries increased from 55% to 77% of total employment (Levy, 1998). Globalization is associated with increased industrialization in Asia and Latin America, rapid communication technologies, liberalization of trade, global financial markets, and increased international competition (Carnoy, 2000).

These structural shifts in the American economy are having a major impact on earnings patterns and the structure of the workplace. Earnings patterns include a decline in real earnings for those without a college education, large numbers of low-wage workers, and increased income inequality. Real earnings declined from 1973 to 2003 for those without a college education. In 2003, almost one-quarter of the labor force earned less than $9.04 per hour, a wage that places a family of four at the poverty line (Mishel, Bernstein, & Allegretto, 2005). Growth in income inequality from 1980–1982 to 2001–2003 is revealed by figures indicating that family income increased by 18.9% in the lowest income quintile compared with 58.5% in the highest income quintile and 84.7% in the top 5%. (Bernstein, McNichol, & Lyons, 2006).

The organization of the workplace structures the opportunities and constraints available within work organizations. The shift from a manufacturing to a service economy and increased international competition have resulted in a complex of interrelated changes in the workplace. These include downsizing and restructuring, job loss and insecurity, nonstandard employment (e.g., part-time, temporary, and contract work), the development of high-performance work systems in which decision making is shared among more workers, an increase in the number of workers who work either long or short hours, and growth in the numbers working nonstandard schedules associated with the development of a 24/7 economy (Applebaum, 2003; Wharton, 2006). Several of these aspects of workplace structure also occur outside the United States; for example, nonstandard employment ranges from 25% to 60% of the workforce among several European countries, Australia, and Japan (Mangan, 2000). These components of the structure of the workplace create the demands, resources, and strategies through which work characteristics experienced by individuals influence family, community, and individual outcomes as proposed in the conceptual model.

In addition to these structural variables, organizational-context variables can be developed by aggregating individual-level variables. These collective properties operate in conjunction with individual-level work characteristics to influence role performance and quality and individual well-being. For example, research has examined organizational-level variables that assess work structure (e.g., gender and racial/ethnic heterogeneity and the number of hours worked in an organizational unit) and the level of supervisor and coworker support in organizational units (Bliese & Jex, 1999; Morris, Shinn, & DuMont, 1999; Wharton, Rotolo, & Bird, 2000).

Family Demographics and Ideology

Over the past several decades, the structure of families and households has changed significantly, thereby altering the family context in which the work–family–community mesosystem operates. Although marriage rates remain high, Americans are marrying later. The median age at first marriage for women increased from 21 years in 1970 to 25 years in 2000. The comparable ages for men were 23 in 1970 and 27 in 2000. Although the divorce rate has decreased slightly since 1980, approximately 50% of first marriages are expected to end in divorce. In addition, women are having fewer children and having their first child at a later age. Mothers from the Baby Boom generation had an average of 3.2 children, compared to 1.9 children for their children's generation. Seventy-four percent of women born in 1938 had experienced a birth by the age of 25, whereas only 50% of women born in 1973 had experienced a birth by age 25 (Casper & Bianchi, 2002). In addition, the percentage of women giving birth while unmarried has increased from 11% in 1970 to 33% in 1999 (Ventura & Bachrach, 2000). These demographic trends have resulted in important changes in household composition. The percentage of married-couple households with children decreased from 40% in 1970 to 24% in 2000, while single-parent families increased from 5% to 9% and persons living alone grew from 17% to 26%. A final important demographic change is the increase in the percentage of the population aged 65 years or older from 10% in 1970 to 12% in 2000 and to a projected 16% in 2020 and 21% in 2050 (Marks, 2006). This has important implications for the growing need to provide care to the elderly among the working-age population.

These changes in family structure have been accompanied by shifts in the social organization of family life, that is, the division of paid and unpaid work by gender. The percentage of married couples in which both spouses are employed increased from 44% in 1967 to 59% in 2001 (U.S. Department of Labor, 2004). Women's employment also increased for married mothers with children under age 6, from 30% in 1970 to 64% in 1997. Many of these mothers of young children were employed full-time, year-round: 33% in 1978 and 54% in 1998 (Casper & Bianchi, 2002). Men and women also have experienced changes in the amount of time they spend in unpaid family work. The average weekly hours spent in household work have decreased for women ages 25–54 from 23 hours in 1976 to 17 hours in 1999, whereas hours for men have increased from 5 in 1975 to 11 in 1999. The number of hours per week spent in child care have remained stable at 7 hours for women and increased from 2 to 4 hours for men (Sayer, Cohen, & Casper, 2004). Thus, the structural context of family life has changed considerably over the past few decades.

Several of these patterns also are occurring in European countries: for example, later marriage and childbearing, decreased fertility, more single parents, an aging population, higher labor force participation for women, and lower labor force participation for men (Carnoy, 2000). However, it is important not to generalize too far. Masako Ishii-Kuntz (1994) has provided several examples in which the nature of the macrosystem differs greatly from that described here. In some countries extended family structures, home-based production, and child labor force participation are relatively important components of family structure and social organization.

Countries also vary according to their cultural and ideological contexts and the role of state in family life: for example, the extent to which the state or individuals are seen as responsible for family welfare; the extent to which families, especially women, are solely responsible for the care of children and the elderly; and the extent of ideological commitment to gender equity in both work and family. Compared to Europe, the United States tends toward individualism, family self-determination, and a residual role for the state regarding work and family issues (Lewis, 1997).

As mentioned earlier, family social organization has moved toward a more gender-neutral division of paid work and unpaid family work in the United States over recent decades. These shifts have been accompanied by changes in the gender ideology that prescribes appropriate behaviors for men and women. The view that married women should not share the provider role with their husbands has declined. For example, the percentages of men and women who agree that men should earn the money and women should take care of the home and children declined from 74% in 1977 to 42% in 2002 for men and from 52% to 37% for women (Bond, Thompson, Galinsky, & Prottas, 2003). In 2000, large majorities of men (66%) and women (94%) expected their partner to work for pay (Radcliffe Public Policy Center, 2000). The belief that husbands of working wives should participate in housework also has grown over the past few decades (Thornton & Young-DeMarco, 2001). Large majorities now believe that men and women should share equally in day-to-day domestic responsibilities (Radcliffe Public Policy Center, 2000).

Similar changes have occurred in norms toward parenting. The percentages agreeing that a working mother can have as just as good a relationship with her child as a nonworking mother have increased from 49% in 1977 to 64% in 2002 for men and from 70% to 78% for women (Bond et al., 2003). In 2000, 79% of men and women strongly agreed that fathers and mothers should share equally in the caretaking of children. Similar percentages reported that men and women should share equally in the caretaking of elder relatives (Radcliffe Public Policy Center, 2000). Such beliefs frame the ways in which individuals view their responsibilities and commitment to work, family, and community.

Community Structure and Participation

The structure and social organization of communities also provide an important context in which the work–family–community mesosystem exists. The overall distribution and extent of residential segregation by income and racial and ethnic status and the practices of public and private community institutions in the broader community determine the conditions and processes that operate in neighborhoods. Local neighborhood contexts include the extent of concentration of affluence and poverty, racial and ethnic isolation, residential stability, land use patterns, population density, extent of family disruption, the availability of jobs, housing affordability, and the level and types of community services (Hanson & Pratt, 1988; Massey, 2001; Sampson, 2001).

These neighborhood contexts in turn are associated with community-level aspects of social organization, for example, the levels of social integration and sense of community, collective efficacy, reciprocity and trust, various types of deviant behavior, and social capital from institutions and networks. These diverse components of community social organization can be captured by the concept of community capacity. Community capacity is an aspect of community social organization in which formal and informal networks and social capital create community results (e.g., neighborhood safety) through shared responsibility and collective competence (Mancini, Martin, & Bowen, 2003).

These structural and organizational contexts also provide a framework within which participation in voluntary associations, informal helping, and social activities takes place. Although participation in voluntary associations generally has been considered high since the time of de Tocqueville, scholars such as Robert Putnam (2000) have proposed that such participation has declined in recent decades. Others, however, have suggested that overall participation has not declined, but that the forms of participation have shifted from large national civic associations (e.g., PTA, Rotary Club, Lions Club) to participation in professional advocacy groups, self-help groups, and volunteer work for schools and social service organizations (Skocpol, 2003). The overall number of group memberships has changed little from 1975 to 1994. In addition, the percentage of individuals volunteering for church, charity, and community groups increased from 44% in 1984 to 58% in 1997. The percentages of individuals belonging to at least one organization and volunteering are higher for Americans than for several European countries (Ladd, 1999).

In addition to formal volunteering, many individuals contribute to their communities by providing informal help (e.g., unpaid assistance such as free babysitting or help with shopping for friends, neighbors, or coworkers) and emotional support (comforting, listening to, or advising friends, neighbors, or coworkers). A recent study indicated that 40% of a national sample had contributed at least 1 hour in the past week to volunteering or providing informal help or emotional support. Those contributing spent an average of 3.6 hours volunteering, 3.4 hours providing informal help, and 2.5 hours giving emotional support to members of the community (Almeida & McDonald, 2005).

Putnam (2000) also has suggested that informal social connections such as social visiting and neighboring have declined between the mid-seventies and the late-nineties. A similar decline in informal socializing has been reported by Robinson and Godbey (1997), who report 8 hours per week in 1965 versus 7 hours in 1985. However, other informal activities such as conversations and sports have shown slight increases over the same time period.

In addition to looking at broad levels and trends, community contexts can be examined by aggregating individual-level community variables. These collective properties operate in conjunction with individual-level characteristics to influence role performance and quality and individual well-being. For example, a recent study examined the community-level effects of deviant behavior and physical discipline on the effects of caretaker control and corporal punishment on child conduct problems (Simons et al., 2002). Another study looked at the mediating role of the density of friendship and acquaintance relationships on the relationship between residential stability and social cohesion (Sampson, 1991). These contextual characteristics of community structure and participation influence the demands, resources, and strategies associated with community life as experienced by individuals in the work–family–community mesosystem.

This discussion of contextual factors suggests that the opportunities and preferences for individuals and family members to negotiate the work–family–community interface vary according to the state of the economy and the workplace; the demographics and ideology associated with family life; and community structure, social organization, and participation. The structural and normative changes associated with the context of work, family, and community life influence the demands, resources, and strategies available to individuals and structure the ways in which they are able to enact their work, family, and community activities and responsibilities. The following chapters articulate processes through which these work, family, and community demands, resources, and strategies influence work, family, community, and individual outcomes.

Social Categories as Context

The four aspects of the macrosystem—economic, workplace, family, and community contexts—operate partly through several intersecting social categories. Social class, race and ethnicity, and gender comprise three of the most important categories. The structure of the economy and the human capital resources of family members are major influences on the opportunities available to families to obtain adequate economic resources. They determine the type of employment and level of income, which, along with education, are major components of social class. Labor-market opportunities and cultural values regarding work, family, and community differ among racial and ethnic groups. Members of various social class and racial and ethnic groups often live in separate communities, which differ in terms of their structure and social organization. Men and women experience different opportunities and constraints in their social roles. Patterns of work, family, and community participation and norms differ for women and men; for example, men spend more time in paid work than women do, whereas women spend longer hours in family work than men do. These categories also intersect with each other; for example, the percentage of individuals earning poverty-level wages in 2003 ranged from 15% for White men and 26% for White women, to 26% for Black men and 34% for Black women, and 36% for Hispanic men and 46% for Hispanic women (Mishel et al., 2005).

In addition to influencing the extent of within-domain and boundary-spanning demands and resources, these social categories may serve as moderators that affect the strength of other relationships proposed in the model presented in Figure 1.2. For example, the strength of relationships between within-domain demands and family role performance and quality may differ by social class, race and ethnicity, and gender. Marks and Leslie (2000) have documented the importance of incorporating social categories in work–family research. These categories need to be considered separately and in combination, for example, the intersection of race, social class, and gender. Unfortunately, little research has examined the effects of these social categories and their intersections on relationships between work, family, and community demands and resources and work, family, and community role performance and individual well-being. Because systematic research is insufficient to serve as the basis for any judgments, these potential moderating effects are not included in the model.

SUMMARY

Over the past two centuries the American economy has moved from an agricultural to an industrial economy and more recently to a postindustrial economy. These shifts have had significant impacts on the domains of work, family, and community and their interrelationships. They also have revealed the connections between work and family, which has led to extensive research on the multiple ways in which work and family life influence each other. More recently, it has become apparent that examinations of work and family should incorporate community. Limited research has shown that work and family life are embedded in the context of the communities in which they operate.

The ecological systems approach provides a useful framework for beginning the conceptual integration of work, family, and community. It suggests that aspects of each domain occur at multiple ecological levels, which are nested within each other according to their immediacy to the developing person. From this perspective, work, family, and community are microsystems consisting of networks of face-to-face relationships. Microsystems are studied by examining relationships between their characteristics (e.g., structure, social organization, norms, support, and orientations), and outcomes (e.g., role performance, role quality, and individual well-being).

This book focuses on the level of the mesosystem, which consists of the interrelationships among the microsystems in which an individual participates. Four mesosystems emerge from the connections among the work, family, and community microsystems—the work–family, work–community, family–community, and work–family–community mesosystems. Figure 1.2 presents a conceptual model for examining mesosystem relationships and linking mechanisms. Economic, workplace, family, and community contexts (the macrosystem) influence the demands, resources, and strategies that are expected to affect work, family, and community role performance and quality and individual well-being. Within-domain and boundary-spanning demands and resources are directly related to work, family, and community role performance and quality and individual well-being.

The model also proposes a chain of relationships through which these direct effects operate. Within-domain demands and resources lead to work–family linking mechanisms (e.g., economic strain and work–family conflict, facilitation, and fit). Linking mechanisms are associated with boundary-spanning strategies, which are proposed to have both mediating and moderating effects on relationships between linking mechanisms and work–family balance. In addition, feedback effects are proposed from boundary-spanning strategies to work, family, and community demands and resources. Work–family linking mechanisms also are expected to be related to work–family balance, which in turn is associated with work, family, and community role performance and quality and individual well-being.

2

Problems With the Worker-Earner Role

The structure of the economy provides a context for work, family, and community life. It determines the extent of opportunity for individuals and family members to obtain adequate employment and income, which are necessary to establish and maintain family life and participate effectively in the community. Providing the basic means of subsistence to its members is one of the major functions of the family. In addition, families aspire to or expect to obtain economic resources beyond the subsistence level. The level of family economic well-being is dependent on both the number of earners and amount of income brought into the family and the needs of the family as determined by family size and composition.

The worker-earner role links the work role in the economy with the earner role in the family. On the individual level, employment and income are the major components of the worker-earner role. Family members generally provide economic resources to their families by earning income through employment, that is, through the worker-earner role. An individual participates in the economy as a worker producing goods and services and as an earner by providing income to meet family needs. Therefore, the need to provide economic resources to the family is a powerful incentive for family members to be employed in jobs that provide adequate earnings. Although traditionally this responsibility has fallen mainly to men, it also is assumed by a majority of women (Voydanoff, 1987).

"Good jobs" that provide employment stability, adequate earnings, and other resources such as decision latitude, social support at work, and psychological rewards have positive effects on family and community role performance and quality and individual well-being. "Bad jobs," which lack some or all of these characteristics, generally have negative consequences for families, communities, and individuals (Grzywacz & Dooley, 2003). These relationships are elaborated more thoroughly in this chapter and in chapters 3 through 6. This chapter considers two aspects of "bad jobs," employment instability and economic deprivation. Other demands associated with "bad jobs" are discussed in chapters 3 and 5, whereas resources associated with "good jobs" are examined in chapters 4 and 6.

This chapter discusses the consequences of employment and income problems associated with the worker-earner role for family and community role performance and quality and individual well-being. Figure 2.1 provides a conceptual model that applies the general model presented in Figure 1.2 to problems with the worker-earner role. It in-

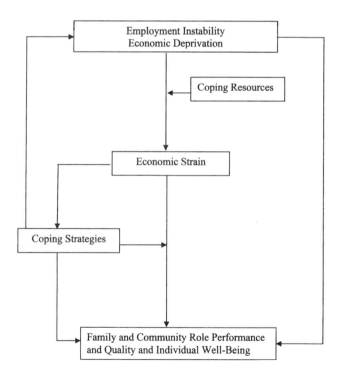

Figure 2.1   A model of problems with the worker-earner role.

corporates propositions from Lazarus and Folkman's (1984) transactional model of the stress process and Patterson's (1988) Family Adjustment and Adaptation Response (FAAR) model. The stress process incorporates stressors (i.e., demands such as chronic strains, life events, and daily hassles) and stress reactions (i.e., the response to a stressor that generally affects individual well-being). These components encompass the stimulus and response approaches to stress. Problems with the worker-earner role (i.e., employment instability and economic deprivation) are stressors that have direct effects on family and community role performance and quality and on individual well-being.

The transactional approach to the stress process posits that psychological stress is "a particular relationship between the person and the environment that is appraised by the person as taxing or exceeding his or her resources and endangering his or her well-being" (Lazarus & Folkman, 1984, p. 19). This approach focuses on appraisal and coping as determinants of whether stressors result in stress reactions. Cognitive appraisal, which mediates between the objective stressor and the stress reaction, is "the process of categorizing an encounter, and its various facets, with respect to its significance for well-being" (p. 31). Encounters can be categorized as positive, stressful, or irrelevant with regard to well-being. The outcome of the appraisal process depends on the relationship between an individual's resources and the demands of the environment.

Economic strain is an appraisal that the financial resources of an individual or family are inadequate in relation to needs. Thus, the perception of economic strain derives from assessing the extent to which financial resources are sufficient to meet demands. The model in Figure 2.1 posits that employment instability and economic deprivation are associated with economic strain, which in turn is negatively related to family and community role performance and quality and individual well-being.

Whether stressors result in stress reactions also depends on the extent to which coping resources and coping behaviors are able to reduce the effects of stressors on outcomes. Personal coping resources include relatively stable personality characteristics (e.g., mastery and self-esteem), intelligence, and knowledge and skills, which affect an individual's ability to deal effectively with stressors. Family coping resources include family system characteristics, such as family adaptability and cohesion, and structural aspects of the family, such as the number of family earners and a manageable family size (e.g., the number of children and other dependents). These are resistance capabilities that reduce the likelihood that stressors will result in negative cognitive appraisals (Patterson, 1988). As indicated in Figure 2.1, coping resources are expected to moderate the effects of employment instability and economic deprivation on economic strain.

Once economic strain occurs, its relationship with outcomes may be affected by coping behaviors or strategies. These strategies include problem-focused coping (e.g., cutting back spending), emotion-focused coping (e.g., redefining goals), and the use of social supports. They are adaptive capabilities that are used to reduce demands, manage meanings and emotions, and maintain or increase resources (Patterson, 1988). Coping strategies also may have feedback effects on employment instability and economic deprivation; for example, the employment of additional family members may reduce economic deprivation in addition to improving family, community, and individual outcomes.

The following sections elaborate the model in Figure 2.1 by reviewing and synthesizing the research that addresses the process and its components. The review reflects the differential extent to which the various aspects have been studied.

EMPLOYMENT INSTABILITY

Problems with the worker-earner role derive from two objective stressors or demands—employment instability and economic deprivation. Employment instability occurs within the context of overall patterns of labor force participation. These patterns are changing for women more than for men. The labor force participation rate for men of prime working age (25 to 54 years) in the United States declined from 93% in 1980 to 90% in 2000, whereas the rate for women in the same age group increased from 67% in 1980 to 79% in 2000. The percentage of women employed full-time, year round increased from 32% in 1980 to 46% in 2000 while approximately 68% of men were employed full-time, year round in 1980 and 2000. Black men have lower rates of labor force participation than other men, whereas Latino women have lower rates than other women (Sayer, Cohen, & Casper, 2004). Overall labor force participation rates for women also increased substantially in several European countries from 1980 to 2001, while remaining stable in Japan (Martin & Kats, 2003).

Trends in Employment Instability

Employment instability includes several important dimensions: unemployment, duration of periods of unemployment, number of periods of employment and unemployment, extent of underemployment and downward mobility, inability of youth to gain entry-level positions, and forced early retirement. This chapter focuses on unemployment and underemployment. Unemployment and underemployment may result from several aspects of the structure and operation of the economy, for example, plant closings, downsizing, mergers and acquisitions, reorganizations, changing technology, outsourcing, and recessions (Probst, 2005). The unemployed are persons who do not have a job, have looked for work in the past 4 weeks, and are available for work. The rate of unemployment varies with economic conditions. During the recession of 1981–1982 in the United States, it peaked at over 10%. Since the fall of 2001, unemployment has decreased from 6.1%, the peak during the past recession, to 5.4% in the 4th quarter of 2004. Approximately 8 million persons were unemployed at this time. The rates in 2004 differed little by gender; however, the rates were higher for Blacks (10.8%) and Hispanics (6.7%) than for Whites (4.6%) (Morisi, 2005). In 2002, the rate of unemployment for workers ages 25–64 was almost three times higher for those with less than a high school diploma (8.7%) than for college graduates (2.9%). (U.S. Department of Labor, 2004). In 2004, the mean duration of unemployment was 20 weeks, the median was 10 weeks, and approximately 3 million persons had been unemployed for 15 or more weeks (Morisi, 2005). In 2002, the U.S. unemployment rate of 5.8% was lower than the average of 7.0% for 18 other industrialized countries (Mishel et al., 2005).

In addition to the unemployed, who are actively seeking employment, in 2004, 4.9 million persons wanted a job but were not currently looking for one. Of these, 1.6 million are considered marginally attached to the labor force because they had looked for a job in the past year and would take a job if one were offered. Approximately 0.5 million of these have given up looking for work because they feel there are no available jobs and are considered discouraged workers. When these marginally attached workers are incorporated in the unemployment rate for the 4th quarter of 2004, it increases from 5.4% to 6.4% (Morisi, 2005).

Although not unemployed or marginally attached to the labor force, a substantial number of persons, 4.8 million at the end of 2003, were considered underemployed because they worked part-time due to their inability to work full-time at their current job or to find a full-time job. When these workers are added to the rate of unemployment and marginal attachment, the labor underutilization rate for the 4th quarter of 2004 increases from 6.4% to 9.5% and includes 14.4 million persons (Morisi, 2005).

Employment Instability, Family and Community Role Performance and Quality, and Individual Well-Being

The model in Figure 2.1 posits direct relationships between employment instability and family and community role performance and quality and individual well-being. Research has revealed that employment instability, usually considered as unemployment, is a demand or stressor with wide-ranging negative consequences for families, communities, and individual well-being. A minimum level of employment stability is needed for family stability and cohesion. Without it, many are unable to form families through marriage, and others find themselves subject to separation and divorce. Several studies in the United States and Europe have reported that unemployment, especially among husbands, is positively associated with the propensity to divorce (Strom, 2003; White & Rogers, 2000). Beyond this, unemployment changes patterns of family life and alters family relationships. Studies in the United States and Europe have shown that unemployment increases the amount of time spent in domestic labor among husbands and wives. These studies suggest that the most egalitarian division of domestic labor is found in couples where the husband is unemployed and the wife is working full-time, whereas the most traditional division of labor occurs when wives are unemployed and husbands are employed full-time (Strom, 2003). Unemployment also is negatively associated with several indicators of marital and family quality (e.g., spouse support, family cohesion, and consensus, communication, and harmony in family relations) and is positively related to marital conflict and stress and spouse abuse (Hanisch, 1999; Voydanoff, 1990).

The effects of unemployment on community role performance and quality operate through two major processes. First, unemployment that occurs as a result of deindustrialization or major plant closings limits the ability of communities to meet the needs of their members. Communities experience a decrease in social and cultural capital. This capital is needed for members to build the social connections and community organizations that are necessary to counteract the negative effects of employment declines (Perrin, 1998). Large-scale unemployment also affects the commercial life of communities and the tax base needed to provide community services. Such changes may alter the sense of community identity experienced by both the employed and unemployed within a community (Newman, 1988).

Unemployment also has negative effects on formal and informal social participation. Employment is a source of social integration and a means of building social and civic skills, which encourage community participation. Unemployment tends to disrupt social relationships and involvement in society. Unemployment is negatively related to volunteering and participating in organizational activities such as clubs (Boraas, 2003; Siddique, 1981). The percentages of unemployed who volunteer are lower among men, women, and Whites and are comparable to rates for the employed among Blacks and Hispanics (Boraas, 2003). Informal social participation (e.g., participating in sporting events and visiting with friends) also is lower among the unemployed and those with unstable work histories (Hanisch, 1999; Siddique, 1981).

Unemployment and underemployment are major life stressors that have diffuse effects on the psychological and physical well-being of the unemployed and their spouses and children. The unemployed and underemployed lose important resources associated with employment, such as time structure, contact with others, contribution to society, personal identity and status, and activity (Hanisch, 1999). Relatively extensive research shows that unemployment is associated with lower psychological well-being among the unemployed as indicated by higher levels of depression, anxiety, psychophysiological distress, and psychiatric illness and lower levels of self-esteem, positive affect, feeling of mastery, and life satisfaction (Hanisch, 1999; Voydanoff, 1990). A recent meta-analysis of 104 empirical studies reported significant effects of unemployment on mental health in both cross-sectional and longitudinal studies (McKee-Ryan, Song, Wanberg, & Kinicki, 2005). Unemployment also is associated with physical health problems including headaches, stomachaches, sleep problems, heart and kidney disease, hypertension, and ulcers (Hanisch, 1999). The McKee-Ryan et al. meta-analysis also revealed a negative relationship between unemployment and physical well-being.

The effects of unemployment on mental health extend beyond the unemployed to their spouses. Strom (2003) cites several studies that reveal negative mental health effects on the spouses of the unemployed. A recent study documents three mechanisms through which the unemployment of one spouse negatively impacts the mental health of the other spouse: Both spouses experience common secondary stressors associated with unemployment (e.g., financial problems or changes in routines), the distress experienced by the unemployed spouse is transmitted to the other spouse through a process of stress transmission or psychological spillover, and the unemployment of one spouse influences the mental health of the other spouse through a disruption in the marital relationship in terms of decreased support and increased marital conflict. These relationships did not differ by ethnicity; however, they were stronger when the husband was the unemployed spouse than when the wife was (Howe, Levy, & Caplan, 2004).

Studies in the United States and Europe report that unemployment also has negative effects on children whose parents experience unemployment. These effects encompass psychological well-being, aspirations and achievement, and physical health. Psychological effects include higher levels of behavior problems such as self-destructive behavior and suicide attempts, and lower levels of mastery and self-esteem. Parental unemployment also is associated with children leaving school early, having lower expectations of finding employment, and being unemployed as adults. Several of these relationships are mediated by higher levels of parent–child conflict and lower parental well-being and parenting skills. Children whose parents have been unemployed also experience physical health problems at higher rates than other children, for example, lower birth weight, shorter stature, higher infant mortality, increased hospital admissions, and higher accident risk (Kahil & Ziol-Guest, 2005; Strom, 2003).

Studies of the effects of underemployment on families, communities, and individuals are sparse. Those working part-time because they cannot find full-time work generally report lower levels of psychological well-being and physical health than the adequately employed do (Dooley, 2003; Friedland & Price, 2003). Probst (2005) cites several studies that suggest that underemployment is associated with lower marital satisfaction, negative effects on children, and social isolation.

ECONOMIC DEPRIVATION

The second objective stressor or demand included in the model, economic deprivation, incorporates two aspects: the inability to meet current financial needs and the loss of financial resources and income over a period of time. The inability to meet financial needs derives from the combination of income level and needs associated with family structure and size, whereas income loss often occurs because of employment instability. Both aspects of economic deprivation affect significant numbers in the United States and have important implications for families, communities, and individuals.

Trends in Economic Deprivation

Earnings form the basis of having an income sufficient to meet a family's financial needs. Patterns of earnings have been uneven over past decades. Real hourly wages have grown between 1973 and 2003 for men with at least some college and declined for those with a high school education or less, whereas wages have increased for women at all educational levels. In 2003, 20% of men and 29% of women earned wages at or below the poverty level for a family of four. These rates were highest for Hispanics, followed by Blacks and Whites (Mishel et al., 2005).

Patterns of family income growth also vary according to demographic and family characteristics. Median family income has increased from $43,210 in 1973 to $52,680 in 2003. However, median family income in 2003 ranged from $34,272 for Hispanics and $34,369 for Blacks to $55,768 for Whites. Median family incomes in

2003 also varied widely for different family types. For married couples, the median family income was $41,122 when the wife was not in the labor force and was $75,170 when she was. For single-parent families, the medians were $26,550 for female-headed and $38,032 for male-headed families (Mishel et al, 2005).

Despite overall increases in family income, many families remain in or near poverty. The overall poverty rate has decreased slightly from 11.4% of families in 1967 to 10.0% in 2003. In 2003, the rate ranged from 8.1% among Whites to 20.8% for Hispanics and 22.3% for Blacks. For families with children, the rate was 7.0% for married couples and 35.5% for female-headed families. The percentages of children under 18 living in poverty in 2003 were 14.3% for Whites, 29.7% for Hispanics, and 34.1% for Blacks. The percentages of families with incomes at or below twice the poverty rate, a level at which families still are likely to have some difficulty meeting basic consumption needs, varied from 25.8% for Asians and 27.7% for Whites to 47.8% for Blacks and 52.0% for Hispanics. In 2000, these rates ranged from 8.2% for college graduates to 67.8% for those with less than a high school education. Although per capita income in the United States in 2000 was slightly higher than the average for 18 other industrialized countries, the United States had higher levels of income inequality, total poverty, poverty among children and the elderly, and long-term poverty (Mishel et al., 2005).

Economic deprivation also is associated with the loss of income because of employment instability. Recession-related and structural unemployment creates economic deprivation for many who previously worked at seemingly secure jobs. The extent of economic deprivation associated with unemployment varies according to prior income level, eligibility for unemployment insurance and other benefits, and the duration of unemployment. During the 2001 recession, average monthly income among the unemployed in the United States was 40% lower than pre-unemployment income. This decrease was reduced by 20% among those receiving Unemployment Insurance (UI). Incomes for UI recipients who had not found work 3 months after their benefits ended were about half what they had been before they began receiving benefits (Smith, 2004). In addition, studies in Britain indicate that wages following unemployment are approximately 6–10% lower than those prior to unemployment (Arulampalam, Gregg, & Gregory, 2001).

Economic Deprivation, Family and Community Role Performance and Quality, and Individual Well-Being

The model in Figure 2.1 proposes that economic deprivation is a demand or stressor that is negatively associated with family and community role performance and quality and individual well-being. This proposition has been supported by extensive research suggesting that low income and income loss have negative impacts on families, communities, and individuals. Economic deprivation is associated with several aspects of family life, including family formation and stability, the division of household labor, and quality of family life. Both men's and women's earnings increase the likelihood of marriage, although the relationships are stronger for men's earnings than for women's. Low income and income loss among men are associated with an increased likelihood of divorce, whereas the findings for women's earnings and divorce probability are mixed. Limited research suggests that these relationships are stronger for Blacks than for Whites. These findings suggest that income provides an economic basis for the formation and stability of family life by providing economies of scale, reduction of economic risk, and income maximization (White & Rogers, 2000). Women's earnings generally are negatively related to the amount of household work they perform. When wives' absolute earnings increase, their absolute levels of time spent in household work decrease. Wives' proportionate share of earnings is positively associated with a relatively balanced distribution of household work. However, the more economically dependent husbands are on their wives, the less household work they perform, especially among low-income families. These findings suggest that wives use their economic resources to reduce their level of household work except when they earn more than their husbands (Coltrane, 2000). Finally, family income has a modest negative relationship with indicators of marital quality such as global marital satisfaction, frequency of interaction, and divorce proneness. These relationships are somewhat stronger when receipt of public assistance is used as the indicator of income (Fein, 2004). A recent study also reported associations between an income-to-needs ratio and debts and family violence against women (Fox, Benson, DeMaris, & Van Wyck, 2002).

Research reveals that economic deprivation is negatively related to some aspects of community participation but not to others. Earnings and family income are positively related to time spent in formal volunteering, but are unrelated to informal helping. This may be related to the different resources required for the two types of participation: human capital and social ties for volunteering, and sense of obligation for informal helping (Wilson, 2000; Wilson & Musick, 1997a). In addition, those experiencing income loss due to unemployment may reduce their informal social participation because of their inability to afford leisure activities or to reciprocate socially (Probst, 2005).

The extensive research on relationships between economic deprivation and the mental and physical health of adults and children generally reveals negative effects. Low income is related to several indicators of psychological distress and physical problems among adults. Low personal earnings and low family incomes are positively associated with depression, anxiety, psychophysiological distress, and a range of physical health problems in the United States and Great Britain (Ecob & Smith, 1999; Sturm & Gresenz, 2002; Voydanoff, 1990). Other studies reveal positive relationships between family income and several aspects of children's adjustment and physical health, such as internalizing and externalizing problems, school achievement, and child health (White & Rogers, 2000). More specifically, studies of family poverty reveal that poverty is associated with a wide array of physical and mental health problems among children and adolescents. Physical health problems include low-birth-weight babies, infant mortality, physical illness, and inadequate nutrition, whereas mental health problems include internalizing and externalizing symptoms such as depression, social withdrawal, and behavioral and conduct problems. Children living in poverty also receive lower grades and lower scores on standardized tests and are less likely to finish high school or attend college. Studies show that several of these relationships are mediated by the home environment and parenting behaviors among poor parents such as being less nurturing and more authoritarian and using inconsistent and harsh physical discipline (Grant et al., 2003; Seccombe, 2000)

COPING RESOURCES

The model presented in Figure 2.1 posits that the effects of employment instability and economic deprivation on economic strain are moderated by individual and family coping resources. These are resistance resources or available assets that prevent employment instability and economic deprivation from being perceived as stressful and creating economic strain. Despite their importance to models of individual and family stress, the role of these resources in reducing the effects of employment instability and economic deprivation on economic strain has not been studied. However, what little is known provides indirect support to the model.

Individual characteristics such as self-esteem and mastery are personal coping resources that affect an individual's ability to deal effectively with stressors. Self-esteem and mastery reduce the relationship between unemployment and psychological distress (Voydanoff, 1990). Family coping resources such as adaptability and cohesion facilitate effective problem solving within families. Research during and since the depression of the 1930s reveals that marital relationships high in empathy and the presence of family adaptability and cohesion prior to unemployment are positively associated with the quality of family relationships during unemployment (Conger, Rueter, & Conger, 2000; Voydanoff, 1990). Family structure characteristics also may serve as resistance coping resources. The employment of multiple family members may reduce the likelihood that the unemployment of one member results in perceived economic strain. In addition, families with relatively few economic dependents such as young children may experience less economic strain as a result of employment instability and economic deprivation than those with greater responsibilities. Unfortunately, research does not examine directly the role of these coping resources in reducing the effects of employment instability and economic deprivation on economic strain.

ECONOMIC STRAIN

Employment instability and economic deprivation are relatively objective indicators of problems associated with the worker-earner role. Economic strain is a subjective evaluation of one's financial situation. It incorporates cognitive assessments of the perceived adequacy of financial resources, financial concerns and worries, and expectations regarding one's future economic situation (Hilton & Devall, 1997; Voydanoff & Donnelly, 1988). Thus, the perception of economic strain derives from assessing the extent to which financial resources are adequate to meet demands. Economic strain also has been referred to as economic pressure (Conger et al., 2000), psychological sense of economic hardship (Barrera, Caples, & Tein, 2001), and financial well-being (Fox et al., 2002).

Sources of Economic Strain and Consequences for Individuals and Families

The model presented in Figure 2.1 proposes that the objective demands, employment stability and economic deprivation, are sources of the subjective demand, economic strain. Economic strain, in turn, is negatively associated with family and community role performance and quality and individual well-being. Indicators of employment instability (e.g., an unstable work history and loss of work or wages) are positively related to economic strain. Several indicators of economic deprivation (e.g., low family income, low per capita family income, high debt-to-asset ratio, and income loss) also show positive associations with economic strain (Barrera et al., 2001; Conger & Elder, 1994; Conger et al., 2000). One study revealed that the effects of low per capita income and income loss on economic strain are comparable for mothers and fathers and for African Americans, European Americans, and Mexican Americans (Barrera et al., 2001).

Research also documents that economic strain is negatively associated with family and community role performance and quality and individual well-being. Economic strain is a cognitive appraisal that influences families, communities, and individuals through a process of psychological spillover in which the strain associated with participating in the worker-earner role is carried over to other domains such that it creates strain in these domains, thereby hindering role performance and reducing quality of life in those domains and limiting individual well-being. Psychological spillover operates through transmission processes in which economic strain is associated with psychological responses, which disrupt close personal relationships in the family and community. Negative transmission processes include negative emotional arousal, interpersonal withdrawal, energy depletion, and stress (Conger et al., 2000; Piotrkowski, 1979; Rothbard, 2001).

The negative psychological spillover associated with economic strain is reflected in consistent and strong positive relationships between economic strain and psychological distress among adults. Economic strain is positively related to anxiety, depression, psychiatric illness, and problems with alcohol. With the exception of alcohol problems, these relationships generally hold for both men and women (Conger et al., 2000; Pierce, Frone, Russell, & Cooper, 1994; Voydanoff, 1990; Wildman, 2003). In addition, the economic strain experienced by one spouse influences the anxiety level of the other spouse (Westman, Etzion, & Horovitz, 2004).

The negative psychological spillover associated with economic strain may generate hostility and decrease warmth in family relationships and role performance. Economic strain also shows consistent negative relationships to marital quality for men and women (Conger et al., 2000; Voydanoff, 1990, 2004d; White & Rogers, 2000). These effects of economic strain on the overall quality of marital relationships generally operate through psychological distress among the partners and problems in the marital relationship such as spousal irritability, behavioral problems, and hostility (Hrba, Lorenz, & Pechacova, 2000), husbands' and wives' emotional distress and marital conflict (Conger et al., 2000; Conger, Rueter, & Elder, 1999), and partners' depression and undermining behavior (Westman, Vinokur, Hamilton, & Roziner, 2004).

Little research has investigated relationships between economic strain and family role performance with the exception of parental behavior. One study, however, revealed that economic strain was negatively to family cohesion but was unrelated to time spent in activities with adolescents (Voydanoff, 2004a). Economic strain generally shows positive relationships to parenting behaviors such as harsh parenting and negative relationships with nurturant and involved parenting. These effects are mediated by parents' emotional distress and marital conflict (Conger & Elder, 1994; Conger et al., 2000).

Finally, economic strain and its associated spillover have negative effects on the well-being of children and adolescents. Most studies document direct positive relationships between parents' economic strain and adolescent problems (internalizing and externalizing symptoms and antisocial behavior) and negative relationships for school achievement (Voydanoff, 2004e). These relationships are mediated by parents' emotional distress, marital conflict, and disrupted parenting (Conger et al, 2000).

Economic Strain as a Mediator

The model in Figure 2.1 also suggests that economic strain mediates the effects of employment instability and economic deprivation on family and community role performance and quality and individual well-being. The findings just cited that document direct effects of employment instability and economic deprivation on economic strain and direct effects of economic strain on outcomes indicate that it is possible for such mediating effects to occur.

Extensive research reveals that economic strain partially mediates the effects of employment instability and economic deprivation on poor health and mental health problems such as depression and anxiety among adults (Avison, 2001; Price, Choi, & Vinokur, 2001; Voydanoff, 1990) and adjustment among adolescents (Whitbeck et al., 1991). Economic strain also partially mediates relationships between employment instability and economic deprivation and parenting efficacy and supportive parenting (Elder, Eccles, Ardelt, & Lord, 1995; Simons, Lorenz, Conger, & Wu, 1992). Findings from several studies in the United States, which reveal that employment instability and economic deprivation influence marital quality through economic strain, have been reviewed and replicated in a study of couples in Finland (Kinnunen & Feldt, 2004).

The Family Stress Model

Thus, the relationships posited in Figure 2.1 of direct and indirect relationships among employment instability and economic deprivation, economic strain, and individual well-being and family role performance and quality generally have been supported in the extant research. Unfortunately, some aspects of individual well-being and family role performance have been neglected, for example, physical health and division of family labor.

In addition, the findings just reported support an extension of the model in Figure 2.1. The family stress model presented in Figure 2.2 proposes a series of linkages among outcomes associated with individual well-being and family role performance and quality for families with adolescent children. The model suggests that economic hardship (employment instability and economic deprivation) influences economic pressure (economic strain), which in turn is linked sequentially to parents' emotional distress, marital conflict, disrupted parenting, and adolescent maladjustment (Conger et al., 2000). This model has been supported for diverse racial and ethnic groups and for boys and girls (Conger et al., 2002; Mistry, Vandewater, Huston, & McLoyd, 2002).

Economic Strain and Community Role Performance and Quality

Because community role performance and quality are not incorporated in the family stress model, they are discussed separately here.

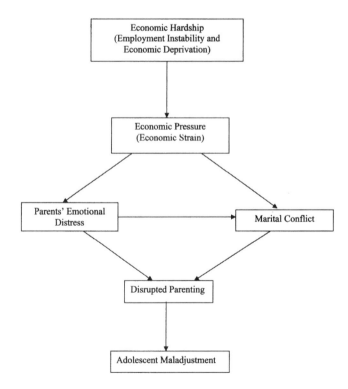

Figure 2.2   Family stress model. Adapted from Conger, Reuter, and Conger (2000), with permission.

Unfortunately, the research in this area is limited. The available research, however, does indicate that the psychological spillover associated with economic strain limits several aspects of community role performance and quality. Those experiencing financial anxiety have lower levels than others of formal (e.g., number of organizational memberships, attendance at club meetings and church, and volunteering) and informal community participation (e.g., time with friends, card playing, and home entertaining) (Putnam, 2000). In addition, economic strain is negatively related to subjective aspects of community life such as trust in others and satisfaction with friends. Satisfaction with friends also mediates the relationship between economic strain and family satisfaction (Voydanoff, Donnelly, & Fine, 1988), whereas parental involvement in school mediates the effects of economic strain on school achievement (Gutman & Eccles, 1999). Finally, economic strain explains relationships between low income and the aspects of community participation discussed earlier, that is, attending club meetings and church, volunteering, spending time with friends, and entertaining (Putnam, 2000). Social engagement is limited more by financial worry than by low income per se.

COPING STRATEGIES

Individuals and families vary in their responses to stressful cognitive appraisals such as economic strain. The use of adaptive coping strategies or behaviors is an important factor influencing the extent to which economic strain detracts from family and community role performance and quality and individual well-being. Coping strategies involve the use of coping resources in an active process of dealing with stressors and their effects. These strategies are undertaken to maintain existing resources, acquire additional resources, reduce demands, and manage tension and meanings associated with experiencing stressors. Major types of coping behaviors include (a) problem-focused coping, which modifies or eliminates the source of the problem, deals with its consequences, or improves the situation; (b) emotion-focused coping, which defines the meaning of the situation or attempts to manage emotions; and (c) the use of social support, which provides instrumental and emotional assistance (Patterson, 1988; Voydanoff, 1990).

Problem-Focused Coping Strategies

Research has documented the use of several problem-focused coping strategies or behaviors designed to maintain or improve the financial situation of families experiencing economic distress. Strategies that involve increasing financial resources include realigning the family work effort, participating in the informal economy, and obtaining financial assistance from the government, community agencies, or friends and relatives. Cutting back on expenditures is designed to reduce financial demands.

Family work effort is the extent of participation of family members in paid employment. When one family member becomes unemployed, others, especially spouses and teenage children, may increase their work effort. The informal economy consists of the exchange of goods and services for cash or by barter. Skills developed through a hobby or on the job, such as sewing or carpentry, are used to save money or earn additional income. In some cases these activities lead to employment in a new occupation. Individuals and families also exchange goods and services such as household items, child care, and transportation. Individuals and families may obtain financial assistance through public assistance such as welfare or food stamps. Although economic strain is related to using these problem-focused coping strategies, their use generally is associated with lower levels of martial and life satisfaction and higher levels of depression and anxiety (Leana & Feldman, 1990; Voydanoff & Donnelly, 1988, 1989).

In addition, economic strain often requires changes in spending patterns to reduce financial demands. These behaviors include cutting expenditures, increasing home production, comparing prices and value when shopping, spending savings, going into debt, or moving to less expensive housing. Although these cuts are effective in improving a family's financial situation, they are not necessarily associated with other positive individual and family outcomes. Cutting spending is related to depression, anxiety, low marital satisfaction, parent–child conflict, and high family tensions and mediates the relationship between unemployment and depression (Broman, Hamilton, & Hoffman, 2002; Voydanoff, 1990; Voydanoff & Donnelly, 1989). When these problem-focused coping strategies are effective, they also may reduce economic deprivation. These feedback effects may lower economic distress, which then reduces the negative consequences of problems with the worker-earner role on family, community, and individual well-being.

Emotion-Focused Coping Strategies

Emotion-focused coping strategies are used to manage the emotions and meanings associated with economic strain. The limited research on emotion-focused coping behaviors has shown that positive comparisons and the devaluation of economic achievements reduce the effects of unemployment on depression, whereas lack of intrusive thoughts has limited buffering effects on relationships between unemployment and mental and physical health. However, avoidance coping, such as denial, keeping feelings to oneself, and eating, drinking, and smoking to relieve tension mediated the effects of financial arguments on stress (Voydanoff, 1990). Unfortunately, these findings do not specifically address relationships between economic strain and outcomes.

The Use of Social Support

Using social support is a third type of coping strategy that may reduce the negative effects of economic strain on family, community, and individual well-being. The use of social support is a complex process involving several dimensions: Support must be available, available support must be used, and the support provided must meet the needs of those receiving it. Social support includes instrumental aid such as money, goods, and services; emotional support; and information such as advice and feedback. It may be used to maintain or increase resources, reduce demands, or manage emotions and meanings. Support may come from several sources: friends, relatives, coworkers, neighbors, self-help groups, and human service professionals.

Studies based on the family stress model discussed earlier reveal that social support can influence the effects of economic strain on several stages of the family stress model, that is, parents' emotional distress, marital conflict, disrupted parenting, and adolescent maladjustment. In some studies, economic strain results in lower levels of social support. However, when support is available, it is negatively associated with adverse outcomes. For example, economic strain is negatively related to support from family and friends, which is negatively associated with depression, especially among women. Economic strain also shows a negative association with father's (mother's) support for the mother (father), which, in turn, is negatively related to the father's (mother's) hostility and explosive discipline (Conger & Elder, 1994). However, in other cases, strain is related to increased support. For example, the effects of economic strain on supportive parenting operate through spouse and social network support (Simons, Lorenz, Wu, & Conger, 1993). In addition, support from adults outside the family buffer the negative effects of economic strain on the psychological well-being of adolescent girls (Conger et al., 2000).

SUMMARY

Problems with the worker-earner role occur when individuals have difficulty maintaining stable employment and earning an adequate income. These objective stressors are negatively associated with family and community role performance and quality and individual well-being. In addition, employment instability and economic deprivation are associated with economic strain, that is, the perception that individual and family financial resources are insufficient and a cause for worry and concern. A conceptual model based on individual and family stress theory suggests that the effects of employment instability and economic deprivation on economic strain are reduced by the presence of individual and family coping resources. When economic strain does occur, it has direct negative effects on family and community role performance and quality and individual well-being. However, the use of coping strategies may limit these negative effects. Economic strain mediates the effects of employment instability and economic deprivation on family, community, and individual well-being.

The extant research generally supports this model. The greatest number of studies has focused on the direct effects of employment instability, economic deprivation, and economic strain on individual well-being and the quality of family life. Another large group of studies has explored the mediating effects of economic strain on relationships between employment instability and economic deprivation and individual and family well-being as well as interrelationships among economic strain, emotional distress, marital conflict, disrupted parenting, and adolescent maladjustment. Relatively little is known about the role of coping resources and strategies or the application of the model to community role performance and quality. In addition, the literature generally is limited to U.S. studies and does not consider possible gender, racial, or ethnic differences in the application of the model.

3

Within-Domain Work, Family, and Community Demands

Chapter 1 presented a general model of the relationships and linkages making up the work–family–community mesosystem. In the second chapter this model was specified and applied to problems associated with performing the worker-earner role. These problems derive from the economic context in which work is performed, that is, the stability of employment and its economic rewards. The next four chapters move beyond this external context to examine demands and resources associated with performing paid work and to extend the analysis by incorporating demands and resources associated with the family and community domains.

The general model presented in Figure 1.2 posits direct relationships between within-domain and boundary-spanning work, family, and community demands and resources and work, family, and community role performance and quality and individual well-being. The model also proposes that within-domain and boundary-spanning demands and resources are associated with work–family linking mechanisms (e.g., work–family conflict and work–family facilitation), which in turn are related to work–family balance and work, family, community, and individual outcomes. The next four chapters discuss these direct effects and the differential ways in which within-domain and boundary-spanning demands and resources are associated with work–family conflict and facilitation. These relationships are summarized in Figure 3.1. The figure indicates that within-domain demands operate through work–family conflict to influence work, family, and community role performance and quality and individual well-being. This chapter addresses these relationships. The figure also proposes that the relationship between within-domain resources and outcomes is mediated by work–family facilitation. Chapter 4 discusses within-domain resources in relation to outcomes and work–family facilitation. In addition, the figure suggests that boundary-spanning demands and resources are related to both work–family conflict and facilitation, which in turn are associated with outcomes. Chapters 5 and 6 address boundary-spanning demands and resources in relation to outcomes, conflict, and facilitation.

Within-domain work, family, and community demands are proposed to show direct relationships to work, family, and community role performance and quality and individual well-being. Work–family conflict is a linking mechanism that is expected to partially mediate or explain relationships between demands and outcomes. Within-domain demands, which are characteristics associated with the structure and content of a domain, are of two types: time-based and strain-based.

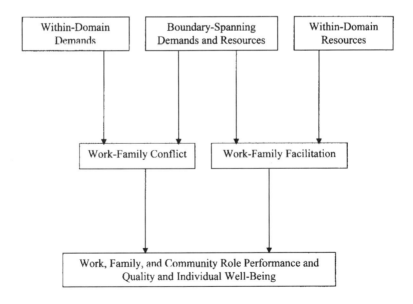

Figure 3.1   The conceptual model of within-domain and boundary-spanning demands and resources.

Time-based demands reflect the idea that time is a fixed resource, that is, time spent in activities in one domain is not available for activities in another domain. Time-based demands are related to outcomes through a process of resource drain in which the time or involvement required for participation in one domain limits the time or involvement available for participation in another domain (Tenbrunsel, Brett, Maoz, Stroh, & Reilly, 1995). This resource drain from one domain limits role performance and quality in other domains, which reduces individual well-being and increases work–family conflict. Time-based demands include the amount of time in paid work (the number and scheduling of work hours), in family work (time caring for children and elderly parents and time in household work), and in community activities (time volunteering and informal helping).

Strain-based demands influence work, family, and community role performance and quality, individual well-being, and work–family conflict through a process of negative psychological spillover in which the strain associated with participating in one domain is carried over to another domain such that it creates strain in the second domain. This strain hinders role performance and quality, thereby reducing individual well-being and increasing work–family conflict. Psychological spillover operates through transmission processes in which conditions in one domain are associated with psychological responses, which are then transferred into attitudes and behavior in another domain. Negative transmission processes include negative emotional arousal, interpersonal withdrawal, energy depletion, and stress (Piotrkowski, 1979; Rothbard, 2001). Strain-based demands include characteristics associated with the social organization of work (job demands and job insecurity), family social organization (marital conflict, children's problems, caregiver strain, and unfairness in household work), and community social disorganization (neighborhood problems and demands from friends). In addition, some time-based demands may produce strain-based demands; for example, the time spent caring for children and elderly parents may create strain-based demands such as role overload. Table 3.1 presents a listing of the time- and strain-based demands discussed here. The list incorporates demands that have been studied relatively often or are thought to be important on theoretical grounds.

Perceived work–family conflict is a linking mechanism through which work and family demands are related to work, family, and community role performance and quality and individual well-being (Voydanoff, 2002). It is a cognitive appraisal of the effects of the work (family) domain on the family (work) domain. According to Lazarus and Folkman (1984), cognitive appraisal is the process of deciding whether an experience is positive, stressful, or irrelevant with regard

TABLE 3.1.   **Within-Domain Work, Family, and Community Demands**

	Work	Family	Community
Time-based demands	Time in paid work Nonstandard work schedules	Time caring for children Time caring for elderly parents Time in household work	Time volunteering Time in informal helping
Strain-based demands	Job demands Job insecurity	Marital conflict Children's problems Caregiver strain Unfairness in household work	Neighborhood problems Friend demands

to well-being. A stressful appraisal occurs when individuals perceive that the demands of the environment exceed their resources, thereby endangering their well-being. Thus, the perception of work–family conflict derives from assessing the relative demands and resources associated with work and family roles. This view of conflict focuses on perceptions rather than objective characteristics that may operate outside the individual's awareness because such perceptions generally mediate the effects of more objective characteristics on outcomes (Edwards & Rothbard, 2005).

Work–family conflict is a form of interrole conflict in which the demands of work and family roles are incompatible in some respect so that participation in one role is more difficult because of participation in the other role (Greenhaus & Beutell, 1985). This conflict can take two forms: work-to-family conflict, in which the demands of work make it difficult to perform family responsibilities, and family-to-work conflict, in which family demands limit the performance of work duties. Although these two forms of work–family conflict are moderately correlated ($r = .48$ in Byron's 2005 meta-analysis), work demands generally are associated with work-to-family conflict, whereas family demands are the proximal sources of family-to-work conflict (Byron, 2005; Voydanoff, 2005f). Similar patterns are found in studies of U.S. and non-U.S. samples (Poelmans, O'Driscoll, & Beham, 2005). Although community demands originate outside the work and family domains, they are expected to influence both work-to-family and family-to-work conflict.

The next section of this chapter discusses relationships between work demands and family and community role performance and quality, individual well-being, and work-to-family conflict. This is followed by an analysis of family demands in relation to work and community role performance and quality, individual well-being, and family-to-work conflict and a discussion of community demands in relation to work and family performance and quality, individual well-being, and work–family conflict. Then the combined effects of demands from different domains are reviewed. The chapter closes with a discussion of the role of work–family conflict as a partial mediator of relationships between within-domain demands and role performance and quality and well-being.

WORK DEMANDS

Time-Based Demands

Time-based demands, that is, demands of time in paid work and nonstandard work schedules, represent a fixed resource in that time spent working may limit time and energy for other activities. Long work hours and nonstandard work schedules place temporal boundaries on workers' physical and psychological availability for participation in family and community life, which may influence family and community role performance and quality and individual well-being. However, potential resources also are embedded in time in paid work. Paid work provides resources such as economic well-being, self-esteem, and social attachment, integration, and support. Although those with the fewest hours in paid work are least likely to have jobs that provide the economic and social resources that enhance family and community role performance and quality and individual well-being, the additional nonwork time provided by short work hours may enhance role performance and quality and individual well-being under some circumstances (e.g., additional time to meet family and community responsibilities). Although working a nonday shift prevents employees from being at home during the afternoon and evening hours when family activities usually occur, such schedules may be compatible with the schedules of other family members. Thus, relationships between work hours and scheduling and role performance and quality, well-being, and conflict may reflect a balance between demands and resources.

Trends in time in paid work and nonstandard work schedules.   The average weekly hours in paid work in the United States have remained stable since 1970. In 2000, the average for men was 43.1 hours week versus 43.5 hours in 1970, whereas women averaged 37.1 hours per week in 2000, unchanged from 37.0 in 1970. For men, the average weekly hours are higher for Whites than Blacks, Hispanics, and Asian Americans, whereas for women, the average is highest for Blacks (Jacobs & Gerson, 2004). This stability contrasts with a decrease for 19 Organization for Economic Cooperation and Development (OECD) countries from an average of 1,870 hours per year in 1979 to 1,602 hours in 2002, while the U.S. numbers changed little (1,838 yearly hours in 1979 vs. 1,815 hours in 2002) (Mishel et al., 2005).

Despite overall stability in working hours in the United States, the percentages of those who work less than 30 hours per week or 50 or more hours per week have increased for both men and women. In 2000, 8.6% of men (up from 4.5% in 1970) and 19.6% of women (up from 15.5% in 1970) worked less than 30 hours per week, whereas 26.5% of men (up from 21.0% in 1970) and 11.3% of women (up from 5.2% in 1970) worked 50 or more hours per week. Men and women in professional, managerial, and technical occupations are more likely to work long hours and less likely to work part-time than are those in other occupations. In addition, the average number of combined weekly hours of married couples has increased from 52.5 to 63.1 from 1970 to 2000. The average for dual-earner couples increased from 78.0 in 1970 to 81.6 in 2000. Thus, the increase for married couples is due mainly to the increase in dual-earner couples from 1970 to 2000 (Jacobs & Gerson, 2004).

When individuals are asked how many hours per week they would like to work, 60% of men and women would prefer to work fewer hours per week than they are currently working, whereas 19% would prefer to work more hours per week. Those working the longest hours are most likely to prefer working fewer hours (80% of men and almost 90% of women working over 50 hours per week), whereas ideal working hours are greater than actual hours for men working less than 40 hours and for women working less than 30 hours per week (Jacobs & Gerson, 2004). Bluestone and Rose (1997) reported than 29% of part-time work is involuntary. Thus, a substantial portion of the working population feels either overworked or underemployed.

Nonstandard work schedules are quite prevalent. In 1997, only 29.1% of employed Americans worked a standard work week of 35 to 40 hours a week, Monday through Friday, on a fixed daytime schedule. One-fifth (19.9%) did not work a fixed daytime schedule, but instead worked fixed evening or night schedules, rotating shifts, or variable hours. One-third (31.7%) performed some of their work on the weekends. Men are slightly more likely to work nonstandard schedules (i.e., a nonday schedule or weekend work) than women are. Blacks are more likely than Whites, Hispanics, and other races (Native and Asian Americans) to work nonday schedules, whereas the rates for working weekends are highest for the combined Native-Asian American group. Those working nonstandard schedules are most likely to be in low-paying service-sector jobs that serve the local economy. A majority of those working nonstandard schedules report that they do so because of employer demands rather than personal choice (Presser, 2003). The percentages of workers 16 years and older who work nonday schedules has remained relatively stable from 1985 (15.9%) to 1997 (16.8%) (Beers, 2000). The percentages of workers in 12 European countries who are employed on nonstandard schedules are either comparable to those in the United States or lower (Presser, 2003).

Although the rates for those working nonstandard schedules in 1997 were slightly lower for married than for unmarried workers, the rates for married workers were still significant (16.4% for nonday schedules and 29.4% for weekend work). However, for two-earner couples, 27.8% included at least one spouse working a nonday schedule, whereas in 44.5% of couples at least one spouse worked on weekends. The comparable rates for two-earner couples with children under 14 were 31.1% for nonday schedules and 46.5% for weekend work. The percentages on nonstandard schedules are higher for women in single-mother families than for married mothers (20.8% versus 16.4% for nonday schedules and 33.2% versus 23.9% for weekend work) (Presser, 2003).

Time in Paid Work.   Evidence regarding the extent to which time in paid work serves as a resource drain in relation to role performance and quality in the family and community domains and individual well-being is mixed. Parents' time in paid work is negatively related to the amount time spent caring for children in some studies and for some activities but not others (Voydanoff, 2004a). Men's paid work hours are negatively related to time spent caring for elderly parents, whereas for women some studies show a negative relationship whereas others report no relationship (Sarkisian & Gerstel, 2004). Paid work hours show stronger relationships to time spent in household work for women than for men. Wives' time in paid work is negatively associated with their time spent in household work and is positively related to husbands' time in household work. Husbands' work hours reveal a modest negative relationship to their time spent in household work in some studies but no relationship in others (Coltrane, 2000). Studies generally report no significant relationships between time in paid work and indicators of marital quality, such as marital happiness, companionship, disagreements, and tension (Barnett, 1998; Voydanoff, 2004d). Other research reveals that parents' time in paid work does not show statistically significant relationships with children's cognitive and social outcomes or adolescent problems and grades (Crouter & McHale, 2005; Voydanoff, 2004e).

The findings for time in paid work in relation to community participation and individual well-being are more consistent. The few studies that have examined relationships between time in paid work and community participation have reported negative associations with time in volunteering and informal helping (Hook, 2004; Wilson & Musick, 1997b). A meta-analysis found that time in paid work has small, but statistically significant, positive mean correlations with mental and physical illness (Sparks, Cooper, Fried, & Shirom, 1997).

In summary, findings for linear relationships between paid work hours and family and community role performance and quality and individual well-being have been weak and inconsistent. This lack of support suggests that the effects of time in paid work on family role performance and quality may be nonlinear. Nevertheless, studies of nonlinear relationships also reveal either little support or inconsistent findings for family role performance and quality and individual well-being (Voydanoff, 2004a, 2004b, 2004c; Voydanoff & Donnelly, 1999b). However, fathers who work full-time and mothers who work part-time are most likely to belong to voluntary and religious associations (Hertel, 1995), whereas women working less than full-time have higher rates of formal and informal community participation than women working full-time (Putnam, 2000).

This research suggests that time in paid work by itself is not a major contributor to family and community role performance and quality and individual well-being. The lack of consistent linear and nonlinear relationships may reflect an overall balance of demands and resources associated with time in paid work. Barnett (1998) has suggested several factors that may influence the relationship between time in paid work and various aspects of well-being, for example, gender, socioeconomic status, substantive job complexity, control over number of hours worked, and the nature and quality of nonwork activities such as household work and child care. Such demands and resources may account for the lack of direct relationships between time in paid work and family, community, and individual well-being.

The model in Figure 3.1 suggests that within-domain demands also are positively related to work–family conflict. Previous research reveals consistent positive relationships between time in paid work and work-to-family conflict (Bellavia & Frone, 2005; Byron, 2005). Time in paid work may be more strongly related to work-to-family conflict than to family and community role performance and quality and individual well-being because work-to-family conflict reflects an appraisal that long paid work hours make it difficult to meet family obligations. Thus, work–family conflict may be a more direct and immediate response to long work hours than family, community, and individual well-being are.

Nonstandard Work Schedules. In addition to time in paid work, the scheduling of that work may serve as a time-based demand. When individuals work during evenings, at night, or on weekends, they are not available to participate in family or community activities that take place during these times, for example, family dinners, meetings of community organizations, and informal socializing with friends and neighbors. This unavailability may be accompanied by decreased role performance and quality in the family and community domains as well as lessened individual well-being and increased work-to-family conflict.

Family role performance and quality (i.e., time caring for children and elderly parents, household division of labor, marital quality, and child well-being) show complex relationships with the work schedules of husbands and wives, the extent of overlap of husbands' and wives' schedules, and weekend work. Mothers who work evenings, nights, or weekends spend less time in activities with their children ages 5–18 than mothers working other schedules (Presser, 2003). Fathers working evenings spend less time with their children than fathers working day or night schedules. Weekend work generally is unrelated to fathers' time with children (Brayfield, 1995; Presser, 2003). Fathers also spend more time caring for their preschool children when their work schedules do not overlap with their wives' schedules and when both spouses work nonday shifts (Brayfield, 1995; Casper & O'Connell, 1998). However, the one available study revealed that nonstandard work schedules were not related to time spent helping elderly parents (Sarkisian & Gerstel, 2004).

Wives spend more time in household work when they work nonday or rotating shifts and their husbands work a day shift, when their work schedules do not overlap with their husbands' schedules, and when their husbands work weekends. Husbands spend more time in household work when they work nonday or rotating shifts and their wives work day shifts, when they are frequently not at work when their wives are, and when they do not work weekends and their wives do (Presser, 2003).

Research on relationships between nonstandard work schedules and marital quality and stability generally reveals weak relationships. However, under specific conditions, nonstandard schedules are negatively associated with marital quality and stability. For example, marital quality is lower for couples working nonday schedules than for couples in which both work day schedules. Working night and rotating shifts increases the likelihood of marital instability, but only for couples with children. Weekend work does not reveal consistent relationships with marital quality and stability (Presser, 2003). However, children whose fathers, mothers, or both parents work nonstandard schedules experience greater emotional and behavioral difficulties and lower educational and cognitive achievements than other children (Crouter & McHale, 2005; Han, 2005; Strazdins, Korda, Lim, Broom, & D'Souza (2004).

These mixed findings suggest that other aspects of family social organization may influence relationships between nonstandard work schedules and family role performance and quality. In future studies, scholars need to examine factors such as the time availability of spouses and parents, the coordination of schedules and family time between spouses, the use of resources such as child care provided by others, and individual characteristics. In addition, it is important to gain understanding of the processes through which nonstandard schedules may affect family outcomes.

Nonstandard work schedules also may influence community role performance and quality, individual well-being, and work-to-family conflict. No studies were located that examined relationships between nonstandard work schedules and community outcomes. Nonstandard work schedules generally show positive relationships to indicators of psychological distress and physical health problems (Totterdell, 2005); however, there are exceptions (Fenwick & Tausig, 2004). In most studies working a nonday schedule was positively associated with work-to-family conflict (Davis, Pirretti, Almeida, & Goodman, 2005; Kinnunen & Mauno, 1998, for women but not men; Voydanoff, 2005f; but see Fenwick & Tausig, 2004).

Strain-Based Demands

Time in paid work and nonstandard work schedules reflect time-based demands. However, strain-based demands also may be important in relation to family and community role performance and quality and individual well-being. These demands involve processes of psychological spillover in which work conditions are associated with psychological responses, which are then transferred into behaviors and attitudes associated with role performance and quality and well-being. In addition, strain-based demands may be associated with work-to-family conflict. Strain-based work demands are diverse and encompass several aspects of the content and security of a job, for example, time pressure, workload pressure, role conflict and ambiguity, emotional demands, and job insecurity.

Time pressure occurs when one does not have enough time to complete assigned work duties. Workload pressure exists when employees work very hard over a period of time to maintain a workload that is considered excessive. Role conflict refers to incompatible requirements or expectations, whereas role ambiguity is a lack of clarity regarding duties or expectations. Emotional demands consist of emotionally demanding interactions with customers and clients (e.g., complaints, impoliteness, and intimidation or dealing with death, sickness, and human suffering). Job insecurity is the perceived likelihood of involuntary job loss. These demands are associated with uncertainty, ambiguity, and lack of control, which may be expected to increase workers' negative emotions, stress, and fatigue (Wichert, 2002). These reactions may spill over into family and community life by limiting employees' interpersonal availability and ability to meet family and community responsibilities. This in turn reduces the quality of life in these domains and reduces individual well-being while increasing work-to-family conflict.

Trends in Job Demands and Insecurity.   The level of several of these perceived strain-based demands has increased over recent decades, for example, job pressure (i.e., time and workload pressure) and job insecurity. In 1997, 68% of workers in a national sample reported that their jobs require them to work very rapdily, compared with 55% in 1977. The percentage reporting that they never have enough time to get everything done on the job increased from 40% in 1977 to 60% in 1997. In 1997, 88% of workers agreed that their job requires them to work very hard, versus 70% in 1977. In 1997, 29% of workers reported that it was very likely or somewhat likely that they would lose their current job in the next couple of years, versus 15% in 1977. The level of job insecurity in 1997 was similar for men and women and for workers across occupational groups (Bond, Galinsky, & Swanberg, 1998). Job insecurity is higher in the United States than it is for the average of 19 mostly European countries belonging to the Organization for Economic Cooperation and Development (OECD) (Burchell, 2002).

Job Demands. The extent to which scholars have investigated the spillover effects of strain-based job demands on family and community role performance and quality, individual well-being, and work-to-family conflict varies according to the job demand and the outcome. Data on relationships between job demands and time in various types of family activity are limited to two studies of job pressure and time with children. These studies reported that job pressure generally was unrelated to mothers' or fathers' time in activities with children (Bass, Grzywacz, Butler, & Linney, 2004; Crouter, Bumpus, Head, & McHale, 2001). However, extensive research has documented that job pressure and stress are negatively associated with marital love, companionship, and adjustment and positively related to marital conflict and tension (Crouter et al., 2001; Haas, 1999; Hughes & Galinsky, 1994). In addition, studies have specified some of the processes through which this negative spillover occurs. For example, poor concentration, job exhaustion, depression, and psychosomatic symptoms mediate the effects of time pressure and role conflict and ambiguity on marital satisfaction for men and women in Canada and Finland (Barling & MacEwen, 1992; Mauno & Kinnunen, 1999).

Job demands generally do not show direct associations with indicators of child well-being (Repetti, 2005). However, they do have indirect effects that operate through job stress, parenting behavior, and parent–child relationships (e.g., fathers' job demands are related to job tension, which is related to parental rejecting behavior, which results in children's shyness) (Stewart & Barling, 1996). A study of mothers revealed a chain of relationships from work pressure to role overload, parent–adolescent conflict, and poor adolescent well-being (Crouter, Bumpus, Maguire, & McHale, 1999). Studies of daily stress transmission also reveal short-term effects of job demands on negative emotional states and irritability, which result in anger and withdrawal from interaction with spouses and children. These effects are greater for those high in negative affectivity, type A behavior, depression, and anxiety (Perry-Jenkins, Repetti, & Crouter, 2000; Repetti, 2005).

Research on strain-based work demands in relation to community role performance and quality is limited to two studies of negative work spillover and time pressure at work. Negative work spillover occurs when work demands create energy depletion, negative emotions, or stress. Men who report having little energy left after work are less likely to donate time to voluntary organizations than are men with a lot of energy left after work (Wuthnow, 1998). However, time pressure at work is positively associated with participating in community projects, attending club meetings, spending time visiting friends, and entertaining at home (Putnam, 2000). These mixed findings provide little guidance regarding the extent to which strain-based work demands limit community role performance and quality.

Extensive research reveals that several job demands (e.g., workload, workpace, and role conflict and ambiguity) are positively associated with psychological distress and physical illness (Marchand, Demers, & Durand, 2005a; van der Doef & Maes, 1999; but see de Lange, Taris, Kompier, & Houtman, 2003, for exceptions). A recent study of European Union countries demonstrated that high levels of job pressure have a negative effect on physical health (Wichert, 2002). Job pressure may have stronger effects on health for workers in lower-skilled than higher-skilled jobs. However, gender and personality factors, with the exception of sense of control, generally do not moderate relationships between job pressure and health (Wichert, 2002).

The psychological spillover associated with job demands also may increase work-to-family conflict by limiting employees' ability to meet family responsibilities. Previous studies show that workload pressure, time pressure, and role conflict and ambiguity are positively related to work-to-family conflict (Bellavia & Frone, 2005; Byron, 2005; Geurts & Demerouti, 2003). Although job demands do not have strong relationships with time in family and community activities, they generally show negative relationships with the quality of family life and individual well-being and positive associations with work-to-family conflict.

Job Insecurity. Perceived job insecurity is a strain-based demand that is expected to have negative effects on family and community role performance and quality and individual well-being because it threatens the economic well-being needed to participate adequately in family and community life. The few extant studies of relationships between job insecurity and family role performance and quality focus on marital quality and children's adjustment. Hughes and Galinsky (1994) reported that job insecurity was related to martial tension. As with job demands, job insecurity is negatively related to marital satisfaction through its relationship to job exhaustion and psychosomatic symptoms (Mauno & Kinnunen, 1999). Fathers' job insecurity also is related to children's shyness through job-related tension and rejecting parental behaviors (Stewart & Barling, 1996). Another study supported a model in which the job insecurity of mothers and fathers was related to children's perceptions of their parents' job insecurity, which in turn was related to children's cognitive difficulties followed by lower grades in school (Barling, Zacharatos, & Hepburn, 1999).

Job insecurity also may have negative effects on community role performance and quality and individual well-being. No studies were found that examined relationships between job insecurity and community role participation or quality. However, a recent meta-analysis revealed consistent positive relationships between job insecurity and mental and physical health problems. These relationships were stronger for mental than physical health problems and for those engaged in manual rather than nonmanual work (Sverke, Hellgren, & Naswall, 2002). However, gender and personality factors, with the exception of sense of control, generally did not moderate relationships between job insecurity and health. Job insecurity exacerbated the negative effects of job pressure on health in a study of nurses in the United States (Wichert, 2002).

Perceived job insecurity is a demand or stressor that may have psychological spillover effects on family life, thereby increasing the extent to which work interferes with family life. Studies show that job insecurity is positively related to work-to-family conflict for men and women (Batt & Valcour, 2003; Kinnunen & Mauno, 1998; Voydanoff, 2005f). Thus, job insecurity has negative consequences for marital quality, children's adjustment, individual well-being, and work-to-family conflict. Information is not available regarding its effects on family role performance or community role performance and quality,

In general, strain-based work demands show more consistent negative associations with family and community role performance and quality and individual well-being than time-based demands do. This may reflect, in part, our more extensive knowledge of the processes through which strain-based demands influence outcomes. It also may be that, because time-based demands may be one source of strain-based demands, the relationships between strain-based demands and outcomes are more direct than those for time-based demands.

FAMILY DEMANDS

As with work demands, family demands can be categorized into two types. Time-based family demands, which may detract from time and attention available for other domain activities, include time spent addressing family responsibilities such as caring for children and elderly parents and performing household work. Strain-based family demands, which may create negative spillover to other domains, are associated with family structure and social organization and include psychological demands from spouses (e.g., marital conflict), children (e.g., children's problems), kin (e.g., caregiver strain), and household work (e.g., perceived unfairness). These demands may limit work and community role performance and quality and individual well-being and increase family-to-work conflict.

Time-Based Demands

A high amount of time spent caring for children and elderly parents or in household work may result in resource drain because it takes time away from other activities. This resource drain may limit work and community role performance and quality and individual well-being and increase family-to-work conflict. However, time in family work also is accompanied by rewards associated with caring for others (e.g., sense of accomplishment and appreciation from others), which may reduce the negative effects of time demands on work, community, and individual well-being and family-to-work conflict. Therefore, the effects of time-based demands may reflect a balance between demands and resources associated with time in family work.

Studies of time-based family demands vary in the extent to which they are based on measures of actual time. Studies of caring for children often use proxy measures such as the number of children in the household and their ages. Some research on caring for elderly parents uses a dummy variable indicating whether any care is given, whereas studies of household work often measure the number or proportion of tasks performed by various family members. The amount of time required to care for children, elderly parents, and households varies according to need and the amount of care provided by others. Therefore, because the extent to which family work results in resource drain depends on the amount of time spent in these activities, this discussion focuses on time spent by husbands and wives in family work.

Trends in Time in Family Work.   Studies of trends in time in primary child care of children under age 18 indicate increases for both mothers and fathers between 1965 and 1998. In a daily diary study, mothers participating in child care reported an average of 100 minutes in 1964 and 135 minutes in 1998, whereas fathers' time increased from 41 minutes in 1965 to 96 minutes in 1998 (Sayer, Bianchi, & Robinson, 2004). These averages are higher than those for Canada, Germany, Italy, and Norway, especially for fathers (Sayer, Gauthier, & Furstenberg, 2004). Approximately one–third of adult children with at least one parent or parent-in-law aged 65 or older provided some type of time-based assistance to at least one of these parents in 1992. The percentages providing help and the average number of hours of help for those providing care in 1992 was about 30% and 100 hours for men and 33% and 150 hours for women (Hill & Yeung, 2003). The amount of time spent in household work has decreased for women from 31.9 hours per week in 1965 to 18.6 hours in 2000. Comparable numbers for men show increases from 4.4 hours in 1965 to 10.0 hours in 2000 (Bianchi & Raley, 2005). Time in household work is similar for White men and women; however, Black men spend more time in household work than White men do (John & Shelton, 1997). A recent study has documented increases in men's time in household work in several European countries over the past few decades (Hook, 2006).

Time Caring for Children.   Little is known empirically about the extent to which time caring for children reduces work and community role performance and quality and individual well-being and increases family-to-work conflict. No studies were found that considered relationships between time caring for children and work and community role performance and quality and individual well-being. One study revealed no relationship between time caring for children and family-to-work conflict (Dilworth & Kingsbury, 2005).

Time Caring for Elderly Parents.   Information on the effects of time caring for elderly parents on work and community role performance and quality, individual well-being, and family-to-work conflict also is sparse. Based on an extensive review and empirical analysis, Hill and Yeung (2003) concluded that time spent caring for elderly parents is not strongly related to several indicators of labor market participation including actual work hours, increases or decreases in work hours, time out of the labor force, time off from work because of the illness of others, and use of vacation time. Another study reported that time caring for elderly parents was not related to job satisfaction (Hammer, Neal, Newsom, Brockwood, & Colton, 2005). No studies were found that looked at community role performance and quality. The one available study of time caring for elderly parents and individual well-being found a positive relationship between time helping and caring for parents and psychological distress and depression, especially for women (Voydanoff & Donnelly, 1999b). Studies of family-to-work conflict report mixed results. Dilworth and Kingsbury (2005) reported a positive relationship between time caring for elderly parents and family-to-work conflict for the Baby Boomer generation (ages 33–51) but not for the younger or older generations, whereas Hammer et al. (2005) found no relationship in their study of those with children at home who also are caring for elderly parents.

Time in Household Work. The limited research on the effects of time in household work reveals mixing findings. Studies of time in household work in relation to work role performance and quality are limited to absenteeism and wages. One study reported that hours of housework were not associated with absenteeism (Erickson, Nichols, & Ritter, 2000), whereas another found that time spent in household work showed stronger negative relationships to hourly wages for women than for men. However, time spent in traditionally female tasks (e.g., cooking, cleaning, and laundry) was negatively related to hourly wages for both women and men. Thus, household tasks that must be performed daily and at specific times that are close in time to market work had negative associations with wages regardless of who performed them (Noonan, 2001). No extant studies have investigated time in household work in relation to community outcomes. In one study, time in household work did not show either linear or curvilinear relationships with psychological distress (Voydanoff & Donnelly, 1999b). However, another study revealed that time in low-schedule-control household tasks (i.e., cooking, cleaning, shopping, and laundry) was positively related to psychological distress for men and women, whereas time in high-schedule-control tasks (i.e., car repair, yard work, gardening, and household repairs) was not (Barnett & Shen, 1997). Once again, the nature of the household tasks was important. Time in household work generally is not related to family-to-work conflict (Dilworth & Kingsbury, 2005; Fu & Shaffer, 2001; Rotondo & Kincaid, 2005).

Thus, limited research indicates that time-based family demands generally do not have strong relationships with work role performance and quality, individual well-being, or family-to-work conflict. When significant relationships are found, however, they indicate negative effects. These findings suggest that family members are able to perform family work with limited adverse consequences for work role performance and quality, individual well-being, and family-to-work conflict. No studies have examined the effects of time in family work on community role performance and quality.

Strain-Based Demands

Strain-based family demands derive from performing the roles of spouse (marital conflict), parent (children's problems), and adult child (caregiver strain), as well as from performing household work (perceived unfairness in household work). Strain-based family demands are expected to reduce work and community role performance and quality and individual well-being and increase family-to-work conflict through processes of negative psychological spillover.

Trends in Strain-Based Demands.   Information from the 1995 National Survey of Midlife Development (MIDUS) indicates that the average respondent reported "some" marital disagreements (i.e., 2.12 on a scale ranging from 1 = *none* to 4 = *a lot*). When asked whether any of their children experienced seven health-related or social problems in the past year, the average number of problems reported was 0.84 (Voydanoff, 2005b). Data from the 1992–1994 National Survey of Families and Households (NSFH) indicate that 39% of mothers of adolescents reported that time in household chores was very unfair or somewhat unfair to them. The comparable figure for fathers was 10% (Voydanoff & Donnelly, 1999a).

Marital Conflict.   Studies of relationships between marital conflict and work role performance and quality address productivity, income, and job satisfaction. Marital conflict is positively associated with lost productivity at work, especially for men in the first decade of marriage. These relationships do not differ by ethnicity or education (Forthofer, Markman, Cox, Stanley, & Kessler, 1996). In a longitudinal study, Rogers (1999) found that increases in marital conflict were associated with increases in wives' income. In contrast, increases in wives' income were not related to husbands' or wives' perceived marital discord. In addition, increases in marital conflict were related to declines in job satisfaction for men and women. These effects were stronger than those from increases in job satisfaction to declines in marital conflict (Rogers & May, 2003).

Only one study was located that examined relationships between marital conflict and community role performance and quality. This study found that marital conflict was negatively associated with perceived support from friends and relatives and unrelated to the frequency of informal social contacts and attendance at club meetings or religious services (Cotton, Burton, & Rushing, 2003).

Studies of marital conflict in relation to individual well-being and family-to-work conflict reveal consistent effects. An extensive literature review has documented that perceived marital conflict and conflictual marital interactions are positively associated with several indicators of poor physical health, including objective health status, physiological data, and self-reported health. These relationships generally are stronger for women than for men. In addition, marital conflict is related to depression, which in turn is related to physical illness (Kiecolt-Glaser & Newton, 2001). Studies of relationships between marital conflict and psychological distress also reveal positive relationships (e.g.,Voydanoff & Donnelly, 1999b), whereas strained marital relationships are negatively associated with life satisfaction and positive mood and positively related to depression and health problems (Walen & Lachman, 2000). Marital conflict also is positively associated with family-to-work conflict (Bellavia & Frone, 2005; Byron, 2005; Geurts & Demerouti, 2003).

Children's Problems.   Another important strain-based demand associated with family life is the extent to which children experience physical, emotional, or behavioral problems. The few studies of the effects of children's problems on their parents' work performance and quality indicate that parents of children with chronic illness or disabilities have poorer self-reported job performance, greater difficulty concentrating at work, and more absenteeism. A recent study also has revealed that parents' emotional problems associated with children's physical health problems are associated with parents' limited productivity at work. This relationship is partially mediated by parents' limited opportunities to meet their own personal needs because of problems associated with their children's illness (e.g., feeding, eating, and sleeping habits). Similar relationships were not found for parents' reduced productivity as a result of physical problems associated with their children's illness (Grzywacz, et al., 2005).

Little empirical research is available regarding children's problems in relation to community role performance and quality or individual well-being. No studies were found of effects on community role performance and quality, whereas limited information suggests that children's emotional and behavioral problems are positively related to anxiety, depression, and psychological distress for men and women (Marchand, Demers, & Durand, 2005b; Roxburgh, 2005; Simon, 1998). In addition, children's physical, social, and behavioral problems and their associated demands on parents are positively associated with family-to-work conflict (Beauregard, 2005; Frone, Yardley, & Markel, 1997; Voydanoff, 2005b).

Caregiver Strain.   Little is known about relationships between caregiver strain and work and community role performance, individual well-being, and family-to-work conflict. No studies were found that looked at work and community outcomes or family-to-work conflict.

However, strain associated with caring for elderly parents is positively related to depression, anxiety, and physical health problems in studies of women (Martire, Stephens, & Atienza, 1997; Roxburgh, 1997; Stephens & Townsend, 1997).

Unfairness in Household Work. Those who feel a relationship is unfair to them are likely to experience anger or lack of control. Those who feel a relationship is unfair to their partners may feel guilty or may fear retaliation and punishment (Mirowsky, 1985). The extent to which perceived unfairness in household work influences work and community role performance and quality and family-to-work conflict is not known. However, one study indicated perceived unfairness in household chores was positively related to psychological distress for wives but not for husbands. Wives' perceived unfairness also exacerbated relationships between hours in household chores and psychological distress (Voydanoff & Donnelly, 1999a).

As with work demands, strain-based family demands are more strongly associated with work and community role performance and quality, individual well-being, and family-to-work conflict than time-based demands are. However, the pattern of the findings is less clear and consistent because many aspects of family demands have not been studied in relation to the outcomes of interest.

COMMUNITY DEMANDS

Community demands and resources differ from work and family demands and resources in that they originate outside of the work family mesosystem. The extent to which they influence work and family role performance and quality, individual well-being, and work–family conflict and facilitation as part of an expanded work–family–community mesosystem depends on the permeability and flexibility of the boundaries among the three domains. Conceptualizing a work–family–community mesosystem that incorporates community demands and resources presumes enough boundary permeability that some carryover from the community domain to the work–family interface exists. However, community demands and resources are not expected to be as strongly related to work and family role performance and quality and work–family conflict and facilitation as work demands and resources are (Voydanoff, 2005c).

Community demands can occur within the context of three aspects of community life: the local community as a whole, the neighborhood as a small geographically based area, and friends who serve as a major source of informal, nonfamily interaction. These demands may be either time based or strain based. Time-based community demands, which are subject to resource drain in relation to other domains, include time spent in formal volunteering and helping neighbors and friends informally. Formal volunteering is assistance provided through organizations and associations. It can be provided through mutual-benefit associations in which the beneficiary is the membership (e.g., professional and union groups) or through community-oriented service organizations that benefit clients or others outside the organization (e.g., church-related or fraternal organizations). Informal helping is assistance given to neighbors and friends. It is comparable to social support: that is, the provision of instrumental aid such as money, goods, and services; emotional support; companionship; and information such as advice or feedback.

Strain-based community demands, which are associated with negative psychological spillover, consist of living in a neighborhood beset with problems and perceived demands from friends. Neighborhood problems encompass high levels of crime and violence, abandoned or run-down buildings, inadequate local institutions such as schools, and lack of respect for rules and laws. Demands from friends include requests for assistance that are seen as excessive; conflictual social interactions; critical, irritating, and unreliable relationships; and negative behavior among children's peers.

Time-Based Demands

Time spent in formal volunteering in the broader community and informally helping neighbors and friends within informal social networks involves time demands that may limit role performance and quality in other domains, reduce individual well-being, and create work–family conflict. Time spent in formal volunteering and informal helping is a fixed resource in that time spent in such activities is unavailable for other activities. In addition, time volunteering and informally helping may be accompanied by other demands such as excessive obligations and lack of reciprocity, which may have negative effects on other domains and well-being. However, these activities also are embedded with resources such as access to instrumental and emotional social support, companionship, value consensus, role models, identity maintenance, and the rewards of helping others and the community. The social embeddedness associated with these resources may generalize to other domains. Therefore, time-based community demands reflect a complex combination of demands and resources. On balance, time-based community demands may not be strongly associated with work and family role performance and quality, individual well-being, and work–family conflict.

Trends in Volunteering and Informal Helping. The percentage of the popula-tion engaged in volunteering increased from 20.4% in 1989 to 27.6% in 2002. The rates are higher in both time periods for women than men, for Whites than for Blacks or Hispanics, and for college gradu-ates than for those with less education (Boraas, 2003; Hayghe, 1991). Although their rates of volunteering are lower, men and Blacks who do volunteer spend relatively high amounts of time volunteering. The an-nual median number of hours spent in volunteering was 52 in 2002. Men's median annual hours of volunteering are 52 compared with 50 for women, whereas Blacks' median hours are 52 compared with 52 for Whites and 44 for Hispanics (Boraas, 2003).

Information on time spent in informal helping is more limited. A 1995 study based on a national sample revealed that those providing informal help in the community averaged 3.4 hours per week, com-pared with an average of 3.6 hours volunteering. Time spent providing informal help in the community was greater for women than for men, for those with above-average incomes than for those with below-aver-age incomes, and for those with some college education than for those with no college education (Almeida & McDonald, 2005).

Time Volunteering. Little is known about the effects of time volunteer-ing on work performance and quality. However, Wilson and Musick's (2003) longitudinal study of women revealed that sustained volun-teering was positively related to occupational status. They suggested that this relationship may be explained by the skill development and social contacts associated with volunteer activity. They viewed paid work and volunteer work as mutually reinforcing. A second study re-ported a negative relationship between time volunteering and job sat-isfaction and no relationship to job stress (Voydanoff, 2005d).

Studies of the effects of time volunteering on family role performance and quality suggest that the results differ by type of volunteering. One study revealed that time volunteering for community-professional or-ganizations was negatively related to time in activities with spouses and adolescents for fathers but not for mothers. Time spent in organized youth activities was unrelated to time in activities with spouses for fa-thers and negatively related to time in activities with spouses for moth-ers. However, time in organized youth activities was positively related to time in activities with adolescents for fathers and mothers (Voydanoff, 2004a, 2004d).

A recent study revealed that overall time spent volunteering was not related to marital satisfaction or risk (Voydanoff, 2005d). However, another study reported that time volunteering in community and pro-fessional organizations was negatively related to marital happiness and unrelated to marital disagreements, whereas time in organized youth activities was not related to marital happiness or disagreements (Voydanoff, 2004d). Buchel and Duncan (1998) reported that frequent volunteer work was positively related to adolescents' educational attainment for fathers but not for mothers. However, parents' time in organized youth activities was not related to adolescents' grades or behavior problems in another study (Voydanoff, 2004e).

Information on relationships between time volunteering and individual well-being and work–family conflict is sparse. Thoits and Hewitt (2001) reported that time in volunteer work was positively associated with physical health and negatively related to depression in a longitudinal study based on a national sample in the United States. No known studies have examined time volunteering in relation to work-to-family or family-to-work conflict.

Time in Informal Helping.   Research on the effects of informal helping on work and family role performance and quality, individual well-being, and work–family conflict is even more limited than the research on time volunteering. No studies were located that examined relationships between time in informal helping and work role performance and quality. Information on time in informal helping in relation to family role performance and quality is limited to two studies. Moderate and high levels of informal helping were positively associated with time in activities with adolescents for fathers. However, informal helping was not related to time with adolescents for mothers (Voydanoff, 2004a). Frequency of informal helping was negatively related to adolescents' educational attainment for fathers but not for mothers (Buchel & Duncan, 1998). No extant studies have examined relationships between time in informal helping and individual well-being and work-to-family and family-to-work conflict.

These mixed findings for time volunteering and informal helping indicate that the balance between time demands and embedded resources varies by type of participation and outcome. In some cases the resources and demands embedded in community participation are either relatively balanced or are tilted toward demands. In others, the voluntary nature of community participation may allow individuals to adjust their participation so that they either maintain a balance between the resources and demands associated with participation or tilt the balance in the direction of resources.

Strain-Based Demands

Two strain-based community demands are relevant to the conceptual model: neighborhood problems and demands from friends. Community structure provides an important context for viewing neighborhood problems as a strain-based community demand. Contextual community factors include community socioeconomic status, population size and density, and levels of residential mobility, ethnic heterogeneity, urbanization, and family disruption. These structural characteristics are associated with community social organization, which is the context in which neighborhood problems and neighborhood cohesion develop. Community social organization incorporates several neighborhood characteristics, for example, physical and social disorder, the ability of a neighborhood to supervise and control teenage peer groups, and informal neighborhood social networks. The extent to which a neighborhood exemplifies these various characteristics influences the level of neighborhood problems and cohesion in a given neighborhood. Neighborhood problems encompass aspects of physical disorder (abandoned and dilapidated buildings, graffiti, noise, and vandalism) and social disorder (crime, drug use, alcohol use, people hanging out, trouble with neighbors, and lack of neighbor surveillance and police protection) (Ross, 2000). The experience and perception of living in a problem-ridden neighborhood is a potential stressor that may carry over to other domains by serving as a concern, a distraction, or a problem requiring concerted effort. This negative spillover may influence work and family role performance and quality, individual well-being, and work–family conflict. Neighborhood cohesion is a community enabling resource that is discussed in the next chapter.

High levels of interpersonal and emotional demands from friends also may spill over to other domains through the transmission of negative emotions, stress, energy depletion, and interpersonal unavailability. Such spillover may limit one's ability to address work and family responsibilities, which in turn reduces work and family role performance and quality and individual well-being and increases work–family conflict.

Trends in Neighborhood Problems and Friend Demands.   Information from the 1995 MIDUS survey indicates that respondents generally feel safe in their neighborhoods (i.e., an average of 1.37 on a scale ranging from 1 = *a lot* to 4 = *not at all*). The average respondent reported that friends "sometimes" make demands on them (i.e., 1.92 on a scale ranging from 1 = *never* to 4 = *often*) (Voydanoff, 2005b).

Neighborhood Problems.   Research on the effects of neighborhood problems on work and family role performance and quality is limited. No studies were located that have investigated the relationship between neighborhood problems and work role performance and quality. Research on relationships between neighborhood problems and family role performance and quality focuses on parental behavior and children's well-being. Neighborhood problems have a negative impact on parental warmth and consistent discipline and a positive effect on harsh interactions with children (Pinderhughes, Nix, Foster, Jones, & The Conduct Problems Prevention Research Group, 2001). In addition, neighborhood problems increase parent-child conflict, which in turn is associated with children's problems (Roosa et al., 2005). Research also has documented that neighborhood problems decrease adolescents' mental and physical health and academic achievement and increase their behavior problems (Aneshensel & Sucoff, 1996; Bowen & Bowen, 1999; Bowen & Chapman, 1996; but see Gerard & Buehler, 2002).

Several studies have revealed positive relationships between neighborhood problems and adults' depression and psychological distress (Cutrona, Russell, Hessling, Brown, & Murry, 2000; Ross, 2000; Steptoe & Feldman, 2001; Voydanoff & Donnelly, 1998). Neighborhood problems also explained the relationship between structural neighborhood disadvantage and depression (Ross, 2000). Another study documented that the relationship between neighborhood problems and physical health is mediated by psychological and physiological distress (Hill, Ross, & Angel, 2005).

Research on neighborhood problems in relation to work–family conflict is limited to one study. A narrow indicator of neighborhood problems (i.e., neighborhood safety) was not related to work-to-family or family-to-work conflict (Voydanoff, 2004c, 2005b). Neighborhood problems generally show negative relationships with those outcomes that have been investigated, that is, parental behavior and adolescent and adult well-being. Additional research is needed on work and family role performance and quality and work–family conflict before definitive conclusions can be drawn.

Friend Demands. As with neighborhood problems, no studies of relationships between friend demands and work role performance and quality are available, and research on family role performance and quality is limited to one aspect, namely, adolescent well-being. Recent studies have reported that adolescents who associate with peers who engage in negative behavior have higher levels of behavior problems and lower levels of psychological adjustment and academic achievement than other adolescents (Dishion, Capaldi, & Yoerger, 1999; Simons, Johnson, Beaman, Conger, and Whitbeck, 1996; Voydanoff & Donnelly, 1999c). Associating with deviant peers mediates the effects of neighborhood problems on children' problems (Roosa et al., 2005). These findings suggest that adolescents generally are quite sensitive to the behavior of their peers. Thus, peers who engage in negative behaviors, such as conduct problems and substance abuse, are likely to have a negative influence on adolescents. The socialization effects of peers through modeling, the sensitivity to evaluation, or a need for affiliation may explain such links. In addition, studies of the effects of friend demands on individual well-being and work–family conflict report that demands from friends are positively related to depression (Umberson, Chen, House, Hopkins, & Slaten, 1996) and work-to-family and family-to-work conflict (Voydanoff, 2004c, 2005b).

Taken together, this literature suggests that community demands are able to influence work and family role performance and quality, individual well-being, and work–family conflict. As with work and family demands, strain-based demands are relatively more important than time-based demands. Important gaps exist in our knowledge of how important these community demands are and the processes through which they influence outcomes.

THE COMBINED EFFECTS OF WORK, FAMILY, AND COMMUNITY DEMANDS

In addition to considering the effects of within-domain work, family, and community demands as separate contributors to cross-domain outcomes, individual well-being, and work–family conflict, it is important to consider how demands from different domains combine to influence outcomes. Many of the studies just discussed included demands from more than one domain as independent sources of a given outcome. This type of analysis implies additive effects of demands from more than one domain on outcomes. Some also have considered the relative importance of demands from more than one domain in relation to outcomes.

It also may be that demands from one domain partially mediate relationships between demands from another domain and work, family, community, or individual outcomes. For example, a work demand such as job pressure may limit participation in family-oriented community activities, which in turn is negatively related to family role performance and quality. No studies were located that examine such relationships.

Demands from one domain also may interact with demands from another domain such that exacerbating effects occur. Studies of moderating effects in which demands in one domain exacerbate relationships between demands in another domain and outcomes are sparse and reveal mixed results. Three studies indicate that family demands exacerbate the effects of job demands on outcomes. For example, in one study, job burnout was more strongly related to absenteeism for employees who had children under 6 in the home or had problems with their child care arrangements (Erickson et al., 2000). In a second study, marital concerns exacerbated the relationship between men's job concerns and psychological distress (Barnett & Marshall, 1992a). A third study revealed that time in household chores exacerbated the relationship between work role ambiguity and work–family conflict for men, whereas time in household chores and time in child care exacerbated the effects of work role conflict on work–family conflict for women (Voydanoff, 1988). In addition, community demands exacerbated relationships between job and family demands and work–family conflict in another study. An unsafe neighborhood exacerbated the effects of job demands on work-to-family conflict, whereas social incoherence exacerbated the relationship between marital disagreements and family-to-work conflict (Voydanoff, 2004a, 2004c). However, relationships between family caregiving demands and depression were not affected by job demands (Stephens & Townsend, 1997). In some of these studies, statistically significant exacerbating effects explained little variance and other effects were not statistically significant.

The results of these few studies suggest that the examination of relationships between within-domain demands and work, family, and community role performance and quality, individual well-being, and work–family conflict can be elaborated further by considering the combined effects of demands from more than one domain. However, the findings reported so far are merely suggestive and require further confirmation.

WORK–FAMILY CONFLICT AS A LINKING MECHANISM

In addition to the direct relationships discussed thus far, the model in Figure 3.1 proposes that within-domain work, family, and community demands are related to work, family, and community role performance and quality and individual well-being through work–family conflict. For this to occur, within-domain demands must be related to work–family conflict, and work–family conflict must be associated with work, family, and community role performance and quality and individual well-being. Previous sections of this chapter have documented the pattern of findings regarding relationships between within-domain demands and work-to-family and family-to-work conflict. This section discusses direct relationships between work-to-family and family-to-work conflict and work, family, and community role performance and quality and individual well-being and reviews the evidence regarding the extent to which work–family conflict is a mediator of relationships between demands and outcomes.

Work–Family Conflict and Role Performance and Quality and Individual Well-Being

The review presented earlier was based on the well-documented proposition that work demands are relatively strongly associated with work-to-family conflict, whereas family demands are relatively important for family-to-work conflict. The assumption regarding the relative importance of work-to-family conflict for family outcomes and family-to-work conflict for work outcomes is less established. Frone et al. (1997) and Greenhaus, Allen, and Spector (2006) have suggested that work-to-family conflict is related to family dissatisfaction or distress, whereas family-to-work conflict is associated with negative work quality. Thus, interference from the originating domain reduces the quality of life in the receiving domain. Others have proposed that work–family conflict is related to negative outcomes in the originating domain rather than the receiving domain. They have suggested that attributing blame for conflict to the originating domain leads to negative affect toward that role; for example, work-to-family conflict is positively related to job stress (Grandey, Cordeiro, & Crouter, 2005; Voydanoff, 2005d; Wayne, Musica, & Fleeson, 2004). Therefore, this section considers the effects of both forms of work–family conflict on both work and family role performance and quality.

Regarding the effects of work–family conflict on work role performance and quality, studies reveal that work–family conflict generally is negatively related to job performance ratings, whereas relationships to absenteeism, tardiness, and leaving work early are inconsistent and vary by the direction of work–family conflict and the attendance-related outcome (Allen, Herst, Bruck, & Sutton, 2000; Boyar, Maertz, & Pearson, 2005; Hammer, Bauer, & Grandey, 2003; MacEwen & Barling, 1994). Extensive research has indicated that work-to-family and family-to-work conflict are negatively related to job satisfaction and positively associated with job stress (Allen et al., 2000; Bellavia & Frone, 2005). Although both directions of work–family conflict generally are negatively related work role performance and quality, the relationships tend to be stronger for quality than for performance.

Relationships between work–family conflict and family role performance and quality have been studied more extensively for quality than for role performance. A few studies reveal that work-to family conflict is positively associated with family absences and tardiness, marital anger and withdrawal, and family withdrawal (Bellavia & Frone, 2005; MacEwen & Barling, 1994), whereas work-to-family and family-to-work conflict show consistent negative relationships to marital and family satisfaction (Allen et al., 2000; Bellavia & Frone, 2005). One study has documented that the negative relationship between work-to-family conflict and marital quality is mediated by psychological distress and the warmth and hostility associated with marital interaction (Matthews, Conger, & Wickrama, 1996).

In addition to the findings cited earlier that both work-to-family and family-to-work conflict are related to job and marital quality, other studies have shown that work-to-family conflict is more strongly related to job quality than family-to-work conflict is, whereas the opposite is true for marital quality—that is, family-to-work conflict is relatively more important in relation to marital quality than is work-to-family conflict (Grandey et al., 2005; Voydanoff, 2005d; Wayne et al., 2004). These findings contrast with the model of Frone et al. (1997), which indicated that work-to-family conflict was related to family dissatisfaction or distress, whereas family-to-work conflict was associated with work dissatisfaction or distress.

No studies were found that examine work–family conflict in relation to community role performance and quality. However, research on relationships between work-to-family and family-to-work conflict and mental and physical illness is extensive and consistent. Both directions of work–family conflict are positively associated with a wide array of indicators of mental and physical illness (e.g., psychological distress, depression, somatic complaints, physical symptoms, somatic complaints, chronic health problems, and obesity). In addition, work–family conflict influences physical health through it effects on mental health and health-related behaviors (Allen et al., 2000; Bellavia & Frone, 2005; Greenhaus et al., 2006).

Work–Family Conflict as a Mediator

Although not all within-domain demands are related to work–family conflict, and both directions of work–family conflict are not related to all aspects of work, family, and community role performance and quality and individual well-being, the dominant pattern of findings indicates that the requirements for the existence of mediating effects of work–family conflict on relationships between within-domain demands and cross-domain outcomes have been met in many situations.

Previous research has examined work-to-family conflict as a cognitive linking mechanism between within-domain work demands and cross-domain outcomes and individual well-being. A recent meta-analysis documented that work-to-family conflict partially mediates the effects time in paid work and a combined measure of several strain-based job demands on family satisfaction (Ford, Kitka, & Langkamer, 2005). One study also documented that work-to-family conflict partially mediated the relationship between job insecurity and marital tension (Hughes, Galinsky, & Morris, 1992), whereas another reported that time in paid work and job demands influenced family role performance and distress through work-to-family conflict (Frone et al., 1997). In addition, work-to-family conflict mediates relationships between a heavy workload and indicators of individual well-being (i.e., depression and health complaints) (Geurts, Kompier, Roxburgh, & Houtman, 2003; Geurts, Rutte, & Peeters, 1999). However, in a longitudinal study, work-to-family conflict did not mediate relationships between cognitive, emotional, and physical job demands and psychosomatic health complaints (Peeters, de Jonge, Janssen, & van der Linden, 2004).

Studies of family-to-work conflict as a mediator of relationships between family demands and cross-domain outcomes and individual well-being are limited. A recent meta-analysis documented that family-to-work conflict partially mediates the effects of total time in child care and household work and marital conflict on job satisfaction (Ford et al., 2005). The Frone et al. study (1997) also showed that children's problems influence job performance and work distress through family-to-work conflict. In addition, relationships between time caring for elderly parents and attendance-related work behaviors operate through family-to-work conflict (Hepburn & Barling, 1996). The mediating role of family-to-work conflict on relationships between other family demands and other aspects of work and community role performance and individual well-being have not been investigated. In addition, no extant studies have explored work–family conflict as a mediator of relationships between community demands and work and family role performance and quality and individual well-being. Despite these gaps, the evidence generally supports the idea that work–family conflict is a linking mechanism between within-domain demands and cross-domain outcomes and individual well-being.

SUMMARY

A portion of the general conceptual model proposes that within-domain work, family, and community demands are negatively related to work, family, and community role performance and quality and individual well-being and positively associated with work–family conflict. Within-domain demands are either time-based or strain-based. Time-based demands are related to outcomes through a process of resource drain in which the time spent in activities in one domain is not available for activities in another domain. Time-based demands include time in paid work (the number and scheduling of work hours), in family work (time caring for children and elderly parents and time in household work), and in community activities (time volunteering and informal helping). Strain-based demands influence outcomes through a process of negative psychological spillover in which the strain associated with participating in one domain is carried over to another domain. Strain-based demands include characteristics associated with the social organization of work (job demands and job insecurity), family social organization (marital conflict, children's problems, caregiver strain, and unfairness in household work), and community social disorganization (neighborhood problems and demands from friends). In addition to these direct effects, work–family conflict is a linking mechanism that is expected to partially mediate or explain relationships between demands and outcomes.

The pattern of findings revealed by research that addresses these aspects of the conceptual model suggests that strain-based demands are more strongly related to role performance and quality, individual well-being, and work–family conflict than time-based demands are. Time-based demands generally are either unrelated to role performance and quality and well-being or show weak negative effects on these outcomes, whereas they tend to show more consistent positive relationships with work–family conflict. The relative weakness of the effects of time-based demands on outcomes may derive from the ability of individuals to maintain a balance between the demands and resources associated with spending time in a given activity. Strain-based demands operate through processes of negative psychological spillover, which may be more difficult to prevent. Findings also reveal that work–family conflict partially mediates relationships between within-domain demands and role performance and quality and individual well-being. However, previous research contains large gaps. Many time- and strain-based demands associated with the family and community domains remain unexplored, and others have been investigated only for a few of the outcomes of interest. These gaps are especially large for community demands. Much additional work is needed to incorporate community demands into the conceptual model.

4

Within-Domain Work, Family, and Community Resources

The preceding chapter discussed within-domain work, family, and community demands in relation to cross-domain role performance and quality, individual well-being, and work–family conflict. This chapter reviews the theoretical and empirical literature regarding how and why within-domain resources are related to role performance and quality, well-being, and work–family facilitation. Figure 3.1 (presented in chap. 3) suggests that within-domain resources are directly related to work, family, and community role performance and individual well-being. Within-domain resources also are predicted to be related to work–family facilitation, which is a linking mechanism that is expected to partially mediate the effects of resources on outcomes.

Within-domain work, family, and community resources engender processes that improve role performance and quality, individual well-being, and work–family facilitation when they are applied across domains. They include enabling resources and psychological rewards. Enabling resources from one domain may generate resources in another domain that provide the means for enhancing participation in the second domain. Enabling resources generally are associated with the structure or content of domain activities, for example, skills and abilities developed through domain activity, behaviors associated with role activities, and the availability of social support from others involved in the domain. Enabling resources in one domain increase the competence and capacities of individuals to perform in other domains. For example, interpersonal communication skills developed at work, at home, or in the community may facilitate constructive communication with members of other domains. In addition, positive participation in domain activities may be associated with energy creation that enhances participation in other domains (Marks, 1977). This improved performance is accompanied by role quality, individual well-being, and work–family facilitation. Enabling resources include job autonomy, skill utilization, and workplace support in the work domain; family adaptation and cohesion and spouse and kin support in the family domain; and formal community support, neighborhood cohesion, and friend support in the community domain.

In early work on psychological rewards, Sieber (1974) proposed that rewards from one domain may facilitate participation in another domain. These rewards included privileges, status security and enhancement, and personality enrichment. Rewards also include psychological resources that are associated with feeling esteemed and valued and intrinsic rewards such as meaningful activities. These rewards may be accompanied by psychological benefits, such as motivation, a sense of accomplishment, self-esteem, and ego gratification. They may affect other domains through processes of positive psychological spillover. Positive transmission processes include positive emotional arousal, interpersonal availability, energy creation, and gratification (Piotrkowski, 1979; Rothbard, 2001). Psychological rewards considered here include meaning, pride, and respect associated with performing work, family, and community activities. A summary of within-domain resources is presented in Table 4.1.

Perceived work–family facilitation is a linking mechanism that connects within-domain resources with work, family, and community role performance and quality and individual well-being. Similar to work–family conflict, it is a cognitive appraisal of the effects of the work (family) domain on the family (work) domain. Work–family facilitation is defined here as a form of synergy in which resources associated with one role enhance or make easier participation in the other role. It can operate from work to family or from family to work. Work–family conflict and work–family facilitation are only slightly correlated with each other. Work-to-family conflict and work-to-family facilitation are either uncorrelated or show weak negative relationships to each other (Voydanoff, 2004d). Comparable weak correla-

TABLE 4.1   **Within-Domain Work, Family, and Community Resources**

	Work	Family	Community
Enabling resources	Autonomy	Family adaptability	Formal community support
	Skill utilization	Family cohesion	Neighborhood cohesion
	Workplace support	Spouse support	Friend support
		Kin support	
Psychological rewards	Meaning	Meaning	Meaning
	Pride	Pride	Pride
	Respect	Respect	Respect

tions are reported between family-to-work conflict and family-to-work facilitation (Voydanoff, 2005b). Grzywacz and Marks (2000) found that the four components of conflict and facilitation formed separate factors in a factor analysis. Thus, work–family conflict and work–family facilitation can be viewed as independent constructs rather than opposite ends of a single continuum.

In contrast to within-domain demands, which were considered in relation to work–family conflict in chap. 3, within-domain resources are expected to be related to work–family facilitation. The differential salience approach of Voydanoff (2004a, 2004b) suggests that within-domain demands and resources are differentially salient in relation to work–family conflict and facilitation. It posits that within-domain demands are positively related to work–family conflict, whereas within-domain resources are positively associated with work–family facilitation. Within-domain demands are relatively salient for work–family conflict because they are associated with processes that limit the ability of individuals to meet obligations in another domain. Within-domain resources are relatively salient for work–family facilitation because they engender processes that improve one's ability to participate in other domains.

The next three sections review work, family, and community resources in relation to cross-domain role performance and quality, individual well-being, and work–family facilitation. This is followed by an analysis of two ways in which demands and resources from different domains may combine to influence outcomes (i.e., resources from two domains and demands and resources from different domains). The final section considers work–family facilitation as a linking mechanism between within-domain resources and cross-domain role performance and quality and individual well-being.

WORK RESOURCES

Enabling Resources

Enabling resources include job design characteristics such as job autonomy and skill utilization and aspects of workplace support, namely, supervisor and coworker support. Job autonomy refers to the extent to which employees are able to decide how to do their jobs. Skill utilization enhances the development of skills and encourages creativity. These characteristics are associated with resources such as time management and problem solving skills, initiative, active learning, and self-confidence. They also contribute to a proactive stance that is associated with energy creation. Workplace support from supervisors and coworkers incorporates aspects of instrumental and emotional social support as well as a sense of community in the workplace. This support provides information and assistance in performing work duties, solidarity, understanding, acceptance, and praise. When enabling resources at work are applied to family and community activities and relationships, they are expected to generate resources that contribute to family and community role performance and quality, individual well-being and work-to-family facilitation.

Trends in Enabling Resources. Chapter 3 reviewed data from a study indicating that within-domain work demands had increased from 1977 to 1997. The same study reveals that job autonomy also has increased during this period. Compared with workers in 1977, more workers in 1997 agreed that they have the freedom to decide what they do on their jobs (74% vs. 56%), that it is basically their responsibility to decide how their jobs get done (86% vs. 80%), and that they have a lot of say about what happens on their jobs (71% vs. 59%). Opportunities for skill utilization also increased between 1977 and 1997. Higher percentages of workers in 1997 agreed that their jobs require them to learn new things (90% vs. 82%), that their jobs require creativity (76% vs. 59%), and that their jobs let them use their skills and abilities (92% vs. 76%). In 1997, over 80% of workers reported that their supervisors keep them informed, have realistic performance expectations, recognize when they do a good job, and are supportive when work problems occur. Large percentages of workers also agreed that they feel part of the group of people they work with (91%) and look forward to being with the people they work with each day (89%). These percentages are comparable to those reported in 1992 (Bond et al., 1998).

Job Autonomy and Skill Utilization. The available evidence regarding the positive effects of job autonomy and skill utilization on family and community role performance and quality, individual well-being, and family-to-work facilitation is quite consistent. Although job autonomy and skill utilization have not been studied in relation to family role performance, job autonomy is consistently related to aspects of the quality of family life, such as marital quality, quality of parent–child interaction, children's cognitive functioning, and fewer behavior problems among children (Greenhaus & Parasuraman, 1999; Perry-Jenkins et al., 2000). Job autonomy and decision latitude also influence parenting behavior and children's well-being through their negative association with psychological mechanisms such as negative mood at work and job exhaustion (Kinnunen & Pulkkinen, 2001; Stewart & Barling, 1996).

Little is known about the effects of job autonomy and skill utilization on community role performance and quality. However, participative work, which involves complex tasks, group decision making, and self-direction, has positive effects on community life. Attitudes, skills, and behaviors learned in participative work carry over into aspects of community life such as involvement in political behavior, leisure activities, and community organizations (Crouter, 1984). More recently, Wilson and Musick (1997b) reported that occupational self-direction was positively associated with volunteering for religious, educational, political, senior citizen, and other organizations.

Job autonomy and skill utilization also are important in relation to individual well-being and work-to-family facilitation. Both show positive associations with mental and physical health (Ettner & Grzywacz, 2001; Marchand et al., 2005a; van der Doef & Maes, 1999) and work-to-family facilitation (Demerouti, Geurts, & Kompier, 2004; Voydanoff, 2004b, 2004c).

Workplace Support. Having supervisors and coworkers that provide support to an individual performing a job also may generate resources that enhance family and community role performance and quality, individual well-being, and work-to-family facilitation. No extant studies have looked at workplace support in relation to family role performance or community role performance and quality. However, in one study, supervisor support was positively related to martial satisfaction through its negative association with job exhaustion and psychosomatic symptoms (Mauno & Kinnunen, 1999). Workplace support shows negative associations with psychological distress and physical illness in most, but not all, studies (de Lange et al., 2003; van der Doef & Maes, 1999). In addition, workplace support is positively related to work-to-family facilitation (Demerouti et al., 2004; Grzywacz & Marks, 2000).

Psychological Rewards

Psychological rewards, such as meaningful work, pride, and respect, are aspects of personality enrichment that increase self-esteem and gratification. The psychological spillover of positive emotions, energy expansion, and interpersonal availability associated with these rewards may contribute to family and community role performance and quality, individual well-being, and work-to-family facilitation.

Trends in Psychological Rewards. In 1997, 90% of workers agreed that the work they do on their jobs is meaningful to them. This is up from 83% in 1977 (Bond et al., 1998). The 1995 MIDUS study found that 88% of workers felt pride in their work and felt that others respected their work. In addition, 91% of respondents in the 2002 National Study of the Changing Workforce reported that they were treated with respect at work (author's calculations).

Meaning, Pride, and Respect.   Little is known empirically about the effects of meaning, pride, and respect at work on family and community role performance and quality, individual well-being, and work-to-family facilitation. A positive evaluation of one's performance as a worker was unrelated to anxiety and depression among a sample of mothers and fathers of young children (Greenberger & O'Neil, 1993). However, limited research reveals that meaningful work, pride, and respect are positively associated with work-to-family facilitation (Voydanoff, 2004b, 2004c). This sparse research literature generally reveals consistent positive relationships between enabling resources and family and community role performance and quality, individual well-being, and work-to-family facilitation. However, a lack of information precludes any empirically based conclusions regarding psychological rewards.

FAMILY RESOURCES

Enabling Resources

Comparable to enabling resources in the work domain, family enabling resources include aspects of family social organization and social support. Enabling resources associated with family social organization include family adaptability and family cohesion. Family adaptability represents the extent to which a family is able to alter its power structure, relationships, and rules in the face of challenges. Family cohesion is an affective component of family life that reflects emotional bonding among family members (Olson, McCubbin & Associates, 1983). These resources facilitate effective problem-solving within families. Instrumental and emotional support from spouses and kin provide empathy, understanding, and practical assistance. Such resources may enhance participation in other domains, thereby improving work and community role performance and quality and individual well-being and increasing family-to-work facilitation.

Trends in Enabling Resources.   Data from parents of adolescents interviewed for the 1992–1994 National Survey of Families and Households indicate that the average respondent reported agreement with items in a scale measuring family cohesion (i.e., means of 4.04 for fathers and 3.97 for mothers on a scale ranging from 1 = *strongly dis-*

agree to 5 = *strongly agree*) (Voydanoff, 2004a). Information from the 1995 MIDUS survey reveals that the average respondent reported receiving relatively high levels of spouse and kin support (i.e., means of 3.56 for spouse support and 3.42 for kin support on scales ranging from 1 = *not at all* to 4 = *a lot*) (Voydanoff, 2005b).

Family Adaptability and Cohesion. Almost no research addresses the consequences of family adaptability and cohesion for work and community role performance and quality, individual well-being, and family-to-work facilitation. The one exception is the finding that family cohesion was negatively associated with anxiety, depression, and psychological distress in two studies (Voydanoff & Donnelly, 1989, 1999b).

Spouse and Kin Support. No studies were found that examined relationships between spouse and kin support and work role performance or community role performance and quality. However, spouse support was positively associated with job satisfaction for men and women in one study (Roxburgh, 1999). In another study, personal and career support from spouses was positively related to career satisfaction for male and female business professionals (Friedman & Greenhaus, 2000).

Spouse and kin support generally are positively related to individual well-being and family-to-work facilitation. Research has revealed that emotional support from spouses is positively related to life satisfaction, positive mood, and regular physical exercise; negatively related to anxiety and depression; and unrelated to health problems (Grzywacz & Marks, 2001; Roxburgh, 1997; Turner & Marino, 1994; Umberson et al., 1996; Walen & Lachman, 2000). In another study, spouse support was negatively related to depression for women but not for men (Schuster et al., 1990). Emotional support from extended kin is positively related to life satisfaction, positive mood, and regular physical exercise; negatively related to depression; and unrelated to health problems (Grzywacz & Marks, 2001; Turner & Marino, 1994; Walen & Lachman, 2000). However, another study found a negative relationship between kin support and depression for women but not for men (Schuster et al., 1990). Emotional support from spouses and kin was positively related to family-to-work facilitation in one study (Voydanoff, 2005b).

Psychological Rewards

Psychological rewards associated with parenting and household work provide meaning, pride, respect, and recognition for parenting activities and housework. Through processes of positive psychological spillover, these rewards may be associated with work and community role performance and quality, individual well-being, and family-to-work facilitation.

Trends in Psychological Rewards. In the 1995 MIDUS study, 84% of respondents reported feeling pride in the work they do at home, 73% reported that others respect the work they do at home, and 81% felt pride for what they have been able to do for their children (author's calculations).

Meaning, Pride, and Respect. Data on the effects of meaning, pride, and respect associated with parenting and household work on community role performance and quality, individual well-being, and family-to-work facilitation is almost nonexistent. Positive evaluations of one's performance as a parent were negatively correlated with anxiety and depression among a sample of parents of young children (Greenberger & O'Neil, 1993), whereas household and parenting rewards were positively related to family-to-work facilitation in another study (Voydanoff, 2005b). Although the meager findings for family enabling resources and psychological rewards generally support the model, much more research is needed to form any firm conclusions.

COMMUNITY RESOURCES

Enabling Resources

Enabling resources in the community are generated through the availability and receipt of formal support from community organizations, neighborhood cohesion, and informal support from friends. Formal support is provided by community organizations and agencies (e.g., health and human service agencies, religious institutions, and schools), whose services are designed to meet the needs of community members. Neighborhood cohesion incorporates aspects of community social organization such as informal neighborhood social networks and a neighborhood's ability to supervise and control teenage peer groups. Support from friends is one type of informal social support, which may include resources such as emotional support, instrumental support, and support in the form of advice or information. Relationships among friends may be positive or negative, that is, they may be supportive or demanding. Supportive and demanding aspects may coexist as independent dimensions within a given relationship.

These enabling resources encompass social and psychological assets such as services from community organizations and agencies and assistance and understanding from caring friends. They provide practical assistance in meeting individual and family needs, access to other resources and support, social embeddedness, individual and group identity, interpersonal connections and attachment, and emotional sustenance. It is proposed that these resources increase the competence and capacity of individuals to meet their work and family responsibilities, thereby improving work and family role performance and quality, individual well-being, and work–family facilitation.

Trends in Enabling Resources. Information from the 1995 MIDUS survey indicates that the average respondent reported relatively high levels of neighborhood cohesion and friend support (i.e., means of 3.42 for neighborhood cohesion and 3.18 for friend support on scales ranging from 1 = *not at all* to 4 = *a lot*) (Voydanoff, 2005b).

Formal Community Support. Little is known about relationships between formal community support and work role performance and quality. A recent study developed a measure of a family-friendly community that incorporates several community features, most of which tap aspects of formal support such as recreational and educational opportunities, churches, and youth-oriented organizations, as well as neighborliness. Living in a family-friendly community was positively related to job and career satisfaction for men and women (Moen, Sweet, & Townsend, 2001).

Research on the effects of formal community support on family role performance and quality is limited to parental behavior, marital and family quality, and children's well-being. Parents' perception of the availability of formal support to obtain advice about a child's problem was associated with parental involvement but not with the frequency of parent–adolescent activities or parental monitoring (Voydanoff & Donnelly, 1998). One study reported that living in a family-friendly community was positively related to men's and women's marital and family satisfaction (Moen et al., 2001).

Information on children's well-being is more extensive. Studies reveal that resources associated with children's and adolescents' participation in organized youth activities influence child and adolescent well-being. Participation in organized youth activities provides supervised activities in a setting that encourages constructive achievement, positive modeling, and interaction with nonfamilial adults and reduces the opportunity for involvement with peers engaged in negative behavior. Children's and adolescents' participation in organized youth activities reveals positive relationships with academic achievement and negative relationships with child and adolescent problems (Eccles, Barber, Stone, & Hunt, 2003; Hofferth & Sandberg, 2001). Other studies report that parents' institutional connections with com-

munity organizations, schools, and religious organizations are positively related to academic achievement and involvement in
constructive social activities among young adolescents but show weak
relationships to psychological adjustment, self-competence, and
problem behavior (Voydanoff, 2001b).

Children spend a majority of their day in school. A positive school
environment encompasses adult relationships, a school climate, and
an absence of negative peer behavior that support academic achievement and psychological adjustment. Such an environment also provides sources of constructive modeling, evaluation, and support.
Thus it is not surprising that children reporting a positive orientation
to school, school connectedness, or perceived school quality are less
likely to engage in problem behavior and more likely to have higher
levels of school achievement and mental health than other children do
(Gerard & Buehler, 2004; Rodgers & Rose, 2002; Voydanoff & Donnelly, 1999c). In addition, a sense of belonging at school explains the
relationship between number of friends at school and fewer depressive symptoms among adolescents in one study (Ueno, 2005).

Little is known about relationships between formal community
support and individual well-being and work–family facilitation. Living
in a family-friendly community is positively related to perceived physical health and energy level (Moen et al., 2001). However, parents' perception of the availability of formal support to obtain advice about a
child's problem was unrelated to parental well-being (Voydanoff &
Donnelly, 1998). No extant studies have examined relationships between formal community support and work–family facilitation.

Neighborhood Cohesion.   Neighborhood cohesion has not been examined in relation to work role performance and quality and studies of
neighborhood cohesion in relation to family role performance and
quality, individual well-being, and work–family facilitation are limited. Neighborhood cohesion was positively associated with involved
parenting and parental acceptance in one study (Wickrama & Bryant,
2003), but relationships with parental warmth, harsh interactions,
and consistent discipline were weak in another (Pinderhughes et al.,
2001). Other studies have revealed that neighborhood cohesion was
negatively related to adolescent problem behavior and positively associated with adolescent depression. It also mediated relationships between neighborhood poverty and problem behavior and depression
(Aneshensel & Sucoff, 1996; Levanthal & Brooks-Gunn, 2000;
Wickrama & Bryant, 2003). In addition, neighborhood cohesion was
positively related to marital satisfaction and negatively related to marital burnout in one study (Stevens, Minnotte, & Kiger, 2005). Neighborhood cohesion also is negatively related to psychological distress

(Cutrona et al., 2000; Ross, Reynolds, & Geis, 2000) but unrelated to work-to-family and family-to-work facilitation (Voydanoff, 2004c, 2005b).

Friend Support. Studies of the effects of friend support on work role performance and quality are limited to one study, which reported that support from friends was not related to job satisfaction but was negatively related to job stress (Voydanoff, 2005d). Research on the effects of friend support on family role performance and quality focuses on its effects on parental behavior and children's well-being. A recent study examined a model proposing that parents' emotional support from their social networks is directly related to child well-being and that this relationship is mediated by parenting behavior and ability. The model was supported for some aspects of parenting and child well-being but not for others. The negative relationship between parents' emotional support and children's behavior problems was mediated by parental efficacy (Marshall, Noonan, McCartney, Marx, & Keefe, 2001). Other studies have revealed that parents' support from friends was negatively related to punitive parental behavior and positively associated with parental involvement (Hashima & Amato, 1994; Voydanoff & Donnelly, 1998). Parents' support also was positively related to several indicators of children's psychological well-being and academic achievement (Furstenberg & Hughes, 1995; Homel, Burns, & Goodnow, 1987), whereas support from peers was negatively related to adolescents' problems and positively associated with school achievement (Gerard & Buehler, 2004; Gonzales, Cauce, Friedman, & Mason, 1996; Rodgers & Rose, 2001). In addition, a few studies have reported that support from friends was positively related to marital satisfaction and negatively related to marital risk (Voydanoff, 2005d). Husbands and wives with overlapping or shared friendship networks had higher marital quality than those who did not Milardo & Allan, 2000).

Studies of the effects of friend support on individual well-being report that emotional support from friends is positively related to life satisfaction, positive mood, and subjective health, negatively related to depression, and unrelated to health problems (Turner & Marino, 1994; Walen & Lachman, 2000). However, friend support was not related to depression for either men or women in another study (Schuster et al., 1990). Limited research also indicates that parents' informal supports are negatively related to depression and positively related to life satisfaction among mothers and fathers (Voydanoff & Donnelly, 1998). In addition, support from friends was positively related to work-to-family facilitation but unrelated to family-to-work facilitation in one study (Voydanoff, 2004c, 2005b).

Psychological Rewards

Psychological rewards associated with the community domain, such as meaning, pride, and respect, derive from participation in community activities and the sense of community that may be associated with such participation. Positive psychological spillover associated with community psychological rewards is expected to create positive relationships between these rewards and work and family role performance and quality, individual well-being, and work–family facilitation.

Trends in Psychological Rewards.   Little data from large representative samples are available that describe trends in psychological rewards. However, the 1995 MIDUS study indicates that 82% of those who do volunteer work feel pride in their work in the community and 78% feel that others respect their work in the community (author's calculations).

Meaning, Pride, and Respect.   Only one known study has examined relationships between community psychological rewards and work and family role performance and quality, individual well-being, or work-to-family and family-to-work facilitation. Psychological rewards associated with being involved in the community (i.e., privileges gained, status security and enhancement, and personality enrichment) were positively related to organizational commitment and unrelated to job satisfaction (Kirchmeyer, 1992).

Although the strength of relationships varies according to dimensions of support and well-being, the findings regarding community resources provide modest support for the model. However, once again, the lack of research on several important dimensions precludes firm conclusions.

THE COMBINED EFFECTS OF WORK, FAMILY, AND COMMUNITY DEMANDS AND RESOURCES

Work, family, and community demands and resources can combine in three ways to form the work–family–community mesosystem. First, they can combine additively in relation to cross-domain role performance and quality, individual well-being, and work–family conflict and facilitation. Alternatively, characteristics from one domain can mediate the effects of other domains on outcomes. In addition, characteristics from one domain can moderate the effects of other domains on outcomes. This section discusses two types of mediating and moderating effects. First, within-domain resources from one domain may mediate or amplify the effects of resources from another domain to influence outcomes. Second, within-domain resources from one domain may mediate or buffer the effects of within-domain demands on outcomes.

The Combined Effects of Resources Across Domains

Research on the mediating and moderating effects of resources from one domain on relationships between resources from another domain on outcomes is sparse. However, one study revealed that a flexible parenting style (i.e., inductive discipline techniques and lack of harsh parenting behavior) mediated the associations of job autonomy with adolescents' self-efficacy for fathers but not for mothers (Whitbeck et al., 1997). Another study found that occupational quality, as indicated by several enabling resources and psychological rewards, influenced participation in community organizations, quality of marital relationships, and sense of personal control, which in turn were negatively related to health risk behaviors and physical illness (Wickrama, Lorenz, Conger, Matthews, & Elder, 1997). A third study examined the extent to which community resources amplify the effects of work and family resources on work-to-family facilitation. The findings revealed three statistically significant amplifying effects: Job autonomy was more strongly related to work-to-family facilitation for those with high support friends; the relationship between work pride and facilitation was stronger for those with a high sense of community; and friend support amplified the positive relationship between spouse support and family-to-work facilitation. These findings were merely suggestive, as none of the interactions explained even 1% of the variance in facilitation and other interactions were not statistically significant (Voydanoff, 2004a, 2004c). Thus, a few studies of a limited range of within-domain resources indicate that resources from one domain may combine with resources from other domains to influence outcomes in ways other than the more commonly studied additive effects.

The Combined Effects of Demands and Resources Across Domains

Much of our understanding of how resources may buffer demands comes from approaches originating in theories of occupational stress and family resilience. A review of these within-domain approaches provides a framework for examining similar relationships that may occur across domains.

Occupational Stress Theory. Occupational stress theory includes two approaches that are relevant to understanding the combined effects of demands and resources on outcomes within the work domain. The most prominent is the job demand-control model, in which job resources are expected to buffer the effects of job demands on job strain and individual well-being. This model is based on the assumption that the level of psychological demands combines with the level of decision latitude to influence psychological strain or physical illness and psychological growth. The strain dimension ranges from low demands–high decision latitude (low strain) to high demands–low decision latitude (high strain), whereas the psychological growth dimension ranges from low demands–low decision latitude (passive) to high demands–high decision latitude (active). Job demands focus on time demands, monitoring demands, and problem-solving demands, whereas decision latitude includes decision or task authority and skill discretion. Most research has focused on the strain dimension, which has been tested either by examining the additive effects of high demands and low decision latitude on psychological strain or physical illness or by considering whether decision latitude buffers the negative effects of psychological demands on strain or illness. Recently, social support has been added to the model as a resource that operates similarly to control in relation to job demands and health outcomes. The research based on this approach generally indicates that the additive effects of job demands, decision latitude, and social support are stronger than the interactive effects (de Lange et al., 2003; van der Doef & Maes, 1999).

The second approach focuses on rewards rather than enabling resources as a potential buffer. The effort–reward approach proposes that an imbalance between work effort and rewards (i.e., situations of high effort and low reward) leads to adverse physical and psychological health consequences. High effort results from the demands of the job or the motivations of workers in demanding situations such as need for control. Rewards include money, esteem, and status control (Siegrist, 1998). According to Theorell (1998), this approach provides the context in which the job demand-control-support model operates. If job demands are not balanced by decision latitude and control, the effort required due to the resulting strain disrupts the effort–reward balance. Research that examines effort–reward imbalance in relation to physical and psychological health outcomes generally supports the model (van Vegchel, de Jonge, Bosma, & Schaufeli, 2005).

Family Resilience Theory.   The family resilience literature views resilience as a process in which risks and protective factors interact in relation to a family's ability to fulfill important family functions such as family solidarity, economic support, nurturance and socialization, and protection. Risks that endanger these family outcomes include nonnormative family demands and the family's shared meanings of these demands. Family protective factors, such as family cohesiveness, flexibility, and communication patterns, may buffer the relationships between risks and outcomes. Individual and community level resources also may serve as protective factors (Patterson, 2002). For example, the family stress model discussed in chapter 2 that proposes linkages among economic pressure, parents' emotional distress, marital conflict, disrupted parenting, and adolescent maladjustment has been expanded to incorporate resilience processes that have additive and protective effects on the relationships in the model. Biological, psychological, and social resources are proposed to have direct effects on the variables in the model and to buffer relationships between variables in the model. R. D. Conger and K. J. Conger's (2002) review of research testing the model indicates that spouse supportiveness buffers the effects of economic pressure on parents' emotional distress, whereas effective problem-solving skills buffer the effects of marital conflict on marital distress. For children, nurturant involved parenting, social support from adults outside the family, and the quality of sibling relationships buffer the effects of variables in the mediational model on child and adolescent maladjustment.

The Buffering Effects of Within-Domain Resources. Few studies have examined the extent to which resources from one domain buffer the negative effects of demands from another domain on work, family, and community role performance and quality, individual well-being, or work–family conflict and facilitation. In addition, only a few of the possible combinations of demands, resources, and outcomes have been considered. Three studies have investigated the buffering effects of cross-domain resources on relationships between work demands and individual well-being. Voydanoff and Donnelly (1998) reported that family (marital happiness) and community resources (informal supports, formal supports, neighborhood resources, and a positive school environment) did not buffer the negative relationship between parents' long work hours and parental well-being. However, family resources (overall marital- and parental-role quality) did buffer the relationship between low job-role quality and psychological distress among men and women in two-earner couples in the other studies (Barnett, 1994; Barnett, Marshall, & Pleck, 1992).

The findings for work resources as buffers of relationships between family demands and individual well-being also are mixed. For example, job satisfaction buffers the relationship between hours spent helping parents and psychological distress for mothers but not for fathers (Voydanoff & Donnelly, 1999b). In addition, job rewards buffer the relationship between overall low parental-role quality and psychological distress among women (Barnett & Marshall, 1992b). However, more specific analyses indicate that the buffering effect is limited to one job resource (job challenge) as a buffer of the relationship between one aspect of parenting demands (disaffection) and distress (Barnett, Marshall, & Sayer, 1992). Stephens and Townsend (1997) found that women's job resources buffered the effect of caregiver strain on depression. However, in another study, women's work satisfaction did not buffer the relationship between caregiver strain and depression or physical health (Martire et al., 1997).

A final study revealed that informal instrumental support (i.e., friends and relatives who provided caregiving assistance or performed chores) buffered the relationship between family caregiving strains and work strains, whereas formal instrumental support and emotional support did not (Pearlin, Aneshensel, Mullan, & Whitlatch, 1996). These mixed findings suggest that within-domain resources may buffer the effects of within-domain demands on outcomes under some conditions. More rigorous research is needed to assess these conditions. Existing studies have used small and specific samples and measures with undetermined psychometric properties.

WORK–FAMILY FACILITATION AS A LINKING MECHANISM

For work–family facilitation to mediate relationships between work, family, and community resources and cross-domain role performance and quality and individual well-being, within-domain resources must be related to work–family facilitation and work–family facilitation must be associated with work, family, and community role performance and quality and individual well-being. The previous sections of this chapter have documented relationships between within-domain resources and work–family facilitation. This section discusses direct relationships between work–family facilitation and work, family, and community role performance and quality and individual well-being and reviews the evidence regarding the extent to which work–family facilitation mediates relationships between resources and outcomes.

Work–Family Facilitation and Role Performance and Quality and Individual Well-Being

Work–family facilitation is expected to be related to work, family, and community role performance and quality and individual well-being because the resources associated with work–family facilitation are thought to enhance role performance, thereby increasing role quality and individual well-being. There are few studies of relationships between work–family facilitation and role performance and quality and individual well-being. However, one study revealed that family-to-work facilitation was not related to two indicators of job performance (Carlson & Witt, 2004), whereas another showed that work-to-family facilitation and family-to-work facilitation were positively associated with job effort. However, although family-to-work facilitation was positively related to family effort, work-to-family facilitation showed an unexpected negative association with family effort (Wayne et al., 2004). The findings for work–family facilitation in relation to job, marital, and family quality were comparable to those cited in Chapter 3 for work–family conflict. Work-to-family facilitation was relatively strongly related to job quality, whereas family-to-work facilitation was relatively important in relation to marital quality (Voydanoff, 2005d; Wayne et al., 2004). No extant studies have examined relationships between work–family facilitation and community role performance and quality. Work-to-family and family-to-work facilitation generally show negative relationships to indicators of mental and physical illness (Grzywacz, 2000; Grzywacz & Bass, 2003).

Work–Family Facilitation as a Mediator

The limited findings presented so far suggest that it is possible for work–family facilitation to partially mediate some relationships between within-domain work, family, and community resources and work, family, and community role performance and quality and individual well-being. However, studies of such relationships are even rarer than those that examine direct relationships between resources and facilitation or facilitation and outcomes. No research was located that examined mediating effects for relationships that originate with work or family resources. One extant study investigated the mediating effects of work-to-family and family-to-work facilitation on relationships between community resources (sense of community, neighborhood attachment, and support from friends) and work and family role quality. Work-to-family facilitation is a more effective mediator in relation to job satisfaction and stress, whereas family-to-work facilitation is relatively important for marital satisfaction and risk. This indicates that not only do community resources have direct effects on job and marital quality, but they also operate through work–family facilitation to influence job and marital quality (Voydanoff, 2005d). These findings represent a relatively stringent test of linkages among the work, family, and community domains. Work–family facilitation is an appraisal of the effects of one domain on the other, rather than characteristics of a single domain. Thus, community resources must penetrate two domains simultaneously to influence job and marital quality through work–family facilitation. Such processes indicate relatively close linkages among work, community, and family life.

SUMMARY

The portion of the general conceptual model discussed in this chapter proposes that within-domain work, family, and community resources have positive associations with cross-domain role performance and quality, individual well-being, and work–family facilitation. Within-domain resources engender processes that are expected to improve role performance and quality, individual well-being, and work–family facilitation when they are applied across domains. They include enabling resources and psychological rewards. Enabling resources in one domain increase the competence and capacities of individuals to perform in other domains. This improved performance is accompanied by increases in role quality, individual well-being, and work–family facilitation. Enabling resources include job autonomy, skill utilization, and workplace support in the work domain; family adaptation and cohesion and spouse and kin support in the family domain; and formal community support, neighborhood cohesion, and friend support in the community domain. Psychological rewards are resources that are associated with feeling esteemed and valued and intrinsic rewards such as meaningful activities. These rewards may be accompanied by psychological benefits, such as motivation, a sense of accomplishment, self-esteem, and ego gratification. They may affect other domains through processes of positive psychological spillover. Psychological rewards include meaning, pride, and respect associated with performing work, family, and community activities. In addition to direct relationships between resources and outcomes, the model proposes work–family facilitation as a linking mechanism that partially explains relationships between resources and outcomes.

Empirical support for this portion of the model is limited. With some exceptions, studies of relationships between enabling resources and work, family, and community role performance and quality, individual well-being, and work–family facilitation document the proposed positive relationships. However, the few studies of the effects of psychological rewards on outcomes form an insufficient base from which to draw conclusions. The findings that resources from one domain can amplify the positive effects of resources from other domains or buffer the negative effects of demands from other domains in relation to outcomes are promising but inconclusive. More definitive information is needed to assess the extent to which work–family facilitation mediates the effects of within-domain resources on role performance and quality and individual well-being. These major lacunae in research on within-domain resources reflect the emphasis on job demands and work–family conflict in the work–family field. Only recently have scholars begun to explore the more positive and constructive aspects of the work–family interface.

5

Boundary-Spanning Work, Family, and Community Demands

Chapters 3 and 4 focused on relationships between within-domain work, family, and community demands and resources and cross-domain role performance and quality, individual well-being, and work–family conflict and facilitation. Chapters 5 and 6 address the effects of boundary-spanning demands and resources, respectively, on these outcomes. Boundary-spanning demands and resources differ from within-domain demands and resources in two ways. First, although both within-domain and boundary-spanning demands and resources may originate in the work, family, or community domains, boundary-spanning demands and resources have characteristics that are inherently part of more than one domain (Voydanoff, 2004b). For example, when individuals work at home or perform family activities at work, they are operating in both domains at the same time. When employers acknowledge and address employees' family needs through a supportive work–family culture and policies, the two domains are partially integrated. Second, boundary-spanning demands and resources influence outcomes through different processes than do within-domain demands and resources. Work–family border theory (Clark

2000), which is a more specific form of boundary theory (Ashforth, Kreiner, & Fugate, 2000; Nippert-Eng, 1996), provides a useful framework for understanding the processes through which boundary-spanning demands and resources influence outcomes.

Work–family border theory views relationships between domains as a continuum ranging from segmentation to integration. At the segmentation end of the continuum, the work and family domains are mutually exclusive categories with distinctive mentalities and no physical or temporal overlap. At the integration end of the continuum, work and family are indistinguishable in terms of the people, tasks, and thoughts involved (Clark, 2000; Nippert-Eng, 1996). Work–family border theory further posits that the extent of segmentation or integration is associated with the degree of permeability and flexibility of the boundaries between domains. Permeability refers to the degree to which elements from one domain enter into another domain, for example, an individual receiving telephone calls from home while at work. Flexibility is the extent to which temporal and spatial boundaries allow roles to be enacted in various settings and at various times, for example, flexible work schedules in which an individual can choose starting and ending times or vary these times to meet family needs. Segmentation is characterized by low permeability and inflexible boundaries, whereas integration is associated with high permeability and flexible boundaries (Clark, 2000).

The next two chapters use work–family border theory as a framework for investigating the effects of boundary-spanning work, family, and community demands and resources on cross-domain role performance and quality, individual well-being, and work–family conflict and facilitation. Despite recent calls from Frone (2003) and Bellavia and Frone (2005), few studies have used work–family border theory as a framework for investigating relationships between boundary permeability and flexibility and performance, quality, well-being, conflict, and facilitation.

Boundary-spanning work, family, and community demands and resources derive from the boundary permeability and flexibility associated with varying degrees of segmentation or integration. Boundary-spanning demands encompass boundary permeability across domains, whereas boundary-spanning resources incorporate boundary flexibility. This chapter addresses boundary-spanning demands, whereas the next chapter discusses boundary-spanning resources. The general model proposes that boundary-spanning work, family, and community demands have direct effects on cross-domain role performance and quality and individual well-being. The model presented in Figure 3.1 also posits that boundary-spanning demands are associated with work–family conflict and facilitation, which in turn are related to outcomes.

Low boundary permeability is accompanied by more difficult transitions across domains, which may result in decreased role performance and quality, individual well-being, and work–family facilitation and increased work–family conflict. Demands associated with difficult role transitions include overnight travel for work, commuting time, and the hours and schedules of community services and schools. High permeability is associated with role blurring or blending, in which distinctions between roles become unclear. Demands associated with role blurring include the performance of work responsibilities at home or family duties at work, permeable work–family boundaries, and work- or family-based community involvement. Table 5.1 provides a summary listing of boundary-spanning work, family, and community demands.

In contrast to the prediction of differential salience of within-domain demands and resources for work–family conflict and facilitation, boundary-spanning demands and resources are expected to have comparable salience for work–family conflict and facilitation. Boundary-spanning demands and resources also are expected to be related to both directions of conflict and facilitation; for example, work-based demands are expected to be associated with both work-to-family and family-to-work conflict and facilitation. Because boundary-spanning demands and resources focus on aspects of role domains that directly address how they connect with each other, the processes relating them to conflict and facilitation are expected to operate similarly in both directions and for both demands and resources.

The next section of this chapter discusses relationships between work-based boundary-spanning demands and family and community role performance and quality, individual well-being, and work–family conflict and facilitation. This is followed by an analysis of family-based demands in relation to work and community role performance and quality, individual well-being, and work–family conflict and facilitation and then by a discussion of community-based demands in relation to work and family performance and quality, individual well-being, and work–family conflict and facilitation. Then the combined effects of within-domain and boundary-spanning demands from different domains are considered. The chapter closes with a discussion of the role of work–family conflict and facilitation as partial mediators of relationships between boundary-spanning demands and role performance and quality and individual well-being.

WORK-BASED DEMANDS

Boundary-spanning demands involve trade-offs deriving from the continuum of segmentation to integration across domains. Segmenta-

TABLE 5.1   **Boundary-Spanning Work, Family, and Community Demands**

	Work	Family	Community
Role transitions	Overnight travel Commuting time	Commuting time	Hours and schedule of community services and schools
Role blurring	Work activities at home Work-to-family boundary permeability	Family activities at work Family-to-work boundary permeability	Work-based community involvement Family-based community involvement

tion is associated with low permeability or blurring between domains and an increased magnitude of the transitions from one domain to another. Integration is accompanied by high permeability or role blurring and relative ease of transitions across domains. Two work-based boundary-spanning demands focus on domain transitions associated with segmentation. They include space- and time-based transitions between work and home (overnight travel for work and time commuting between home and work). The work demands derived from the integration end of the continuum include role blurring associated with various aspects of working at home and work-to-family boundary permeability.

Role Transitions

Traveling overnight for work and spending time commuting between work and home increase the segmentation between the work domain and the family and community domains. This segmentation increases the difficulty of transitions across domains, which may limit role performance and quality across domains, decrease individual well-being and work–family facilitation, and increase work–family conflict.

Trends in Overnight Travel and Commuting Time.   In 1997, 21% of workers were away from home at least one night on business travel over the past 3 months. The percentage for men (27%) was higher than that for women (15%). The average was two nights away from home on business in the past three months (Bond et al., 1998). These figures are similar to a 1987–1988 study, which reported that 22% of workers had traveled overnight for business over the past 12 months, 30% of men and 13% of women. The median number of nights away on business for the past 12 months was 12 (Presser & Hermsen, 1996). In 2000, the average travel time to work was 25.5 minutes per day, up slightly from 22.4 minutes in 1990 and 21.7 minutes in 1980. Men had longer commutes in 2000 than women did, an average of 27.2 minutes for men versus 23.6 minutes for women (U.S. Census Bureau, 2004).

Overnight travel for Work.   Traveling overnight for work reduces the accessibility of employees to family members during trips and may create difficult transitions from one domain to another when leaving and returning. Frequent overnight travel also limits the availability of employees for family and community activities and may disrupt the rhythm of family life.

Little is known about the effects of overnight travel for work on family and community role performance and quality. However, a couple of studies provide some clues regarding family life. A qualitative study of women who travel revealed that the family division of labor was adjusted to accommodate their travel. Women prepared for their absence by activities such as preparing meals ahead of time and making to-do lists for other family members. During wives' absence, husbands and children performed household work ordinarily done by wives when they were home. Fathers also became more engaged in parenting activities. The women generally reported that family functioning was maintained rather than improved or decreased by their travel (Zvonkovic & Peters, 2003). A second study found that travel frequency was negatively associated with marital satisfaction for women but not for men (Roehling & Bultman, 2002). This research reveals adjustments in family functioning associated with overnight travel but provides little insight into effects on the quality of family life and no information on community role performance and quality.

Studies of relationships between overnight travel for work and individual well-being and work–family conflict and facilitation reveal mixed results. Two studies did not find a relationship between overnight travel and depression and psychological distress (Glass & Fujimoto, 1994; Voydanoff, 2005a). However, Humble and Zvonkovic (2005) cited studies that documented positive relationships between extended travel of 90 days or more and depression and health problems among travelers and their family members. Some studies have shown positive relationships between overnight travel and work-to-family conflict (Humble & Zvonkovic, 2005; Voydanoff, 2005a), whereas others have not (Batt & Valcour, 2003; Rotondo & Kincaid, 2005). In addition, research has not shown a relationship between overnight travel and family-to-work conflict (Voydanoff, 2005f) or work-to-family facilitation (Rotondo & Kincaid, 2005). Thus, the demands associated with traveling overnight for work appear to be limited in their effects on individual well-being and work–family conflict and facilitation.

Commuting Time.   Commuting time reflects the duration of the daily transition between work and the family and community domains. It has been viewed both as a time constraint and as a useful transition time. Commuting time reduces the amount of time available for other activities and makes it more difficult to leave one domain quickly to address needs in another domain. However, the time spent commuting also may serve as a decompression period after leaving one domain and a time for preparing to enter another.

Few studies have examined the effects of commuting time on family and community role performance and quality. However, one study reported that the relative commuting times of husbands and wives influenced time in household chores. Although wives spent more time in household chores than husbands regardless of commuting patterns, the gap between husbands and wives was largest when husbands had long commutes and wives had short commutes and smallest when husbands had short commutes and wives had long commutes. This study also found that commuting time was negatively related to family satisfaction for wives but not for husbands (Hofmeister, 2003).

Some studies have documented negative relationships between commuting time and individual well-being and work–family facilitation and positive associations with work–family conflict, whereas others have not. One study reported that commuting time was not related to psychological distress (Nomaguchi, Milkie, & Bianchi, 2005), whereas another found a positive relationship (Voydanoff, 2005a). Voydanoff (2005a, 2005f) found that commuting time was positively related to work-to-family conflict and unrelated to family-to-work conflict. Hofmeister (2003) reported a positive relationship between commuting time and work-to-family conflict for wives and a positive effect of wives' long commutes on husbands' family-to-work conflict. Another study found no relationship between commuting time and work-to-family facilitation (Rotondo and Kincaid, 2005). These findings do little to clarify the extent to which time demands accompanying long commutes are more important than commuting as a period of preparation and decompression in relation to role performance and quality, well-being, conflict, and facilitation.

The existing research on overnight travel for work and commuting time reveals similar patterns of findings. Both are associated with modest adjustments in family functioning and lower quality of family of life for women but not for men. The findings for individual well-being and work–family conflict and facilitation are mixed for both overnight travel and commuting time. No information is available for community role performance or quality for either demand.

Role Blurring

At the integration end of the continuum, work and family activities overlap, boundaries are flexible and permeable, and role blurring is high. For example, various aspects of performing paid work activities at home (regularly working at home, bringing work home, and being contacted about work at home) sometimes are considered as mechanisms for increasing flexibility regarding the temporal and spatial dimensions of work. However, performing paid work at home also may create role blurring, interruptions, and distractions (Ashforth et al., 2000; Nippert-Eng, 1996; Rau & Hyland, 2002), which may be negatively associated with family and community role performance and

quality, individual well-being, and work–family facilitation and positively related to work–family conflict.

Although one may posit that performing paid work at home is associated with role blurring, more direct assessments of blurring are
possible. These include three aspects of work-to-family boundary
permeability. First, performing work in the family setting may create
role blurring by creating situations in which work and family duties
converge such that individuals perform both at the same time (i.e.,
multitasking). Performing work activities at home also may increase
distractions such as psychological preoccupation with work while at
home and behavioral interruptions of work by family members. Thus,
the effects of other aspects of working at home (doing regular work at
home, bringing work home, and receiving contacts from work while at
home) may operate through their effects on work–family multitasking
and distractions. In addition, role permeability may be assessed by
asking individuals the extent to which their work, family, and community roles are segmented or integrated. This cognitive assessment of
boundary permeability also may partially explain the effects of behavioral indicators of role blurring on cross-domain role performance
and quality, individual well-being, and work–family conflict and
facilitation.

Trends in Work Activities at Home and Work-to-Family Boundary Permeability.   In 2002,
9% of workers from the National Study of the Changing Workforce reported working some or all of their regularly scheduled hours at home,
22% brought work home at least once a week, 21% were contacted about
work-related matters outside normal work hours at least once a week,
and 13% engaged in work–family multitasking at home often or very often (author's calculations).

Work Activities at Home.   Work activities can be performed at home in
several ways. Workers may work at home on a regular basis, may
bring work home with them at the end of the day or on weekends, or
may be contacted at home by supervisors, coworkers, or clients. Little
is known about the extent to which performing work activities at home
influences family and community role performance and quality. However, one study suggested that telework (working at home on a regular
basis via computer) has mixed effects on family life. It may facilitate
the management of household tasks and child care arrangements
(e.g., by overlapping household chores with work duties), increase interaction with family members, and facilitate dealing with minor family crises. However, the role blurring associated with teleworking also
may have negative consequences for family relationships. The study
indicated that both types of responses occurred (Hill, Hawkins, &

Miller, 1996). Other studies have found that those who work at home spend more time in household chores than those who do not (Hill, Ferris, & Martinson, 2003; also see Noonan, Estes, & Glass, in press, for a review). However, studies also have shown that for those only doing some of their regular work at home, the amount of time working at home is not related to time in household work for women or men (Noonan et al., in press; Silver & Goldscheider, 1994). One study has reported mixed findings for the effects of mothers' doing regular work at home on parenting and children's well-being. The number of regular weekly work hours worked at home was positively associated with the amount of time available to children on weekdays and shared meals but was not related to the frequency of mother-child activities, mothers' child-oriented community activities, discipline style, maternal warmth, or children's behavior problems (Estes, 2004, 2005). No information is available regarding the effects of bringing work home or being contacted at home on family and community role performance and quality.

Available studies suggest that the effects of performing work activities at home on individual well-being and work–family conflict and facilitation vary according to the way in which one performs work at home. Two studies reported that doing regular work at home was not related to psychological distress (Nomaguchi et al., 2005; Voydanoff, 2005a). Another found no relationship between doing regular work at home and work-to-family conflict; however, it was positively associated with family-to-work conflict and work-to-family and family-to-work facilitation (Hill, 2005).

Other studies have shown positive relationships between bringing work home and perceived stress (Hyman, Baldry, Scholarios, & Bunzel, 2002; Voydanoff, 2005a). Voydanoff (2005f) also reported that bringing work home was positively associated with both work-to-family and family-to-work conflict, whereas Roehling, Moen, and Batt (2003) found that bringing work home was positively related to both directions of work–family conflict and facilitation. In addition, job contacts at home are positively related to perceived stress and work-to-family conflict (Clark, 2002; Voydanoff, 2005a). Thus, it is important to distinguish among the different ways in which individuals work at home. When individuals work at home on a regular basis, they may establish structures and routines that prevent conflict and stress and create facilitation. These routines may be less prevalent for those who bring work home or receive job contacts at home in a less structured way.

Work-to-Family Boundary Permeability.   Only a limited number of studies have examined aspects of work-to-family boundary permeability (i.e., multitasking, distractions, and perceived work-to-family boundary permeability) in relation to the outcomes of interest here. Voydanoff (2005a) found that multitasking on work and family activities at home was positively associated with psychological distress and work-to-family conflict. It also partially mediated the negative effects of bringing work home and job contacts at home on distress and conflict. Another study reported that a combined measure of psychological distractions and behavioral interruptions from work while at home was negatively related to job satisfaction and unrelated to perceived family performance (Cardenas, Major, & Bernas, 2004).

Scholars are just beginning to develop measures of perceived work-to-family boundary permeability and examine its effects. A recent study used a measure of work-to-family boundary permeability that included questions about various aspects of working at home and distractions. It found that high boundary permeability was unrelated to perceived job performance and positively related to psychological strain, work-to-family conflict, and family-to-work conflict (Hecht & Allen, 2004a, 2004b). A second study reported that work-to-family boundary permeability was positively to work-to-family conflict (Clark, 2002).

These findings suggest that it is important to consider the processes through which various types of working at home influence family and community role performance and quality, individual well-being, and work–family conflict and facilitation. For example, work–family multitasking partially mediates the effects of bringing work home and job contacts at home on psychological distress and work-to-family conflict (Voydanoff, 2005a). This suggests that multitasking is one mechanism through which working at home influences individual well-being and work–family conflict. Future research may document additional aspects of work-to-family boundary permeability that influence the effects of working at home on outcomes.

FAMILY-BASED DEMANDS

As with work-based boundary-spanning demands, family-based demands can be considered in terms of the difficulty of role transitions and the extent of role blurring. These demands are comparable to those discussed earlier as work-based demands. Family-based role transitions include commuting time, whereas role-blurring demands consist of the performance of family activities at work and family-to-work boundary permeability. These demands may limit work and community role performance and quality, individual well-being, and work–family facilitation and increase work–family conflict.

Role Transitions

The last section considered commuting time as a work-based demand with relationships to family role performance and quality, individual well-being, and work–family conflict and facilitation. However, it also is possible to view commuting time as a family-based demand. A daily commute begins with a trip to work in which an individual may decompress from preparatory family activities and prepare to enter the work domain. The trip home may serve the same purposes in the reverse direction. The duration of the commute may have effects on both domains. As a work-based demand, commuting time was shown to have modest effects on family role performance and quality. As a family-based demand, it also may have effects on work performance and quality. However, no studies were found that examined effects on work. It is possible that one direction of a commute is more difficult than the other in terms of the amount of traffic and time, the level and type of decompression and preparation, and auxiliary activities such as errands performed on the way to work or on the way home. In this case the direction of commute may have different effects on individual well-being and work–family conflict and facilitation. Once again, no information is available on this issue.

Role Blurring

Similar to work-based role blurring, the performance of family activities at work and family-to-work boundary permeability may have negative consequences for work and community role performance and quality, individual well-being, and work–family conflict and facilitation.

Trends in Family Activities at Work and Family-to-Work Boundary Permeability. No information based on large representative samples was located that reported trends in family activities at work and family-to-work boundary permeability.

Family Activities at Work. Although workers may be more likely to engage in work activities at home than family activities at work, several types of family activities may be performed at work, for example, receiving telephone calls and e-mails from family members, discussing family issues with coworkers, and performing family activities such as paying bills, making appointments, and online shopping. However, only one known study has examined relationships between these activities and the outcomes of interest. This study reported that a boundary management scale that focused mainly on addressing family and personal issues at work showed a statistically significant positive relationship to family-to-work conflict and a nonsignificant positive association with work-to-family conflict for a sample of professional workers (Kossek, Lautsch, & Eaton, 2006).

Family-to-Work Boundary Permeability. Family-to-work permeability includes three components comparable to those for work-to-family permeability: multitasking at work, distractions, and perceived family-to-work boundary permeability. Almost no information is available on relationships between these aspects of boundary permeability and work and community role performance, individual well-being, and work–family conflict and facilitation. No known studies have examined the consequences of multitasking at work. One study that used a combined measure of psychological distractions and behavioral interruptions from family members while at work found the measure was unrelated to perceived job performance (Cardenas et al., 2004). Another study, which measured family-to-work boundary permeability with items addressing psychological distractions and behavioral interruptions by family members at work, found that high boundary permeability was negatively related to perceived job performance, positively related to family-to-work conflict, and unrelated to work-to-family conflict (Hecht & Allen, 2004a, 2004b). Another study also reported that family-to-work boundary permeability was not related to work-to-family conflict (Clark, 2002).

The findings of these few studies are not consistent enough to draw conclusions about the consequences of family-based boundary spanning demands. The effects of these demands on work performance and quality and work–family conflict are mixed. No studies have examined family-based demands in relation to community role performance and quality, individual well-being, or work–family facilitation.

COMMUNITY-BASED DEMANDS

Community-based boundary-spanning demands focus on the interface between the community and other domains rather than on characteristics specifically associated with community activities. They involve trade-offs deriving from the continuum of segmentation to integration across domains. At the segmentation end of the continuum, community, work, and family roles are quite separate, boundaries are impermeable, and role blurring is low. For example, when the hours of community service organizations and schools are incompatible with paid work hours, working families find it difficult to access services and to provide care for their children outside of school hours. This incompatibility may have negative effects on work and family role performance and quality, individual well-being, and work–family conflict and facilitation. At the integration end of the continuum, community and work or family activities overlap, boundaries are permeable, and role blurring is high. For example, participating in community activities that are integrated with work or family activities (e.g., work-based volunteering or participation in organized youth activities) may facilitate transitions across domains. However, the time involved may interfere with other work and family duties, and psychological involvement, preoccupation, and interruptions may spill over across domains (Ashforth et al., 2000; Nippert-Eng, 1996).

Trends in Community-Based Demands

Information on trends in hours and schedules of community services and schools in relation to work and family schedules is limited. In 2001, 20% of kindergarten through eighth-grade children spent time alone or were cared for by nonparents before school, whereas 50% spent time alone or with nonparents after school. The average time per week in these arrangements was 4.7 hours before school and 9.0 hours after school (U.S. Department of Education, 2004). No information was located regarding trends in work-based community involvement. In 1997, children between the ages of 6 and 12 spent an average of 3.2 hours per week participating in organized activities (e.g., sports, cultural pursuits, religiously sponsored activities, and groups such as Girl Scouts). Participation was higher among children whose mothers had at least a college education. Participation in several activities has grown between 1985 and 1997, for example the amount of time in sports has increased 35% (Weininger & Lareau, 2002). Weininger and Lareau estimate that each hour of a child's participation involves at least 40 minutes of work on the part of the child's mother.

Role Transitions

Despite anecdotal information, few empirical studies have examined the consequences of the mismatch of hours and schedules across the work, family, and community domains for work, family, and individual outcomes. Barnett and Gareis (2006) have reported that the amount of time children spend unsupervised after school hours, which is a function of the mismatch of work and school schedules, is positively correlated with parental concern about after-school time (PCAST). PCAST is an aspect of family-to-work conflict consisting of parents' concerns about their ability to have contact with their children after school while they are still at work, the safety and productivity of their children's time after school, and the logistics and quality of their children's after school arrangements.

Role Blurring

Role blurring occurs when community activities pervade or intrude on work or family activities. For example, although work-based volunteering generally is considered beneficial to work organizations, extensive volunteering may limit the ability of the individuals involved to perform other work duties. Participation in family-based community activities, such as children's sports and other organized activities, may make it difficult to limit the influence of the activity on family life. Such blurring may make it more difficult to coordinate work and family activities, thereby negatively affecting work and family role performance and quality, individual well-being, and work–family conflict facilitation.

No studies were located that specifically examined such relationships. However, qualitative studies have documented that children's participation in organized youth activities is extensive, especially in middle-class families, and is associated with crowded schedules and time pressures on both children and parents. In addition, parents, especially mothers, were involved in remembering schedules, providing transportation, and seeing that supplies and equipment were available (Lareau, 2000). This research provides initial glimpses into the multiple ways in which community-based boundary-spanning demands may influence the combined effects of the work, family, and community domains on work and family role participation and quality, individual well-being, and work–family conflict and facilitation.

THE COMBINED EFFECTS OF WITHIN-DOMAIN AND BOUNDARY-SPANNING DEMANDS

Within-domain and boundary-spanning work, family, and community demands and resources can combine in three ways to form the work–family-community mesosystem. First, they can combine additively in relation to cross-domain role performance and quality, individual well-being, and work–family conflict and facilitation. Several of the studies cited in earlier sections of this chapter have considered the combined effects of within-domain and boundary-spanning demands on outcomes. These studies reveal that both types of work demands combine additively to influence outcomes, for example, paid work hours, nonday work schedule, workload pressure, job insecurity, overnight travel for work, commuting time, and bringing work home, are positively related to work-to-family conflict (Voydanoff, 2005f). Second, within-domain and boundary-spanning demands from one domain may mediate the effects of demands from other domains on outcomes. In addition, demands from one domain may exacerbate the effects of demands from other domains on outcomes. Only one study looked at such effects. Sonnentag and Bayer (2005) found that long work hours and work pressure were positively associated with preoccupation with work while at home, which in turn was negatively related to positive mood and positively related to fatigue at bedtime. Moreover, work pressure exacerbated the positive relationship between psychological preoccupation and fatigue.

WORK–FAMILY CONFLICT AND FACILITATION AS LINKING MECHANISMS

If boundary-spanning demands are related to work–family conflict and facilitation, and conflict and facilitation are related to work, family, and community performance and quality and individual well-being, it is possible that conflict and facilitation mediate relationships between boundary-spanning demands and outcomes. Although these direct relationships have been documented earlier in this chapter, little is known about the extent to which mediating effects occur. However, one study has shown that the effects of commuting time and work–family multitasking on perceived stress are reduced to nonsignificance when work-to-family conflict is included in the regression equation (Voydanoff, 2005a).

SUMMARY

This chapter addresses the portion of the conceptual model that proposes that work-, family-, and community-based boundary-spanning demands are negatively related to work, family, and community role performance and quality and individual well-being. It also predicts that these relationships are partially mediated by work–family conflict and facilitation. Boundary-spanning demands differ from within-domain demands in that they are inherently part of more than one domain. They are proposed to influence role performance and quality, well-being, and conflict and facilitation through processes associated with the extent of cross-domain segmentation and integration. Segmentation creates difficulty in making transitions from one domain to another, whereas integration is accompanied by cross-domain role blurring. Boundary-spanning demands associated with role transitions include overnight travel for work, commuting time, and the hours and schedules of community services and schools. Role blurring demands consist of the performance of work activities at home and family activities at work, work-to-family and family-to-work boundary permeability, and work-based and family-based community involvement.

Few studies have examined relationships between boundary-spanning demands and cross-domain role performance and quality, individual well-being, or work–family conflict and facilitation. Existing research suggests that the effects of work-based role transition demands on role performance and quality are modest. Findings for individual well-being and work–family conflict and facilitation are mixed. Some studies indicate that role transition demands are positively associated with work–family conflict and negatively related to individual well-being and work–family facilitation, whereas others report no significant relationships. More consistent information is available for work-based role blurring demands. Although performing work at home on a regular basis generally is not related to family role performance and quality, individual well-being, or work–family conflict and facilitation, several characteristics associated with working at home are. These include bringing work home, receiving job contacts at home, multitasking work and family activities at home, experiencing distractions while working at home, and perceiving high work-to-family boundary permeability. More definitive conclusions regarding the consequences of work-based boundary-spanning demands for work, families, communities, and individuals await further study. Moreover, the lack of information about the effects of family-based and community-based boundary-spanning demands precludes informed discussion regarding their effects.

6

Boundary-Spanning Work, Family, and Community Resources

Chapter 5 discussed boundary-spanning work, family, and community demands in relation to cross-domain role performance and quality, individual well-being, and work–family conflict and facilitation. This chapter reviews the theoretical and empirical literature regarding how and why boundary-spanning resources are related to role performance and quality, well-being, and work–family conflict and facilitation. Boundary-spanning resources are expected to be directly associated with work, family, and community role performance and individual well-being. In addition, Figure 3.1 suggests that boundary-spanning resources influence work–family conflict and facilitation. These linking mechanisms are expected to partially mediate relationships between resources and outcomes.

Boundary-spanning resources address how work, family, and community domains connect with each other in terms of boundary flexibility. Boundary flexibility refers to the degree to which temporal and spatial boundaries permit role activities to be performed in various settings and at various times, that is, flexibility regarding when and where activities are performed. Work-based boundary-spanning resources include the availability of workplace policies and programs that enhance the flexibility of the temporal boundary between work and family. These policies and programs may improve flexibility in two ways: work supports and family supports (Drago & Hyatt, 2003; Glass & Finley, 2002; Lambert, 1993). Work supports (e.g., flexible work schedules and dependent care benefits) help employees accommodate their family responsibilities without reducing work hours or the amount of work that is performed. Family supports (e.g., parental leave, the ability to take time off from work for family responsibilities, and part-time work) enhance flexibility by reducing an individual's time at work. In addition, normative support can increase boundary flexibility by providing organizational support for workers to use these policies and programs to coordinate work and family obligations and activities.

Family-based and community-based boundary-spanning resources also include work supports, family supports, and normative support. Spouses and kin can increase the ability of individuals to meet the temporal demands of their work roles by performing additional dependent care and household work activities, which frees up time for work activities. In addition, one spouse may be the major provider so that the other spouse can devote more time to family activities. Community programs (e.g., child-care and after-school programs) provide a similar type of support by caring for family members when individuals are at work. Family and community members and friends also may provide normative support to individuals who are attempting to combine work and family activities by acknowledging the value of such attempts and giving instrumental and emotional social support. Boundary-spanning resources may enhance cross-domain role performance and quality, individual well-being, and work–family facilitation and reduce work–family conflict through increased flexibility of the temporal boundary between work and home, legitimacy for the use of work–family policies, spouse and kin assistance, community-based programs, and normative work–family support from family, community, and friends. Boundary-spanning resources are summarized in Table 6.1.

As with boundary-spanning demands, the conceptual model indicates that boundary-spanning resources have comparable salience for work–family conflict and facilitation. Boundary-spanning resources are expected to be negatively related to work–family conflict and positively associated with work–family facilitation. Boundary-spanning resources may reduce work–family conflict and increase work–family facilitation through interrelated processes that enhance workers' perceived control over managing the work–family boundary and legitimize the use of work–family policies. Because

TABLE 6.1   **Boundary-Spanning Work, Family, and Community Resources**

	Work	*Family*	*Community*
Work supports	Flexible work schedules	Spouse and kin dependent care	Child-care programs
	Dependent care benefits	Spouse and kin household work	After-school programs
Family supports	Time off for family	Spouse employment	
	Part-time work		
Normative support	Supportive work-family culture	Spouse and kin work-family support	Community work-family support
	Supervisor work-family support		Friend work-family support

boundary-spanning resources encompass the boundaries across the work and family domains, they also are expected to influence both di rections of work–family conflict and facilitation.

The next section of this chapter discusses relationships between work-based boundary-spanning resources and family and community role performance and quality, individual well-being, and work–family conflict and facilitation. This is followed by an analysis of family-based resources in relation to cross-domain role performance and quality, individual well-being, and work–family conflict and facilitation and then by a discussion of relationships between community-based resources and cross-domain performance and quality, well-being, and conflict and facilitation. Then the combined effects of within-domain demands and resources and boundary-spanning resources from different domains are considered. The chapter closes with a discussion of the role of work–family conflict and facilitation as partial mediators of relationships between boundary-spanning resources and role performance and quality and individual well-being.

WORK-BASED RESOURCES

Work Supports

Research on the effects of the availability of a range of work–family policies on family role performance, individual well-being, and work–family conflict and facilitation has revealed mixed results. Some studies have found negative relationships with perceived stress (Hill, 2005; Tang & MacDermid, 2005) and work-to-family conflict and facilitation (Allen, 2001; Hill, 2005; Judge, Boudreau, & Bretz, 1994; Thompson, Beauvais, & Lyness, 1999), whereas others have reported no relationship to time in household work, perceived stress, or work–family conflict and facilitation (Batt & Valcour, 2003; Estes, Maume, & Noonan, 2005; Hill, 2005; Jahn, Thompson, Kopelman, & Prottas, 2001; O'Driscoll et al., 2003; Silver & Goldscheider, 1994; Thompson & Prottas, 2006). However, by incorporating a broad range of policies into one measure, the findings may mask the effects of different types of policies on outcomes. The results become more consistent when a distinction is made between work support and family support policies and programs. Therefore, these findings are discussed separately here.

Trends in Flexible Work Schedules and Dependent Care Benefits. The percentage of workers who reported being able to periodically change their starting and quitting times within some range of hours (traditional flextime) increased from 29% in 1992 to 45% in 1997 and 43% in 2002.

In addition, 23% of workers in 2002 stated that they were able to change their schedules on a daily basis compared with 25% in 1997 and 18% in 1992 (Bond et al., 1998, 2003). In 1997, education and income were negatively related to the availability of traditional flextime, whereas being Black also was negatively associated with the availability of daily flextime. Women had slightly higher levels of flextime availability than men did (Swanberg, Pitt-Catsouphes, & Drescher-Burke, 2005). In 2000, the percentage of workers with variable start and end work times in the EU ranged between 7% in Greece and 30% in the Netherlands and the United Kingdom. The average was 22% (Demerouti, 2006).

The percentage of workers reporting that their employers offer child care services was 10% in 1992, 11% in 1997, and 10% in 2002, whereas the percentage of workers reporting child care resource and referral services through their employers was 18% in 1992, 20% in 1997, and 18% in 2002. However, the percentage reporting elder care resource and referral services at work increased from 11% in 1992 to 25% in 1997 and 24% in 2002 (Bond et al., 1998, 2003). Although the percentages reporting child care services, child care resource and referral services, and elder care resource and referral services varied little by gender in 1992, they were consistently higher for professional and technical workers (15%, 26%, and 15% respectively) than for nonprofessional workers (7%, 16%, and 8% respectively) (Jacobs & Gerson, 2004).

Flexible Work Schedules.   Although no studies have examined the effects of the availability of flexible work schedules on family and community role performance and quality, two studies of relationships between the use of flexible work schedules and family and community role performance and family quality revealed mixed results. When mothers used flexible work schedules, they spent less time and their husbands spent more time in household work; however, flexible scheduling was not related to weekly hours in child care for either mothers or fathers (Noonan et al., in press). Mothers' use of flexible work schedules was positively related to the frequency of mother–child activities, negatively associated with firm and flexible parental discipline, and unrelated to the amount of time available to children on weekdays, shared meals, and mothers' child-oriented community activities (Estes, 2005). The use of flexible schedules was not directly related to children's behavior problems; however, flexible scheduling influenced behavior problems indirectly through its positive relationship to mother–child activities and negative relationship to warm and responsive parenting (Estes, 2004). The second study showed that marital and family satisfaction were higher among women who used flexible work schedules when there no children in the home and lower when children were present. Men reported lower family satisfaction when their wives used flexible work schedules if there were children in the home (Roehling, Moen, & Wilson, 2004).

Most studies of relationships between flexible work schedules and individual well-being and work–family conflict and facilitation have reported that a flexible work schedule is not related to perceived stress (Lapierre & Allen, 2006; Parasuraman, Purohit, Godshalk, & Beutell, 1996;Voydanoff, 2005a) or work–family conflict or facilitation (Lapierre & Allen, 2006; Markel, 2000; Roehling et al., 2003; Sullivan & Hoole, 2005; Voydanoff, 2005a). However, others found relatively weak negative relationships between schedule flexibility and somatic complaints (Thomas & Ganster, 1995) and work-to-family conflict (Anderson, Coffey, & Byerly, 2002).

Dependent Care Benefits.   Only one study was found that examined the effects of the availability of dependent care benefits on family or community role performance and quality. Thompson and Prottas (2006) found that dependent care benefits were unrelated to family satisfaction. Research relating dependent care benefits to individual well-being and work–family conflict and facilitation has found that such benefits are not related to perceived stress (Ganster & Bates, 2003; Voydanoff, 2005a) or work-to-family or family-to-work conflict (Anderson, et al. 2002; Batt & Valcour, 2003; Voydanoff, 2005a).

Family Supports

Family support policies increase boundary flexibility by allowing workers to take time off during the workday to meet personal or family needs or providing part-time work arrangements. These policies are oriented toward making it easier for employees to accommodate family responsibilities by reducing work time, either on a daily or more long-term basis. They may enhance family and community role performance and quality, individual well-being, and work–family facilitation and reduce work–family conflict by limiting time-based work demands and creating time resources within the family. The availability of time-based family support policies may be related to outcomes through a process in which the availability of policies increases the perceived flexibility of temporal boundaries between work and family life. Research suggests that the availability of family support policies enhances employee perceived control and symbolizes corporate concern regardless of whether an employee uses the policies (Batt & Valcour, 2003; Grover & Crooker, 1995). This perceived flexibility and control may reduce time-based demands, thereby reducing negative outcomes and increasing positive outcomes. Because work support policies are more limited in their approach to accommodating family responsibilities, they may be less effective in relation to outcomes than family supports are.

Trends in Time Off for Family and Part-Time Work. In 2002, 63% of employees said that it is "not too hard" or "not hard at all" to take time off during the workday for personal or family reasons. The ability to take time off did not differ by gender, earnings, or occupational category (Galinsky, Bond, & Hill, 2004). The comparable figure of 66% in 1997 was unrelated to gender, race, and education. However, those in the lowest earnings category were less able to take time off than those in the highest category were (Bond et al., 1998; Swanberg et al., 2005). In 2002, 47% of workers reported access to part-time work at their workplaces compared with 45% in 1992. The 1992 figure differed little by gender or occupational status (Galinsky et al., 2004; Jacobs & Gerson, 2004).

Time Off for Family. No extant studies have examined the effects of being able to take time off during the workday to meet family needs on family and community role performance and quality. However, limited research has reported that the ability to take time off during the workday was negatively related to perceived stress (Voydanoff, 2005a) and work-to-family and family-to-work conflict (Major, Klein, & Ehrhart, 2002; Markel, 2000; Voydanoff, 2004b) and positively related to work-to-family facilitation (Voydanoff, 2004b).

Part-Time Work. The available research on relationships between part-time work and family and community role performance and quality is limited. One study found that part-time work among Canadian women was positively associated with perceived family competence and that the relationship operated through decreased perceived job overload (Kelloway & Gottlieb, 1998). Two studies of parents also provide relevant information. Mothers who worked part time spent more time and their husbands spent less time in household work than those who worked full-time. However, part-time work was not related to weekly hours in child care for either mothers or fathers (Noonan et al., in press). Mothers' part-time work was positively associated with shared meals and mothers' child-oriented community activities but was unrelated to time available to children on week days, frequency of mother–child activities, firm and flexible discipline, or children's behavior problems (Estes, 2004, 2005). In a second study, 86% of managers and professionals reported that working part-time had positive effects on their children and their relationship with them (Lee, MacDermid, Williams, Buck, & Leiba-O'Sullivan, 2002.)

Studies of part-time work in relation to individual well-being and work–family conflict and facilitation also are sparse. However, Ettner and Grzywacz (2001) documented a positive relationship between part-time work and health. In addition, Kelloway and Gottlieb (1998) reported that part-time work among women was negatively related to perceived stress and that this relationship was mediated by perceived job overload, whereas Higgins, Duxbury, & Johnson (2000) found no relationship between women's part-time work and perceived stress or depression. The Higgins et al. study also indicated that women's part-time work was negatively associated with work-to-family and family-to-work conflict. Kinnunen and Mauno (1998), however, found that part-time work was negatively related to work-to-family conflict for women but not for men and was unrelated to family-to-work conflict for both men and women. Another study, which looked at the ability to change between full and part time work, found no relationship to either perceived stress or work-to-family conflict (Voydanoff, 2005a).

Normative Support

The third type of work-based boundary-spanning resource consists of having a work–family culture and supervisors that support employee efforts to meet family needs and do not exact career penalties for using work and family support programs. Those studying the effects of available work–family policies on employees and their families have discovered that these policies need to be accompanied by a work–family culture that supports their use. A supportive work–family culture counters the common perception that career penalties are associated with work and family support policies, thereby increasing the likelihood that employees will use them to coordinate their work and family obligations. It enhances employee flexibility in coordinating work and family responsibilities by legitimizing employee efforts to meet family needs and by creating a perception that career penalties are not associated with using available policies. This legitimatization provides implicit permission to use work–family policies. Supervisors may provide more explicit support to employees. When supervisors respond positively to discussing and accommodating employees' family obligations, employees are likely to feel comfortable using available work–family policies. Organizational work–family support that acknowledges and legitimizes the importance and value of coordinating work and family responsibilities is expected to be positively associated with family and community role performance and quality, individual well-being, and work–family facilitation and negatively related to work–family conflict.

Trends in Supportive Work—Family Culture and Supervisor Work—Family Support.   Work er perceptions of the supportiveness of the work–family culture and of supervisors improved somewhat from 1992 to 2002. The percentage of workers agreeing that there was an unwritten rule at their workplace that employees could not take care of family needs on company time decreased from 36% in 1992 to 30% in 1997 and 32% in 2002. The number of workers reporting that their supervisors were fair in responding to employees' personal or family needs increased from 78% in 1992 to 84% in 1997 and 82% in 2002, whereas 65% of workers felt comfortable bringing up personal or family issues in 1992 compared with 76% in 1997 and 73% in 2002 (Bond et al., 1998; Bond et al., 2003).

Supportive Work—Family Culture.   Few studies were found that link a supportive work–family culture to family or community role performance and quality. However, two studies indicated that a supportive work–family culture was positively related to perceived family functioning and marital and family satisfaction (Desrochers & Sargent, 2005; Hill, 2005), whereas another found no relationship between culture and family satisfaction (Thompson & Prottas, 2006).

Findings for relationships between a supportive work–family culture and individual well-being and work–family conflict and facilitation generally are more consistent. A supportive work–family culture is negatively related to perceived stress (Ganster & Bates, 2003; Voydanoff, 2005a) and work-to-family and family-to-work conflict (Allen, 2001; Allen, Greenhaus, & Foley, 2005; Behson, 2002b; Ganster & Bates, 2003; Thompson & Prottas, 2006; Thompson et al., 1999; Voydanoff, 2004b). Two studies of a supportive work–family culture in relation to work–family facilitation found a positive relationship (Colton, Hammer, & Neal, 2002; Voydanoff, 2004b), whereas another did not (Thompson & Prottas, 2006).

Supervisor Work—Family Support.   Three studies investigating relationships between supervisor work–family support and family and community role performance and quality reported mixed results. In the first study, mothers' supervisor work–family support was positively associated with shared meals, firm and flexible discipline, and warm and responsive parenting but unrelated to time availability to children on weekdays, frequency of mother–child activities, and child-oriented community activities (Estes, 2005). Supervisor work–family support was negatively related to children's behavior problems indirectly through its association with mothers' personal control and depression (Estes, 2004). The second study found that supervisor work–family support was positively related to satisfaction with home activities and family cohesion for those with less than two dependents but not for those with two or more dependents, and for those in single-earner marriages but not those in dual-earner marriages (Clark, 2001). A third study reported positive relationships between supervisor work–family support and marital and family satisfaction (Hill, 2005).

Little is known about relationships between supervisor work–family support and individual well-being. One study found that supervisor work–family support was unrelated to individual stress (Hill, 2005). In other studies, supervisor work–family support was negatively related to work-to-family conflict (Allen, 2001; Batt & Valcour, 2003; Thomas & Ganster, 1995; Voydanoff, 2004b; but see Hill, 2005) and family-to-work conflict (Allen et al., 2005; but see Hill, 2005) and positively associated with work-to-family and family-to-work facilitation (Hill, 2005; Voydanoff, 2004b).

Work-based boundary-spanning resources oriented to boundary flexibility may influence cross-domain role performance and quality, individual well-being, and work–family conflict and facilitation through work–family policies and a work–family culture and supervisors that provide practical assistance to workers attempting to coordinate work and family responsibilities. Overall, the findings suggest that it is important to make distinctions among and within the categories of boundary-spanning resources, that is, work, family, and normative support policies and programs. Little is known about the effects of these supports on family and community role performance and quality, and the few findings are not consistent enough to permit any conclusions. Although the availability of family support policies may be more effective than work support policies, work support policies, especially flexible work schedules, may still have a modest effect on role performance and quality, well-being, and conflict and facilitation. Family supports, especially the ability to take time off during the workday to address family responsibilities, and normative support generally are positively associated with individual well-being and work–family facilitation and negatively related to work–family conflict.

Although few studies investigate relationships between work-based resources and both work–family conflict and facilitation, there is some support for the comparable salience approach. Work supports generally are unrelated to both conflict and facilitation. For family supports, time off for family is related to both conflict and facilitation, whereas no studies examined relationships between part-time work and facilitation. The two types of normative support are negatively related to conflict and positively associated with facilitation in most studies; however, the pattern of relationships is not always consistent.

FAMILY-BASED RESOURCES

Chapter 4 discussed within-domain family resources that were expected to have positive consequences for work and community role performance, individual well-being, and family-to-work facilitation. These resources included instrumental and emotional support from spouses and kin. This chapter focuses on a specific type of spouse and kin support, that is, support focused on the intersection of the work and family domains. Such support is oriented toward spouses and kin improving the ability of another family member to coordinate work and family activities. Comparable to work-based boundary-spanning resources, family-based resources are of three types: work supports, family supports, and normative support. Family-based work supports encompass dependent care and household work provided by spouses and other family members. Such supports are expected to enhance role performance across domains by facilitating or reducing family work while the employee maintains a comparable level of participation in work duties. Family-based family support occurs when one spouse serves as the major family provider so that the other spouse may engage more extensively in family activities. This type of support is expected to improve role performance across domains by adjusting the level of work involvement to accommodate family responsibilities and activities. In addition, family members are likely to coordinate their work and family responsibilities more effectively when they receive work–family normative support from spouses and kin. Such support provides cohesion and legitimacy to a family's efforts to combine work and family life and assists family members by supporting their decisions and efforts. All three types of support are expected to be positively related to work and community role performance and quality, individual well-being, and work–family facilitation and to be negatively associated with work–family conflict.

Work Supports

Few studies have examined spouse and kin dependent care and household work in relation to work and community role performance and quality, individual well-being, and work–family conflict and facilitation. Research summarized by Bellavia and Frone (2005) indicated that spouse and kin dependent care and household work are negatively related to family-to-work conflict (but see Dilworth, 2004). However, with one exception, this research does not assess whether this dependent care and household work is performed to facilitate the coordination of work and family responsibilities of another family member. One study has reported that household work performed by one family member to assist another family member meet work responsibilities was negatively related to family-to-work conflict but unrelated to work-to-family conflict and mental and physical well-being (Lapierre & Allen, 2006). Therefore, it is not possible to determine the extent to which it serves as a boundary-spanning resource or how much influence it has as a boundary-spanning resource for work and community role performance and quality, individual well-being, and work–family conflict and facilitation.

Family Supports

Husbands and wives may coordinate their work commitments in several ways in order to combine their work and family responsibilities more effectively. Moen and Sweet (2003) present five categories of work-hour arrangements for dual-earner couples: high commitments (both work more than 45 hours a week), dual moderates (both work 39–45 hours per week), neotraditionalists (husband works more than 45 hours a week, wife does not), crossover commitments (wife works more than 45 hours a week, husband does not), and alternative commitments (neither works long hours; one works reduced hours). In addition, in single-earner couples, one spouse works and the other does not. The extent to which the spouse who works more hours (e.g., neotraditionalists, crossover commitments, alternative commitments, or single-earner couple) does so in order to support the family effort of the spouse who works fewer hours isn't clear. However, in the Moen and Sweet study, the total percentages in the neotraditionalist, crossover commitment, and alternative commitment categories ranged from approximately 70% for those with children in the home to between 40% and 55% for nonparents and empty nesters. This suggests that family responsibilities influence the extent to which one spouse works more hours than the other. For all family categories, the percentage of neotraditionalists is larger than the percentages of crossover commitments. A second study indicated that the husband rather than the wife was the primary breadwinner for two-thirds of a small sample of middle-class dual-career couples in which one spouse was the primary breadwinner with a career and the other held a less demanding job (Becker & Moen, 1999). No studies were located that provided a systematic analysis of the effects of these family support resources on work and community role performance and quality, individual well-being, and work–family conflict and facilitation.

Normative Support

Research summarized in chapter 4 indicated that spouse and kin emotional support generally is positively related to work role quality, individual well-being, and family-to-work facilitation. In addition, Bellavia and Frone's (2005) review indicated a negative relationship between spouse and kin support and family-to-work conflict. However, once again, it is not possible to determine the extent to which such general emotional support serves as a boundary-spanning resource by incorporating normative support for work–family role coordination or as such how it influences work and community role performance and quality, individual well-being, and work–family conflict and facilitation. Family-based boundary-spanning resources generally remain unexplored and little understood; however, they provide an important area for future investigation. Such resources may be important in coordinating work and family responsibilities across domains.

COMMUNITY-BASED RESOURCES

Boundary-spanning community resources are of two types: work supports and normative supports. Community-based work supports encompass community-based services that may facilitate work–family role coordination. They provide services to working families that enable them to maintain their work obligations and commitment while also meeting their family responsibilities. Among the most important are child care and after-school programs. In addition, family members may be better able to coordinate their work and family responsibilities when they receive normative support from community members and friends regarding how they combine their work and family activities. Such support reinforces a family's efforts to combine work and family life and assists family members by supporting their decisions and efforts. These community-based resources are expected to be positively associated with work and family role performance and quality, individual well-being, and work–family facilitation and negatively related to work–family conflict.

Work Supports

Trends in Community-Based Child Care and After-School Programs. In 2002, 24% of preschool children of employed mothers were cared for in organized child care facilities such as a day care center or nursery school, compared with 25% in 1985 (U.S. Census Bureau, 2005). In 2001, 20% of kindergarten through eighth-grade children spent time alone or were cared for by nonparents before school, whereas 50% spent time alone or with nonparents after school. Of these children, one-fifth were cared for in centers or school-based programs before school and two-fifths after school. More than half of these programs were conducted in public schools, whereas approximately 10% each were located in private schools, community centers, or separate buildings (U.S. Department of Education, 2004).

Community-Based Child Care and After-School Programs.   Little is known about the effects of community-based child-care and after-school programs on work and family role performance and quality, individual well-being, or work–family conflict and facilitation. Barnett and Gareis (2006) found that children's participation in after-school programs was negatively related to parental concerns about after-school time (PCAST). PCAST is an aspect of family-to-work conflict consisting of parents' concerns about their ability to have contact with their children after school while they are still at work, the safety and productivity of their children's time after school, and the logistics and quality of their children's after-school arrangements.

Normative Support

In addition, family members may be better able to coordinate their work and family responsibilities when they receive normative support from community members and friends regarding how they are combining their work and family activities. Such support may enhance a family's efforts to combine work and family life and assist family members by supporting their decisions and efforts. The support associated with these resources is expected to improve work and family role performance and quality, individual well-being, and work–family facilitation and decrease work–family conflict. No known studies have explored this issue. Much more study is needed to better understand the role of community-based boundary-spanning resources in facilitating work–family role coordination.

COMBINED EFFECTS OF WITHIN-DOMAIN DEMANDS AND RESOURCES AND BOUNDARY-SPANNING RESOURCES

Boundary-spanning resources may combine with within-domain demands and resources in several ways to form a work–family–community mesosystem. They may influence cross-domain role performance and quality, individual well-being, and work–family conflict and facilitation in an additive fashion or they may mediate or moderate the effects of within-domain demands and resources on outcomes. For example, resources such as after-school programs may buffer the relationship between work hours and work-to-family conflict or amplify relationships between work resources and work-to-family facilitation. Unfortunately, only three known studies have examined such relationships. Woolf and Adams (2005) found that the use of a range flexible work options buffered the relationship between work hours and work-to-family conflict, that is, the relationship between hours and conflict was weaker for those using flexible work options. Moreover, Tucker and Rutherford (2005) showed that work schedule autonomy buffered the relationship between paid work hours and physical health symptoms. However, Major et al. (2002) reported that being able to take time off for family during the work day did not buffer the effects of work hours on work-to-family conflict.

The implications for work–family policy differ for additive and moderating effects. When demands and resources have additive effects on role performance and quality, individual well-being, and work–family conflict and facilitation, resources reduce negative outcomes but do not address the negative effects of demands on outcomes. Thus, the negative consequences associated with demands remain unchanged, whereas resources have independent compensating effects on outcomes. However, if resources buffer the effects of demands on outcomes, the negative effects of demands are reduced or eliminated. Thus, demands no longer contribute to outcomes and increasing resources is sufficient to protect against the negative effects of demands. When additive effects occur, policies that only increase resources are insufficient to reduce the negative effects of demands on well-being. Thus, it is important to investigate such relationships further.

WORK–FAMILY CONFLICT AND FACILITATION AS LINKING MECHANIMS

If boundary-spanning resources are positively associated with work–family conflict and facilitation and conflict and facilitation are related to cross-domain role performance and quality and individual well-being, it is possible that work–family conflict and facilitation mediate relationships between boundary-spanning resources and role performance and quality and well-being. This chapter has documented associations between several boundary-resources, especially work-based resources, and work–family conflict and facilitation. Chapters 3 and 4 documented negative relationships between work–family conflict and role performance and quality and individual well-being, and positive relationships between work–family facilitation and these outcomes. Thus, statistically speaking, mediating effects are possible. Because boundary-spanning resources also have direct beffects on role performance and quality and individual well-being, work–family conflict and facilitation are expected to have partial rather than full mediating effects.

Several studies have indicated that work-to-family conflict partially mediates relationships between work-based boundary-spanning resources and individual well-being, whereas no known studies have examined mediating effects for other outcomes or for work–family facilitation. Work-to-family conflict partially mediated relationships between flexible work schedules and stress-related outcomes in two studies (Anderson et al., 2002; Thomas & Ganster, 1995). Work-to-family conflict mediated the effects of time off for family on perceived stress, whereas work-to-family conflict (but not family-to-work conflict) mediated the relationship between part-time work and psychological well-being (van Rijswijk, Bekker, Rutte, & Croon, 2004). Work-to-family and family-to-work conflict also mediated the effects of a supportive work–family culture and supervisor work–family support on psychological and physical health (Allen et al., 2005; Voydanoff, 2005a).

SUMMARY

The portion of the conceptual model examined in this chapter proposed that boundary-spanning work, family, and community resources are positively associated with cross-domain role performance and quality, individual well-being, and work–family facilitation and negatively related to work–family conflict. It also predicts that work–family conflict and facilitation partially mediate relationships between boundary-spanning resources and role performance and quality and individual well-being. Boundary-spanning resources are expected to have positive effects on outcomes by increasing the flexibility of the temporal boundary between the work and family domains, by reducing time demands in one domain such that time resources are increased in another domain, by providing assistance in one domain that facilitates performance in another domain, and by providing work–family normative support that strengthens the ability of individuals to coordinate activities in the work and family domains.

These supports are of three types: work supports, family supports, and normative support. Work supports include flexible work schedules and dependent care benefits in the work domain, spouse and kin dependent care and household work in the family domain, and child care and after-school programs in the community domain. Family supports encompass being able to take time off from work to perform family activities or to work part time and having one spouse be the major provider so that the other spouse can devote more time to family activities. Normative support consists of a supportive work–family culture and supervisor work–family support in the work domain and spouse, kin, community, and friend work–family support in the family and community domains.

Research on this aspect of the model has focused almost exclusively on work-based boundary-spanning resources. In general, the availability of family supports such as time off for family and part-time work are more strongly related to cross-domain role performance and quality, individual well-being, and work–family conflict and facilitation than work supports such as flexible work schedules and dependent care benefits are. A supportive work–family culture and supervisor work–family support also show relationships to role performance and quality, individual well-being, and conflict and facilitation. In addition, a few studies indicate that work-to-family conflict mediates relationships between work-based resources and individual well-being. Although a few studies support the model for family-based and community-based boundary-spanning resources, the evidence is too sparse to formulate any conclusions.

7

Work–Family Fit and Balance as Linking Mechanisms

The previous four chapters have considered perceived work–family conflict and work–family facilitation as linking mechanisms between work, family, and community demands and resources and work, family, and community role performance and quality and individual well-being. This chapter incorporates two additional linking mechanisms—perceived work–family fit and work–family balance. It presents conceptualizations of both mechanisms and proposes a model that links them to within-domain and boundary-spanning demands and resources, to each other, to boundary-spanning strategies, and to work, family, and community role performance and quality and individual well-being.

Similar to work–family conflict and facilitation, work–family fit and balance are cognitive appraisals of the effects of the work and family domains on each other. They derive from assessing the relative demands and resources associated with work and family roles. Community demands and resources also are relevant. However, because of a lack of information about their role, they are not considered here. Based on person–environment fit theory, two dimensions of perceived work–family fit are formulated: work demands–family resources fit and family demands–work resources fit. Work–family balance is a global assessment of the extent to which work and family resources are sufficient to meet work and family demands (Voydanoff, 2005e).

Based on the general model presented in chapter 1, Figure 7.1 provides a conceptual model that links within-domain and boundary-spanning demands and resources to work, family, and community role performance and quality and individual well-being through work–family fit and balance. Work, family, and boundary-spanning demands and resources are associated with the two dimensions of fit, which combine with boundary-spanning strategies to influence work–family balance, which in turn affects role performance and quality and individual well-being. The model provides a framework for clarifying and integrating previous conceptualizations, measures, and empirical research regarding work–family fit and balance as linkages between the work–family interface and outcomes.

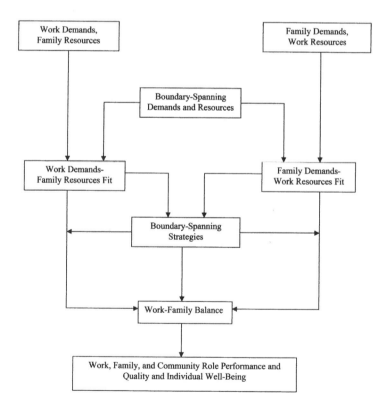

Figure 7.1   The conceptual model of work-family fit and balance.

The next section of this chapter presents a conceptualization of work–family fit and balance. It ties the conceptualization to other uses of the concepts of fit and balance as well as to work–family conflict and facilitation. This is followed by a discussion of the proposed effects of work, family, and boundary-spanning demands and resources on work–family fit. Next, the effects of work–family fit on work–family balance are reviewed, followed by a discussion of the mediating and moderating effects of boundary-spanning strategies on the relationship between work–family fit and balance. Then the consequences of work–family balance for work and family role performance and quality are considered.

A CONCEPTUALIZATION OF WORK–FAMILY FIT AND BALANCE

Work–Family Fit

Work–family fit is conceptualized from the perspective of the person–environment fit approach to occupational stress. The basic tenet of person–environment fit theory is that stress arises from the lack of fit or congruence between the person and the environment rather than from either one separately (see Edwards, Caplan, & Harrison, 1998, and Edwards & Rothbard, 2005, for reviews of occupational stress research based on this approach). Fit is of two types: demands–abilities and needs–supplies. Demands include quantitative and qualitative job requirements, role expectations, and group and organizational norms, whereas abilities include aptitudes, skills, training, time, and energy that may be used to meet demands. Fit occurs when the individual has the abilities needed to meet the demands of the environment. Strain is expected to increase as demands exceed abilities. Needs encompass biological and psychological requirements, values, and motives, whereas supplies consist of intrinsic and extrinsic resources and rewards that may fulfill the person's needs, such as food, shelter, money, social involvement, and the opportunity to achieve. Fit exists when the environment provides the resources required to satisfy the person's needs, whereas stress occurs when needs exceed supplies.

Misfit, which occurs when demands and needs exceed abilities and supplies, results in strains and illness as well as coping behavior and cognitive defense to improve fit, whereas fit can create positive mental and physical health outcomes. Evidence regarding the effects of abilities and supplies exceeding demands and needs on strain is inconclusive. As abilities and supplies exceed demands and needs, strain may decrease, increase, or level off (Edwards & Rothbard, 2005). Although this formulation of person–environment fit generally is applied to the work domain, Edwards and Rothbard (1999) have extended it to the analysis of fit in the family domain. They have documented that work supplies–needs fit for autonomy, relationships, and security is relatively strongly associated with work satisfaction, whereas family fit on the same dimensions is more strongly related to family satisfaction.

Others have extended the principles of the person–environment fit approach from the fit of demands and resources within either the work or family domain to the consideration of fit across these domains. Pittman (1994) and Barnett, Gareis, and Brennan (1999) focused on family demands–work resources fit. Pittman's conceptualization of fit suggested that family members weigh the demands on them with the benefits that the job and work organization provide. His measure included questions about the extent to which the military provides a good environment for childrearing, satisfaction with living conditions, and organizational sensitivity to the needs of family members. Barnett et al. considered fit in terms of the ability of employees to develop and optimize strategies to meet family needs in the workplace. They measured fit by asking a series of questions about how well the number and distribution of physicians' and their partners' work hours and work-schedule flexibility met their own, their partners', and their children's needs.

Expanding on this approach, DeBord, Canu, and Kerpelman (2000) and Teng (1999) proposed a two-dimensional model of work–family fit. The first dimension conceives of fit as the match of work demands with family abilities or expectations regarding meeting work demands, whereas the second dimension is the match of work supplies or rewards with family needs or goals. Work demands and family needs consist of time-based and strain-based work and family demands. Family abilities or expectations and work supplies or rewards focus on organizational and social rewards at work and family coping abilities. Teng developed measures of both the work demands–family abilities and the work rewards–family needs dimensions of fit. The measure of work demands–family abilities fit included questions regarding concern about several work demands, whether family members feel these demands are more difficult than expected, and how well family members are dealing with the demands. This dimension consists of an additive combination of demands and abilities. The work rewards–family needs items asked how well the rewards and benefits of the job meet individual and family needs. This is a measure of an individual's direct appraisal of work rewards–family needs fit. This previous work provides some conceptual and empirical support for a demands and resources approach to work–family fit.

Building on this previous work, this chapter defines work–family fit as a form of interrole congruence in which the resources associated with one role are sufficient to meet the demands of another role such that participation in the second role can be effective. Work–family fit has two dimensions: Work demands–family resources fit in which family-related resources are adequate to meet the demands of the work role and family demands–work resources fit in which work-related resources are sufficient to satisfy family demands. The two dimensions range from fit in which demands and resources are equivalent to misfit in which there is a discrepancy between demands and resources. For example, a fit scale could range from -4 (demands are less than resources) through 0 (demands and resources are equal) to +4 (demands are greater than resources).

Drawing on the demands and resources approach articulated in Chapters Three through Six, the first stage of the model presented in Figure 7.1 proposes that work demands and family resources are related to work demands–family resources fit, whereas family demands and work resources are associated with family demands–work resources fit. Boundary-spanning demands and resources are related to both types of fit.

Work–Family Balance

Work–family balance is the global assessment that work and family resources are sufficient to meet work and family demands such that participation is effective in both domains. It combines the appraisals that family resources are adequate to meet work demands and that work resources meet family demands with the effects of boundary-spanning strategies to yield an overall appraisal of the extent of harmony, equilibrium, and integration of work and family life. It ranges from high levels of balance to high levels of imbalance.

Most empirical studies have used a single item asking respondents about their level of satisfaction or success with the balance between their work and family lives, demands, or responsibilities. Valcour and Batt (2003), however, developed a scale based on items asking the level of satisfaction with the division of time and attention between work and personal life, ability to balance needs across domains, ability to perform job and home duties adequately, and fit between work life and personal or family life. In addition, the Hill, Martinson, Ferris, and Baker (2004) scale included items on the extent to which work resources such as flexibility and time away from work are sufficient to maintain balance as well as questions regarding overall balance. These measures provide an overall assessment or appraisal of the extent to which the balance of demands and resources permits adequate role performance in work and family life.

In the second stage of the model, the two dimensions of fit are proposed to result in an overall assessment of work–family balance, either directly or through the use of boundary-spanning strategies. The premise of a direct relationship between fit and balance is consistent with the model of Edwards and Rothbard (2005), who proposed that work and family person–environment fit have additive effects on strain. In addition, Teng (1999) combined measures of work demands–family abilities fit with family needs–work supplies fit to create an overall measure of fit. The final stage of the model proposes that work–family balance is related to work and family role performance and quality and individual well-being.

Implications of the Conceptualization

The inconsistent use of the concepts of fit and balance in previous research creates confusion in the literature. The model in Figure 7.1 places these previously disparate conceptualizations of work–family fit and balance in a broader context that reveals how they are related to each and how they might be integrated. Some previous definitions of fit are similar to the one used here, for example, the extent to which family abilities meet work demands and work supplies meet family needs (DeBord et al., 2000) or the relationship between demands and efforts to meet the demands (Clarke, Koch, & Hill, 2004). Other definitions, however, are comparable to definitions of balance as used here, for example, fit as the overall level of integration of work and family life (Hill, Hawkins, Martinson, & Ferris, 2003) or the assessment of balance between families and work organizations (Pittman, 1994).

Similar variations occur in definitions of work–family balance. Some scholars use a definition much like the one used here, that is, an overall assessment of equilibrium or harmony (Clarke et al., 2004; Joplin, Shaffer, Lau, & Francesco, 2003). Others use definitions comparable to the definition of work–family fit used here, for example, considering success in balancing work and family life in terms of role demands, available resources, and the fit between them over the life course (Moen, Waismel-Manor, & Sweet, 2003) or defining work-life balance as the stability resulting from the balance between changing demands and environmental and personal resources (Crooker, Smith, & Tabak, 2002). Other definitions focus on managing demands without explicitly incorporating resources, for example, work–family balance as the ability to balance work and family demands and responsibilities (Hill et al., 2004; Tausig & Fenwick, 2001). In addition, some have defined role balance as full engagement in the performance of each role in an individual's total role system (Marks & MacDermid, 1996) or the extent to which individuals experience equal time, involvement, effectiveness, and satisfaction in work and family roles (Greenhaus, Collins, & Shaw, 2003). This last conceptualization does not view work–family balance as a cognitive appraisal. The conceptualization and model presented here provide guidance for future conceptual and empirical work by providing useful distinctions between fit and balance and by locating existing work in a broader framework.

In addition to work–family fit and balance, work–family conflict and work–family facilitation are linking mechanisms between work and family demands and resources and role performance and quality and individual well-being. Work–family conflict was defined in Chapter Three as a form of inter-role conflict in which the demands of work and family roles are incompatible in some respect so that participation in one role is more difficult because of participation in the other role. Work–family facilitation was defined in Chapter Four as a form of synergy across role domains in which the resources associated with one role enhance or make easier participation in the other role. Work and family demands generally are related to work-to-family and family-to-work conflict respectively, whereas work and family resources are associated with work-to-family and family-to-work facilitation respectively. In contrast, work–family fit and balance are derived from the extent to which resources associated with one role are sufficient to meet the demands of another role. Thus, work–family conflict, facilitation, fit, and balance are cognitive appraisals that reflect work and family demands and resources in different ways. Conflict and facilitation are useful for understanding the differential or independent effects of demands and resources, whereas fit and balance address the intersection or joint effects of demands and resources. Thus, the two types of linking mechanisms are useful for addressing different questions. For example, if one were concerned about the effects of time caring for young children on job performance, family-to-work conflict would be a useful appraisal to examine. If one were interested in whether job autonomy would be helpful in meeting the demands associated with caring for young children, it would be more important to assess family demands–work resources fit. The part of the general model considered in this chapter focuses on fit and balance rather than on conflict and facilitation.

Some scholars also have defined work–family fit and balance in terms of work–family conflict and facilitation, rather than as separate concepts. For example, Grzywacz and Bass (2003) viewed work–family fit as multiple dimensions of work–family conflict and facilitation. They stated that work–family conflict maps onto the concept of demands, whereas capabilities are relevant for facilitation. Rather than assessing demands and capabilities directly, however, they developed a framework in which fit "represents the extent to which work–family facilitation can eliminate experiences of work–family conflict, or the extent to which work–family facilitation creates an environment that can tolerate experiences of work–family conflict" (p. 250). They used indicators of work–family conflict and facilitation to measure work–family fit. In addition, several scholars have defined work–family balance as the absence of work–family conflict (Buffardi, Smith, O'Brien, & Erdwins, 1999; Clark, 2001; Saltzstein, Ting, & Saltzstein, 2001), whereas others have defined it as low levels of work–family conflict and high levels of work–family facilitation (Frone, 2003). Either reducing work–family conflict or increasing work–family facilitation increases balance. On the basis of this conceptualization, Fisher-McAuley, Stanton, Jolton, and Gavin (2003) have developed a measure of work–family balance using items that assess work interference with personal life, personal life interference with work, and work/personal life enhancement, whereas a measure presented by Huffman, Payne, and Casper (2004) uses items that tap facilitation and lack of conflict. No independent measures of work–family fit and balance are used, thus confounding fit and balance with conflict and facilitation. This chapter argues that the sources and consequences of work–family fit and balance are better understood when specific demands and resources are examined rather than relying on appraisals of conflict and facilitation as representations of fit and balance. When measures of conflict and facilitation are used as indicators of fit, the analysis is one step removed from the demands and resources associated with work and family roles (e.g., it is not clear which demands are creating the conflict or which resources are associated with facilitation).

A DEMANDS AND RESOURCES APPROACH TO WORK–FAMILY FIT AND BALANCE

Demands, Resources, and Work–Family Fit

The conceptual model presented in Figure 7.1 extends the analysis of work and family person–environment fit as formulated by Edwards and Rothbard (1999, 2005) to a cross-domain approach in which work demands are compared with family resources and family demands are compared with work resources. This approach yields two types of work–family fit: work demands–family resources fit and family demands–work resources fit. Fit occurs when work (family) resources meet, offset, or satisfy family (work) demands. The model suggests two types of demands and resources that are associated with work–family fit: within-domain work and family demands and resources and boundary-spanning demands and resources. These demands and resources have been discussed in the previous four chapters as sources of role performance and quality, individual well-being, and work–family conflict and facilitation.

Within-domain demands and resources are expected to be differentially salient for the two dimensions of work–family fit. Within-domain work demands and within-domain family resources combine to influence work demands–family resources fit, whereas family demands and work resources are relevant for family demands–work resources fit. The extent to which enabling resources and psychological rewards in one domain meet or counteract the time-based and strain-based demands in the other domain determines the level of fit. For example, spouse and kin support may contribute to work demands–family resources fit by helping employees deal with work demands such as job pressure and insecurity. Job autonomy and meaningful work may increase family demands–work resources fit by making it easier for individuals to address strain-based family demands emanating from spouse, children, or kin.

It also is possible that resources from the work (family) domain may combine with resources from the family (work) domain to influence work demands–family resources (family demands–work resources) fit. For example, job autonomy may be useful in increasing work demands–family resources fit. The differential salience approach does not preclude such crossover effects. Instead it emphasizes that the dominant pattern of effects is for work (family) demands and family (work) resources to influence work demands–family resources (family demands–work resources) fit (Voydanoff, 2004b).

Research that examines the effects of the within-domain demands and resources considered in Chapters Three and Four on the two types of fit is sparse. Pittman (1994) found that husbands' and wives' satisfaction with the husbands' work hours was positively associated with a measure of family demands–work resources fit that addressed the extent to which the military provides a good environment for childrearing, satisfaction with living conditions, and organizational sensitivity to the needs of family members. Barnett et al. (1999) showed that paid work hours were negatively related to a measure of family demands–work resources fit based on a series of questions about how well the number and distribution of physicians' and their partners' work hours and work-schedule flexibility met their own, their partners', and their children's needs. In addition, Pittman reported that work–family fit mediated relationships between husbands' and wives' satisfaction with the husbands' work hours and marital tension, whereas Barnett et al. found that fit mediated the relationship between work hours and burnout.

In contrast to within-domain demands and resources, work-based and family-based boundary-spanning demands and resources are expected to be associated with both dimensions of fit. Boundary-spanning demands (e.g., commuting time and overnight travel for work) limit the ability of individuals to make transitions between the work and family domains. This increases the level of demands both at work and at home, which decreases both types of fit. Boundary-spanning demands that create role blurring across domains (e.g., bringing work home and family interruptions and distractions at work) also decrease both types of fit by increasing both work and family demands. Boundary-spanning resources may have positive effects on both dimensions of work–family fit. Workplace policies that facilitate the coordination of work and family responsibilities and normative support for such policies provide additional resources to meet the demands of work and family life. For example, flexible work schedules may improve work demands–family resources fit by adjusting the timing of work, thereby improving the match between a work demand and a family's ability to meet the demand. Flexible schedules also may facilitate a family's ability to care for children or other relatives, thereby increasing family demands–work resources fit. No studies were located that investigated relationships between boundary-spanning demands and resources and indicators of either type of work–family fit.

Relationships Between Work–Family Fit and Work–Family Balance

In the present model, work–family balance is considered as a global assessment that work and family resources are sufficient to meet work and family demands such that participation is effective in both domains. These demands and resources operate through the two dimensions of work–family fit to influence balance. The model proposes that the two dimensions of work–family fit have additive effects on work–family balance. However, the relative importance of the two dimensions may vary among individuals. The extent to which the work or family role is relatively salient may influence these relationships (see Greenhaus & Powell, 2006, for a similar argument regarding relationships between resources and work–family enrichment).

No known studies have assessed relationships between work–family fit as defined here and work–family balance. Some insight into the factors associated with work–family balance can be obtained, however, by reviewing research that uses a demands and resources approach in the examination of direct relationships between work and family demands and resources and work–family balance. Studies of the additive effects of work and family demands and resources on work–family balance generally support the model. Within-domain and boundary-spanning demands such as long work hours, job demands, job monitoring intensity, elder care responsibility, and job-related travel generally were negatively related to work–family balance, whereas the relationship between balance and young children at home was statistically significant in some studies but not others (Buffardi et al., 1999; Hill et al., 2003; Keene & Quadagno, 2004; Valcour & Batt, 2003). Within-domain and boundary-spanning resources such as job autonomy and complexity, part-time work, supervisor work–family support, and a supportive work–family culture generally showed positive relationships to work–family balance, whereas flexible work schedules and on-site child care were unrelated to balance (Ezra & Deckman, 1996; Keene & Quadagno, 2004; Lyness & Kropf, 2005; Saltzstein et al., 2001; Valcour & Batt, 2003).

MEDIATING AND MODERATING EFFECTS OF BOUNDARY-SPANNING STRATEGIES

In addition to having direct relationships to work–family balance, the model in Figure 7.1 suggests that work–family fit may operate through boundary-spanning strategies to influence work–family balance. Boundary-spanning strategies are actions taken on the part of individuals and families to reduce or eliminate misfit between work and family demands and resources. This concept is adapted from Moen and Wethington's (1992) family adaptive strategies. They defined family adaptive strategies as "the actions families devise for coping with, if not overcoming, the challenges of living, and for achieving their goals in the face of structural barriers" (p. 234). Viewed from the perspective of stress theory, boundary-spanning strategies are comparable to coping strategies, responses, or behaviors on both the individual and family level (Voydanoff, 1990). Barnett (1998) also adapted the concept of family adaptive strategies in her discussion of a work/social system strategy. A work/social system strategy is used by workers to meet their needs and aspirations, which reflect commitments and responsibilities to themselves, their families, and others in their social systems. A related approach was used by Kossek, Noe, and DeMarr (1999), who defined work–family role synthesis as the personal strategies used to manage the joint enactment of work and family roles and to cope with role conflict. Such strategies also have been referred to as work–family adaptive strategies, adjustments, trade-offs, accommodation, and scaling back.

Some strategies change work, family, and community roles so that time-based and strain-based demands are reduced, for example, cutting work hours, reducing work responsibilities, limiting dependent care and household work, and performing less volunteer work and informal helping. When time and strain demands are reduced in one domain, enabling resources and psychological rewards in another

domain are better able to meet these lowered demands. Other strategies increase resources, for example, taking a more enriching job,
gaining job flexibility by becoming self-employed, hiring dependent
care and household services, and using community services. These
strategies provide additional resources for individual and family efforts to meet demands in another domain. Table 7.1 provides a list of
the most commonly discussed boundary-spanning strategies.

Depending on the timing, these strategies may prevent work–family
misfit in the first place; for example, using flextime may reduce the
need to cut work hours. Thus, a given strategy can have a positive relationship to work–family fit (a preventive effect), or can be positively related to work–family balance (a therapeutic effect), or can have a
buffering effect on the relationship between work–family fit and
work–family balance (Bowen, 1998). Bowen's study of leader support
documented that all three types of relationships can exist simultaneously (see Greenhaus & Parasuraman, 1994, for a comparable approach that views social support as stress-preventing,
health-sustaining, and buffering in relation to stress and well-being).

Preventive strategies are encompassed by the resources discussed in
chapters 4 and 6 as predictors of work, family, and community role
performance and quality and individual well-being, for example, supportive supervisors, coworkers, and family members and the availability of quality child care. This chapter focuses on the mediating and
moderating effects of therapeutic strategies. These strategies may mediate negative effects such that misfit leads to the use of strategies,
which in turn improves balance. Strategies also may moderate the effects of fit on balance by buffering the negative effects of misfit on balance. In this situation, the negative relationship between misfit and
balance decreases when boundary-spanning strategies are used. For
example, the negative relationship between work–family misfit and balance may be weaker for those who cut work hours, increase work–family support, or use community services such as after-school programs.

When work–family fit occurs, boundary-spanning strategies may
be unnecessary. However, some individuals who experience
work–family fit may increase resources as an additional source of satisfaction and well-being, for example, taking a more enriching job,
hiring household services, or using community services. These strategies may have direct effects on balance or they may amplify positive relationships between work–family fit and balance.

Boundary-Spanning Strategies and Work–Family Fit and Balance

No known studies have examined the effects of boundary-spanning
strategies on relationships between work–family fit and work–family

TABLE 7.1   Work, Family, and Community Boundary-Spanning Strategies

	Work	Family	Community
Reduce time-based demands	Cut work hours	Miss family occasions	Reduce volunteer time
	Refuse overtime	Do less dependent care	Reduce informal help
	Change work schedule	Limit childbearing	
	Refuse travel	Do less household work	
Reduce strain-based demands	Take less demanding job		Change neighborhood
	Refuse promotions		Change school
	Refuse work assignments		
Increase resources	Increase work hours	Hire dependent care	Use community services
	Increase earnings	Hire household services	
	Take more enriching job	Increase employment of family members	
	Become self-employed	Increase work-family support	

balance. Two studies, however, have reported that strategies oriented to reducing family demands (e.g., missing a family occasion) are negatively related to balance, whereas the effects of reducing work demands (e.g., cutting back on work) are mixed (Keene & Quadagno, 2004; Milkie & Peltola, 1999). This limited research does not support the idea that boundary-spanning strategies are effective in increasing work–family balance. It may be that using boundary-spanning resources such as work and family supports as preventive mechanisms in relation to work–family fit is more effective than using boundary-spanning strategies to increase balance. Additional research with a longitudinal design is needed to explore such relationships.

Thus, there is limited empirical support for the proposition that boundary-spanning strategies mediate or moderate relationships between work–family fit and work–family balance. This is due largely to a dearth of studies; however, other issues may be involved. For example, a qualitative study (Roy, Tubbs, & Burton, 2004) describes the proactive use of strategies that stagger and decrease obligations and expand resources among low-income families. However, when demands are extremely high, the use of these strategies is accompanied by psychological and physical health costs. Moreover, boundary-spanning strategies may be helpful to some members of a family but not others (Moen & Wethington, 1992). Some have suggested that coping strategies may be effective only under certain conditions and strategies such as avoidance or defensive behavior may exacerbate rather than reduce the effects of role strain on outcomes (Greenhaus & Parasuraman, 1987). Thus, limiting work hours or job-related travel may reduce work–family misfit if a person's or family's career goals also are modified but may not if the changes are seen as a necessary but not desired adjustment to work–family role misfit. In addition, an individual's or family's choice of strategies is limited by structural conditions, for example, the nature of available jobs, cognitions such as gender roles norms, and economic need (Moen & Yu, 2000). Therefore, effective strategies are not always available to individuals and families.

Boundary-Spanning Strategies and Work–Family Conflict and Facilitation

The general conceptual model presented in chapter 1 suggests that boundary-spanning strategies mediate and moderate relationships between work–family linking mechanisms and work–family balance. Thus, it is expected that boundary-spanning strategies also should influence the effects of work–family conflict and facilitation on balance. Once again, no studies were found that examined such relationships. However, one study found that cutting back on work and family activities did not mediate relationships between work-to-family conflict and distress (Guelzow, Bird, & Koball, 1991). A second study reported that family-to-work conflict was positively associated with reducing work demands to accommodate family, which in turn buffered the effects of conflict on work stress (Behson, 2002a). These results are inconclusive with regard to the hypothesized relationships.

Feedback Loops

The model presented in chapter 1 also proposes that boundary-spanning strategies have feedback effects on within-domain and boundary-spanning demands and resources. The successful use of these strategies may change within-domain and boundary-spanning demands and resources such that they can prevent work–family conflict and promote work–family fit and facilitation. For example, reducing work hours may create enhanced spouse support, thereby increasing work–family fit. A similar approach is proposed in Barnett's (1998) model, in which work–family fit mediates relationships between distal and proximal conditions and outcomes. Her model includes feedback from outcomes to distal and proximal conditions. Types of feedback include national policies regarding child care, health care, and parental leave; employment policies regarding work hours, job redesign, and promotion; time allotment between work and family; and individual aspirations, health, and job performance. Although Barnett does not consider these feedback mechanisms as boundary-spanning strategies, they include changes in individual orientations and work- and family-related behaviors that may prevent work–family conflict or increase work–family fit and facilitation.

RELATIONSHIPS BETWEEN WORK–FAMILY BALANCE AND ROLE PERFORMANCE AND QUALITY AND INDIVIDUAL WELL-BEING

The final stage of the model proposes that work–family balance is positively associated with work, family, and community role performance and quality and individual well-being. A global assessment of balance between the work and family domains is posited to improve performance and quality in both domains as well as to have positive effects on community role performance and quality and individual well-being. Positive behaviors and psychological spillover associated with high levels of work demands–family resources fit and family demands–work resources fit influence work–family balance, which in turn is associated with high work, community, and family role performance and quality and individual well-being. It also is possible that role performance is a precursor of role quality. Greenhaus and Powell

(2006) propose that performing well in a role is likely to be reflected in increased positive affect. No known studies have examined the consequences of work–family balance as conceptualized here.

SUMMARY

Drawing on person–environment fit theory, this chapter formulates a demands and resources approach that serves as a framework for understanding the role of perceived work–family fit and balance as linking mechanisms between within-domain and boundary-spanning demands and resources and work, family, and community role performance and quality and individual well-being. The conceptual model proposes that work, family, and boundary-spanning demands and resources combine to create two dimensions of work–family fit. Work demands–family resources fit derives from work demands, family resources, and boundary-spanning demands and resources, whereas family demands–work resources fit results from family demands, work resources, and boundary-spanning demands and resources. The two dimensions of work–family fit combine with boundary-spanning strategies to influence work–family balance. Work–family balance then affects work, family, and community role performance and quality and individual well-being.

The elaboration of the model documents the role of work–family fit and balance as linking mechanisms between within-domain and boundary-spanning demands and resources and work, family, and community role performance and quality and individual well-being. It clarifies the meaning of the concepts of work–family fit and balance by integrating disparate approaches and by suggesting how fit and balance may operate together in relation to work and family role performance and quality. It provides guidance for the development of measures of work–family fit and balance and suggests directions for empirical research. In addition, it serves as a first step in developing a more dynamic approach to understanding work–family linkages that may lead to a more nuanced approach to understanding how the efforts of workplaces and families can contribute to improved work and family role performance and quality.

Research on the linkages proposed in the conceptual model is sorely lacking. The few studies of relationships between demands and resources and work–family fit are limited to a few predictors with small nonrepresentative samples. No known studies have examined direct relationships between work–family fit and work–family balance or considered boundary-spanning strategies as mediators or moderators of such relationships. Similarly, no studies were located that investigate work–family balance as conceptualized here in relation to work, family, and community role performance and quality and individual well being.

The bulk of the research that has been conducted focuses on work and family demands and resources in relation to work–family balance without considering the intervening linkages of work–family fit or boundary-spanning strategies. The results of this research show that relationships between work, family, and boundary-spanning demands and resources and various measures of work–family balance sometimes differ across studies. The most consistent findings are found for the negative relationships between work hours and job demands and work–family balance. Having young children in the home is negatively related to work–family balance in some studies but not in others. For resources, job autonomy, supervisor work–family support, and a supportive work–family culture are positively related to work–family balance. Work-support policies generally are not related to balance. This research suffers from several limitations, however. The generalizability of the findings is limited because many of the studies included a large number of predictors without ruling out the possibility of multicollinearity among them. The selection of predictors needs to be guided explicitly by theoretical considerations. In addition, most of the studies used measures of work–family balance whose psychometric properties have not been assessed. These limitations reflect the early stage of development of research on work–family fit and balance.

8

Directions for Future Research

This book uses ecological systems theory as a basis for the development of a conceptual model of linkages through which work, family, and community characteristics influence work, family, and community role performance and quality and individual well-being. The most general form of the model is presented in Figure 1.2 in chapter 1. The top of the model indicates that economic, workplace, family, and community contexts influence the demands, resources, and strategies that are expected to impact work, family, and community role performance and quality and individual well-being. The remainder of the model proposes several ways in which work, family, and community demands and resources are related to work, family, and community role performance and quality and individual well-being. First, the model posits that within-domain and boundary-spanning demands and resources are directly related to work, family, and community role performance and quality and individual well-being. This general proposition is the basis for much of the extant research on relationships among work, family, and community life. Second, the model serves as a framework for proposing a chain of relationships through which these direct effects may operate. Demands and resources lead to work–family linking mechanisms (i.e., economic strain and work–family conflict, facilitation, and fit), which mediate relationships between demands and resources and work–family balance and work, family, and community role performance and quality and individual well-being. Linking mechanisms also are associated with boundary-spanning strategies, which are proposed to have both mediating and moderating effects on relationships between linking mechanisms and work–family balance. In addition, feedback effects are proposed from boundary-spanning strategies to work, family, and community demands and resources. Using this model as a framework, the preceding chapters have summarized and integrated the theoretical and empirical research and scholarship that has examined the complex interconnections between work, family, and community life. Based on this review and analysis, this chapter presents an agenda for future research.

The model presented in Figure 1.2 is based on our current state of knowledge. Because the amount and quality of research vary considerably for the various aspects of the model, our knowledge base is inadequate for the construction and elaboration of a completely developed model. Additional research undoubtedly will generate a revised conceptual model. Because of the lack of a strong research base for the model, much needs to be done. The extensive agenda for future research focuses on three main areas of improvement. First, the review in the previous chapters indicates that several of the relationships in the model have not been examined, that the extant studies often do not include all of the relevant variables needed to document a predicted relationship, and that the measures used in many studies are inadequate. These problems must be addressed in future studies. Second, future research needs to view the model as a temporal process that requires longitudinal research. Last, it is important for future studies to specify the conditions under which relationships occur in terms of individual characteristics and social categories, social context and cross-cultural variation, and couples and families as units of analysis.

EXAMINE RELATIONSHIPS MORE COMPLETELY WITH BETTER MEASURES

The conceptual model provides a series of relationships that address the nature and functioning of the work–family–community mesosystem. Each of these proposed relationships requires systematic empirical testing with studies that meet high methodological standards. This section provides recommendations for additional testing of the major relationships proposed in the model, that is, relationships between within-domain and boundary-spanning work, family, and community demands and resources and cross-domain role performance and quality and individual well-being; work–family linking mechanisms as mediators of these relationships; and the relationship between work–family fit and work–family balance.

Relationships between Within-Domain and Boundary-Spanning Demands and Resources and Role Performance and Quality and Individual Well-Being

Additive Relationships.   The most basic component of the model is the prediction that within-domain and boundary-spanning demands and resources influence work, family, and community role performance and quality and individual well-being. This proposed relationship provides the rationale for much of the existing research on the work–family–community mesosystem. Most of the research presumes that the effects of various demands and resources across domains are additive; that is, each demand or resource has an independent effect on the aspects of role performance and quality or individual well-being being examined. In most studies, some demands and resources are more strongly related to outcomes than others, and some demands and resources have no effects on outcomes. Despite this, in general, the expectation of additive effects of demands and resources on role performance and quality and individual well-being is supported.

However, our understanding of this general proposition could be enhanced by expanding this part of the model in two directions. First, it may be important to examine nonlinear relationships. This suggestion is based on the fact that some characteristics that are considered as demands (e.g., time-based demands) actually incorporate aspects of both demands and resources; for example, paid work hours reduce the time available for family activities while bringing needed income into the home. This suggests that work hours may have positive effects on family life by providing resources to the family; however, when work hours reach a threshold level, the resource drain associated with long work hours may reduce family and community role performance and quality and individual well-being. The same may hold for boundary-spanning demands such as commuting time. Perhaps a moderate time spent commuting serves as a period of decompression and preparation, whereas long commutes create difficult transitions between domains. Testing for nonlinear relationships would be useful in this regard.

Additional conceptual work regarding the nature and operation of demands and resources also is needed. More detailed and focused measures could shed additional light on how the mixture of demands and resources associated with within-domain and boundary-spanning demands and resources influence outcomes. For example, it would be theoretically useful to be able to separate out the demand and resource components of demands such as working at home and informal social support. Both appear to contain elements of demands (role blurring and emotional demands) and resources (performing family activities while working at home and emotional support).

The second extension of the general proposition that demands and resources show additive relationships with role performance and quality and individual well-being involves examining the processes through which these effects occur. Because of a lack of comprehensive information, these mediating effects are not specified in the conceptual model. However, some of the studies reviewed in earlier chapters have provided examples of how such processes may operate. For example, chapter 3 discussed studies revealing that job demands (e.g., job insecurity) influence marital quality and children's well-being through their effects on job tension, psychosomatic symptoms, negative emotional states, and destructive parenting behaviors. Chapter 4 documented that job resources influence role performance and quality and well-being through their negative associations with these mechanisms. In addition, chapter 5 indicated that working at home influences psychological distress through the mechanism of multitasking. Further knowledge of such processes is important for a more complete understanding of how the model operates.

Although the model proposes that within-domain and boundary-spanning demands are directly related to work, family, and community role performance and quality and individual well-being, it also would be useful to extend this analysis by exploring interrelationships among the various outcomes. It is difficult to compare directly the effects of a given demand or resource on the diverse outcomes included in the model because few studies include the multiple outcomes needed to make such comparisons. In addition, it would be informative to examine relationships among the diverse outcomes. For example, Figure 2.2 presents a research-based model in which economic pressure is associated with a sequence of family outcomes, namely, parents' emotional distress, marital conflict, disrupted parenting, and adolescent maladjustment. Other studies propose a more general causal order among the types of role performance and quality and individual well-being considered in earlier chapters; for example, individual well-being has been considered both as causally prior to and as a consequence of the quality of work and family life. Others have proposed that performance in a given domain is causally prior to the perceived quality of life experienced in that domain (Greenhaus & Powell, 2006).

Interactive Relationships.   Although the general model assumes additive relationships among the demands and resources, earlier chapters also discussed the limited research that addresses the extent to which demands and resources have interactive effects on outcomes. Demands from one domain may exacerbate the effects of demands from another domain, resources from one domain may amplify the effects of resources from another domain, or resources from one domain may buffer the effects of demands from another domain. The extant findings are merely suggestive with regard to these moderating effects. Studies that have examined such effects generally report mixed results; that is, some effects are statistically significant whereas others are not. Moreover, even when effects are statistically significant, they generally explain little variance in the dependent variables. Despite these limited findings, the theoretical rationale underlying interactive effects suggests they are a promising area of study.

More Variables and Better Measures. In addition to these expansions of the model, research is needed that examines more of the proposed relationships with a more comprehensive range of demands and resources. Moreover, measurement issues must be addressed. Chapters 3 through 6 revealed that the effects of work demands and resources on role performance and quality and individual well-being have been studied more extensively than family and community demands and resources. Despite this, more complete information on work-based demands and resources is needed in several areas. Other potentially important demands and resources should be examined, for example, emotional demands, work-role conflict and ambiguity, psychological involvement, performance feedback, and psychological rewards such as status enhancement and personality enrichment. Measures of some frequently studied work demands and resources need improvement, such as dummy variables that lack specificity (e.g., working at home and the availability of flexible work schedules). Much of the previous research also has lumped together aspects of work characteristics that are proposed to be differentially related to outcomes in the proposed model. For example, many studies examine the effects of the number of available boundary-spanning resources rather than constructing separate measures for work support and family support policies and programs. Similarly, many measures of social support combine support from friends, relatives, and coworkers rather than examining each type separately.

Several aspects of the model have not been explored with reference to family demands and resources. In addition, when studies incorporate family demands and resources, they often do not include the full range of relevant demands and resources. Because previous research is so limited, it is difficult to specify possible similarities or differences across four types of family role or activity, that is, spouse, household, parenting, and kin. The marital relationship and household activities are core aspects of family life, whereas relationships with children and extended kin are more variable among diverse types of families. Few studies incorporate all four types of family demands and resources. In general, research has focused on time-based and strain-based family demands and spouse and kin support. Research on family adaptability and cohesion and family-based psychological rewards, boundary-spanning demands, and boundary-spanning resources is sparse.

Moreover, more relevant measures of family roles and activities are needed. More specific information could be obtained by having detailed measures of the amount of time spent in the four family activity arenas. Studies need to develop measures of parenting and elder care demands that move beyond proxy measures of the number and ages and children and whether or not one is caring for an elderly parent. Children's problems are only one aspect of the demands associated with parenting over the life course. In addition, measures of parenting rewards are limited. Measures that assess the range of parenting demands and resources would incorporate the diversity associated with rearing children of different ages. Additional research is needed that includes a more comprehensive range of variables that can assess more specifically the processes associated with each role dimension in relation to linking mechanisms and outcomes.

Studies that include community demands and resources are even more limited than those for family demands and resources. The examination of community factors in relation to the work–family interface is in its early stages. The conceptual model includes community demands and resources that are associated with three aspects of community life: the local community as a whole, the neighborhood as a small geographically based area, and friends who serve as a major source of informal, nonfamily interaction. Within this context, studies have focused on a few aspects of community life, for example, time-based and strain-based community demands and community-based enabling resources. However, other community demands and resources may be relevant to work and family role participation and quality and individual well-being. These include the lack of compatibility between work hours and the schedules of community services and schools, psychological rewards associated with community participation (e.g., sense of accomplishment, mastery, and self-esteem), community-based programs and services needed by working families (e.g., child and elder care and community-based transportation to and from work and after-school programs), and a physical layout that makes it easy to access needed services. Additional studies should explore the influence of these community demands and resources on outcomes.

Indicators of community participation could be improved by measuring participation in specific types of volunteer work such as work-related professional and community organizations and family-related or youth organizations. Aspects of neighborhood and friend contact could be distinguished; for example, time in informal socializing with friends and neighbors could be examined separately from time in direct assistance, such as transportation and child care. All of the proposed relationships regarding the role of community demands, resources, and strategies require examination through studies that are methodologically sound and incorporate a range of community characteristics. This is needed for an analysis of the relative importance of the various community factors and the processes through which they influence linking mechanisms and outcomes.

Work–Family Linking Mechanisms as Mediators

The general conceptual model proposes that work–family linking mechanisms (i.e., economic strain and work–family conflict, facilitation, and fit) mediate relationships between work, family, and community demands and resources and work–family balance. Work–family balance in turn is associated with work, family, and community role performance and quality and individual well-being. Because of significant gaps in the research, the more specific models discussed in chapters 2 through 6 focused on linking mechanisms as mediators of the effects of demands and resources on role performance and quality and individual well-being rather than work–family balance.

For mediating effects to occur, demands and resources must be associated with linking mechanisms, which in turn are associated with outcomes. Research reviewed in chapter 2 documents these direct relationships and mediating effects for economic strain. Chapters 3 through 7 review direct and mediating effects for work–family conflict, facilitation, and fit. The research for these linking mechanisms reveals a relatively complex pattern of findings. The elaboration of relationships between within-domain demands and resources in chapters 3 and 4 proposed that within-domain demands were differentially salient for work–family conflict, whereas within-domain resources were relatively important in relation to work–family facilitation. In addition, chapters 5, 6, and 7 proposed that boundary-spanning demands and resources have comparable salience for work–family conflict, facilitation, and fit. Although limited research has supported these propositions, additional theoretical and empirical work is needed to understand the mechanisms and processes through which this may happen and to document the extent to which and the conditions under which it occurs.

In addition to the distinction between differential and comparable salience, the discussion in previous chapters proposed that work-based within-domain demands are related to work-to-family conflict whereas family-based within-domain demands are associated with family-to-work conflict. Much research supports this idea. However, boundary-spanning demands and resources are expected to be related to both directions of conflict and facilitation. The research discussed earlier generally provides more support for this idea than for the comparable salience of boundary-spanning demands and resources. It is difficult to draw conclusions about either proposition because so little research has examined work–family facilitation.

Increased understanding of the role of work–family conflict, facilitation, fit, and balance as linking mechanisms between work, family, and community demands and resources and cross-domain role performance and quality and individual well-being is dependent on improved conceptualization and measurement of these linking mechanisms. Of the four mechanisms, conceptual and empirical work is most developed for work–family conflict. A great deal of research has examined the sources and consequences of work–family conflict. Moreover, as part of this research, several relatively comprehensive and reliable measures of work–family conflict have been developed (see Tetrick & Buffardi, 2005, for an analysis and critique of measures of work–family conflict).

However, the conceptualization and measurement of work–family facilitation are in their early stages. This book has conceptualized work–family facilitation in terms of resource generation and positive psychological spillover. Others have used similar approaches; for example, Greenhaus and Powell (2006) elaborate instrumental and affective paths through which resources in one role enhance performance in another role. However, neither the conceptualization nor measurement of work–family facilitation has been adequate to generate extensive research of the sources and consequences of facilitation. Two current measures of work–family facilitation used in national surveys have limited range and reliabilities. An adequate measure must include items that address both resource generation and positive psychological spillover. The National Study of the Changing Workforce measure consists of items regarding mood and energy, which focus on spillover and one aspect of resource generation. However, additional items are needed that include other aspects of resource generation such as work behaviors, attitudes, and skills. The measure used in the National Survey of Midlife Development in the United States includes items that address resource generation but not positive psychological spillover. More comprehensive measures, which incorporate both research generation and psychological spillover, have been developed recently by Carlson, Kacmar, Wayne, and Grzywacz (2006), Geurts et al. (2005), and Hanson, Hammer, and Colton (in press). Future research based on these and other new measures will improve our understanding of facilitation.

Work–Family Fit and Balance

Chapter 7 presented a model of the sources and consequences of work–family fit and balance. However, the review of previous measures and empirical research on work–family fit and balance reveals unresolved issues and suggests directions for further development. Most generally, additional work on the development and testing of the model is needed. The limited and problematic research reviewed in chapter 7 does not allow an adequate evaluation of the efficacy of the model. Scholars need to test the various relationships proposed in the model and to consider alternative paths. First, it is important to compare the ways in which demands and resources may combine in relation to work–family fit. Is it useful to compare demands and resources across domains on the basis of the person–environment fit approach in which distinctions are made between demands-abilities and needs-supplies? Or is it sufficient to examine the overall additive effects of work, family, and boundary-spanning demands and resources on fit? Do demands and resources combine to influence fit in other ways—for example, do resources buffer the negative effects of demands on fit?

Furthermore, improved model development requires better measures of work–family fit and more adequate studies that examine the relationships proposed in the model. Measurement of work–family fit is quite undeveloped. The most comprehensive measure of work–family fit has been developed by Teng (1999). Her measures of the two types of fit, however, are not comparable to each other. The measure of work demands–family abilities fit consists of the additive combination of several work demands and family abilities, whereas the work rewards–family needs items are a direct appraisal of work rewards–family needs fit that asks how well several benefits of the job meet individual and family needs. Two other measures of work–family fit assess specific aspects of family demands-work resources fit. Barnett et al. (1999) focus on the extent to which work hours and scheduling meet individual and family needs, whereas Pittman (1994) addresses whether the military is responsive to family needs. Bakker (2005) uses a similar approach with a measure that reflects within-domain work demands–abilities fit by using items such as "I am well able to meet the demands of my work" and "I have sufficient skills to carry out my work tasks properly." Similar questions could be designed that address work demands–family resources and family demands–work resources fit, for example, "To what extent does support from your spouse help you handle demands from your employer to work overtime?"

Most studies of work–family balance use a single-item measure that assesses individual appraisals regarding the level of satisfaction or success with the balance between work and family life or the balance of work and family demands or responsibilities. Such measures provide useful global assessments of work–family balance. When the question references balancing work and family demands or responsibilities rather than overall work and family life, however, the consideration of resources as part of the process is implied but not directly considered. It is encouraging to note that multi-item scales of work–family balance are under development. Some are more relevant to the demands and resources approach presented in chapter 7 than others, however. Perhaps the most compatible are those that assess individual abilities to perform activities in both the work and family domains effectively. For example, the Valcour and Batt (2003) scale assesses the level of satisfaction with the way respondents divide their time and attention between work and personal or family life, how well their work and personal or family life fit together, their ability to balance the needs of their job with their personal or family life, and their opportunity to perform their job well and yet be able to perform home-related duties adequately. A scale being developed by Joplin et al. (2003) includes subscales measuring equilibrium (I feel fulfilled in all aspects of my life), control (e.g., I manage all aspects of my life effectively), and synchrony (My personal life and my work life are complementary). Such approaches hold promise for more comprehensive measures of fit and balance.

CONCEPTUALIZE THE MODEL AS A TEMPORAL PROCESS

Another critical need is to further specify the model as a temporal process. This requires a methodology that is qualitative, at least initially, and longitudinal. Particular aspects of the work–family–community mesosytem, that is, specific combinations of work, family, and community characteristics, need to be studied over time. Tracking the effects of a change in work, family, or community characteristics on work, family, and community role performance and quality and individual well-being would be useful, for example, changes in work hours or scheduling, the birth of a child, or moving to a new neighborhood. (See, for example, Holtzman and Glass's 1999 longitudinal study of the factors associated with changes in job satisfaction following the birth of a child.)

Within-domain and boundary-spanning demands and resources have been conceptualized as creating or preventing work–family conflict, facilitation, and fit, whereas boundary-spanning strategies are proposed as responses to conflict, facilitation, and fit. This formulation needs to be tested in studies using a longitudinal design. For example, changes in employment or community conditions (e.g., work hours or scheduling, neighborhood or school situation, or use of community services) could be tracked over time to assess their effects on conflict, facilitation, and family well-being. Greenhaus and Parasuraman (1999) propose a similar approach when they suggest viewing the occurrence of work–family conflict as a "stress episode." (Also see Thoits, 1995, for a discussion of "stress sequences.")

Longitudinal data also are needed to address the thorny problems discussed in chapter 7, namely, the role of preventive versus therapeutic boundary-spanning strategies. The model's use of boundary-spanning strategies as mediators and moderators of relationships between the two dimensions of work–family fit and work–family balance also requires additional conceptual and empirical work. The model proposes that boundary-spanning strategies are used to reduce the negative effects of work–family misfit on work–family balance (a therapeutic effect). This is an oversimplification, however. In some cases strategies may prevent work–family misfit in the first place (a preventive effect). In addition, preventive strategies are comparable to the availability of boundary-spanning resources as discussed in chapter 6, whereas therapeutic strategies are similar to the use of work–family policies. Studying the use of policies rather than their availability has been problematic because causal direction is difficult to establish. In cross-sectional research one cannot distinguish between policies that are ineffective and situations in which those with the most demanding family situations are most likely to use the policies (Batt & Valcour, 2003). Only longitudinal research can document these distinctions empirically.

A longitudinal approach can be extended further by considering processes underlying responses to the work–family–community mesosystem over the life course. For example, Kofodimos (1990) discusses a "spiraling imbalance" between work and family over the careers of executives as they increasingly make decisions favoring work over family responsibilities. In addition, Han and Moen (1999) refer to the turning points and transitions involved in couples' meshing of work and family careers over the life course. Swisher, Sweet, and Moen (2004) have taken a first step in this direction in the area of community by examining differences in perceptions of community family-friendliness for families in different life course stages.

SPECIFY THE CONDITIONS UNDER WHICH RELATIONSHIPS OCCUR

Although it is desirable to propose and elaborate a model that is generalizable across diverse situations, it also is important to examine the conditions under which relationships occur to verify that the model is in fact appropriate in a variety of circumstances. These include the extent to which relationships hold across variations in individual characteristics and social categories, social contexts, and cultures, and for couples and families as well as individuals.

Incorporate Individual Characteristics and Intersecting Social Categories

Until recently, researchers have given little attention to the extent to which individual characteristics may influence relationships among demands and resources, linking mechanisms, strategies, and outcomes. However, several recent studies have documented their relevance and the need for further examination. For example, Parasuraman and Greenhaus (2002) have reviewed studies that document the influence of stable dispositional traits such as negative affectivity on how individuals appraise their environment. Stress associated with negative affectivity also affects work–family conflict. The value of considering a broad picture of personality has been shown by Wayne et al. (2004), who examined the Big Five personality traits (conscientiousness, neuroticism, extraversion, agreeableness, and openness to experience) in relation to work–family conflict and facilitation. The pattern of results revealed that some traits were related to both conflict and facilitation, whereas others were related to either conflict or facilitation. It would be useful to extend this analysis to other outcomes and to consider personality traits as moderators of relationships in the model.

In addition, relationships in the model may differ according to several social categories to which individuals belong. Marks and Leslie (2000) have provided a provocative discussion of the need for considering intersecting social categories in multiple roles research. They include five social categories: social class, gender, race, household structure, and sexual orientation. Research designs and samples need to be broadened to include enough data so that relevant social categories can be examined across the full range of variability. For example, although qualitative research reveals that low-income families experience more severe work and community demands with fewer resources, few studies have made systematic comparisons across social classes. These social categories may serve as important moderators of relationships between demands and resources and linking mechanisms and the usefulness of boundary-spanning strategies may vary across social categories. They were not included in the model here, however, because the available data are inadequate to illustrate or specify their operation in the model.

Consider Social Context and Cross-Cultural Variation

In addition, the relationships proposed in the model operate within a larger social context. According to ecological systems theory, mesosystems and microsystems are influenced by the larger macrosystem in which they are embedded. The macrosystem includes shared belief systems, social and economic resources, opportunity structures, hazards, and patterns of social interaction. Dimensions of the macrosystem can be incorporated into analyses of work and family relationships through the use of contextual variables, for example, rates of unemployment, divorce, and female employment; organizational size and composition; community social organization and capacity; norms regarding gender roles; and the supply of family-support services. The use of these contextual variables is based on the assumption that individuals evaluate the demands and benefits of their work and family roles in terms of these broader contexts. Despite their importance, little research has included contextual variables.

These aspects of macrosystems vary both within a society and cross-culturally. Thus, it is important to test the model cross-culturally. Initial steps have been taken in this direction and large-scale cross-cultural studies are underway. For example, several studies that examine aspects of work–family conflict in a cross-cultural context are presented in a recent book edited by Steven Poelmans (2005). Limited studies have documented variation in macrosystem characteristics; for example, the rate of female employment varies considerably in different societies. However, the extent to which relationships and processes differ is less evident. Perhaps a given condition has similar effects even though the conditions vary in different societal or cultural contexts. For example, although women generally do paid work for fewer hours per week than men do, the effects of long work hours on family and community role performance and quality and individual well-being may be similar for men and women.

Examine Couples and Families as Units of Analysis

Last, the model needs to be examined on both the individual and couple or family levels of analysis. Although the formulation of the model focuses on the individual level of analysis, the ways in which work, family, and community demands and resources combine to influence linking mechanisms and outcomes operate within the context of a couple or family. For example, the combined work hours and schedules of both partners provide the context in which the need for child care, after-school, and elder-care services arise. Or, the effects of overnight travel on work–family conflict or marital quality may be greater for families in which both partners travel than for those in which only one partner travels. Husbands and wives make joint decisions regarding the division of paid work, household work, and dependent care. In addition, the demands and resources of one partner are likely to have crossover effects on the other partner; for example, the unemployment and economic strain experienced by one partner have negative effects on the individual well-being of the other. Considering the family as the unit of analysis also includes giving more attention to diverse family forms, for example, single-parent families, remarried families and stepfamilies, families with shared custody of children, and childless families with extensive elder care responsibilities (Parasuraman & Greenhaus, 2002). Extending the model to couples and families would incorporate the complexities involved within families as they attempt to coordinate the work and family responsibilities of several members. In addition, the resources brought to bear to address work, family, and community demands and the boundary-spanning strategies used to decrease demands or increase resources are developed and used within the context of the entire family constellation. It is important for studies to begin to formulate research questions in terms of couples and families and to develop useful strategies for answering them.

MOVING FROM RESEARCH TO POLICIES AND PROGRAMS

The relationships proposed in the conceptual model provide implicit implications for policy and practice. Insufficient testing of the model, however, precludes the development of explicit policy and practice recommendations based solely on the model. Nevertheless, it is possible to formulate a broad strategy regarding policies and programs that would encourage the integration of the work, family, and community domains so that they operate together to assist working families coordinate and fulfill their work, community, and family obligations in a way that enhances role performance and quality and individual well-being.

For example, the model reveals the importance of examining not only the demands that may reduce role performance and quality individual well-being but also the resources that may enhance them. Thus, policies and programs should include the enhancement of work, family, community, and boundary-spanning resources as well as the reduction of work, family, community, and boundary-spanning demands. Both can occur either by developing policies and programs that reduce demands and increase resources independently (e.g., by reducing work hours or increasing job autonomy) or by designing policies that address demands and resources jointly (e.g., by creating a supportive work–family culture that focuses on flexibility in meeting family demands such as caregiving for children or parents).

A strategy based on the development of the resources and the reduction of the demands associated with work, family, and community role performance and quality individual well-being represents a preventive rather than a therapeutic approach. For this preventive approach to be effective, work, family, and community demands must be limited and resources must be adequate and accessible to working families. When these conditions do not exist, boundary-spanning strategies are needed that reduce work–family conflict and misfit after it occurs. However, these are viewed as secondary in importance to the preventive approach.

A special emphasis on boundary-spanning demands and resources is warranted because they represent a critical point of intervention for policies and programs designed to enhance role performance and quality and well-being in the context of the work–family–community mesosystem. By addressing the intersection of two domains simultaneously, reducing boundary-spanning demands or increasing boundary-spanning resources is more likely to influence outcomes than altering within-domain demands or resources.

We also need to understand the work context in which boundary-spanning community demands and resources operate. For example, how do boundary-spanning community resources (e.g., after-school and elder-care programs) combine with within-domain work demands (e.g., long work hours) and boundary-spanning work resources (e.g., time off work for family needs or flexible work schedules) to reduce work–family conflict and enhance family well-being?

Work-based policies and programs are a critical part of a strategy designed to enhance family well-being. These policies include increasing the flexibility of work, for example, by developing more flexible employment schedules, providing dependent-care assistance, and creating opportunities for family leave and time off from work to address family needs. Others have reported that these work–family policies are necessary but not sufficient to reduce work–family conflict and increase work–family facilitation. It also is essential to reduce the level of within-domain work demands. Rapoport and her colleagues (2002) have documented the importance for work–family integration of job design efforts that increase worker autonomy and decrease work stress. In addition, Bookman (2004) emphasizes the importance of work organizations' efforts to facilitate community participation among employees and by supporting family support services in the community.

This book has presented a relatively comprehensive framework of the ways in which work, family, and community demands, resources, and strategies affect cross-domain role performance and quality and individual well-being. The formulation and testing of theoretically based hypotheses and the documentation of specific interrelationships among work, community, and family are needed to increase our understanding of how to enhance the integration of work, community, and family life. This additional work also will provide conceptual and empirical grounding for the development of workplace, community, and government policies and programs that enhance rather than hinder the well-being of working families.

SUMMARY

Using a general conceptual model as a framework, this book has summarized and integrated the theoretical and empirical literature that has examined the relationships comprising the work–family–community mesosystem. Despite relatively extensive analysis of parts of the conceptual model, additional conceptual and empirical work is needed to further our understanding of the model and its implications for policies and programs. An agenda for future research includes investigating more of the relationships proposed in the model, incorporating more demands and resources in the analysis, improving measures of the variables being examined, exploring the model as temporal process using longitudinal research, and specifying the individual, contextual, and family circumstances under which the relationships in the model occur.

References

Allen, T. D. (2001). Family-supportive work environments. *Journal of Vocational Behavior, 58,* 414–435.

Allen, T. D., Greenhaus, J. H., & Foley, S. (2005, April). *Family-supportive work environments: Further investigation of mechanisms and benefits.* Paper presented at the Annual Meetings of the Society for Industrial and Organizational Psychology, Los Angeles.

Allen, T. D., Herst, D. E. L., Bruck, C. S., & Sutton, M. (2000). Consequences associated with work-to-family conflict: A review and agenda for future research. *Journal of Occupational Health Psychology, 5,* 278–308.

Almeida, D. M., & McDonald, D. A. (2005). The national story: How Americans spend their time on work, family, and community. In J. Heymann & C. Beem (Eds.), *Unfinished work: Building equality and democracy in an era of working families* (pp. 180–203). New York: New Press.

Anderson, S. E., Coffey, B. S., & Byerly, R. T. (2002). Formal organizational initiatives and informal workplace practices. *Journal of Management, 28,* 787–810.

Aneshensel, C. S., & Sucoff, C. A. (1996). The neighborhood context of adolescent mental health. *Journal of Health and Social Behavior, 37,* 293–310.

Applebaum, E. (2003). *The transformation of work and employment in the U.S.* Working paper, Center for Women and Work, Rutgers.

Arulampalam, P., Gregg, P., & Gregory, M. (2001). Unemployment scarring. *The Economic Journal, 111,* F577–F584.

Ashforth, B. E., Kreiner, G. E., & Fugate, M. (2000). All in a day's work. *Academy of Management Review, 25,* 472 – 491.

Avison, W. R. (2001). Unemployment and its consequences for mental health. In V. W. Marshall, W. R. Heinz, H. Krueger, & A. Verma (Eds.), *Restructuring work and the life course* (pp. 177–200). Toronto: University of Toronto Press.

Bakker, A. B. (2005). Flow among music teachers and their students. *Journal of Vocational Behavior, 66,* 26–44.

Barling, J., & MacEwen, K. E. (1992). Linking work experiences to facets of marital functioning. *Journal of Organizational Behavior, 13,* 573–583.

Barling, J., Zacharatos, A., & Hepburn, C. G. (1999). Parents' job insecurity affects children's academic performance through cognitive difficulties. *Journal of Applied Psychology, 84,* 437–444.

Barnett, R. C. (1994). Home-to-work spillover revisited: A study of full-time employed women in dual-earner couples. *Journal of Marriage and the Family, 56,* 647–656.

Barnett, R. C. (1998). Toward a review and reconceptualization of the work/family literature. *Genetic, Social, and General Psychology Monographs, 124,* 124–182.

Barnett, R. C., & Gareis, K. C. (2006). Antecedents and correlates of parental after-school stress: Exploring a newly identified work–family stressor. *American Behavioral Scientist, 49,* 1382–1399.

Barnett, R. C., Gareis, K. C., & Brennan, R. T. (1999). Fit as a mediator of the relationship between work hours and burnout. *Journal of Occupational Health Psychology, 4,* 307–317.

Barnett, R. C., and Marshall, N. L. (1992a). Men's job and partner roles: Spillover effects and psychological distress. *Sex Roles, 27,* 455–472.

Barnett, R. C., & Marshall, N. L. (1992b). Worker and mother roles, spillover effects, and psychological distress. *Women & Health, 18,* 9–40.

Barnett, R. C., Marshall, N. L., & Pleck, J. H. (1992). Men's multiple roles and their relationship to men's psychological distress. *Journal of Marriage and the Family, 54,* 358–367.

Barnett, R. C., Marshall, N. L., & Sayer, A. (1992). Positive-spillover effects from job to home: A closer look. *Women & Health, 19,* 13–41.

Barnett, R. C., & Shen, Y. (1997). Gender, high- and low-schedule-control housework tasks, and psychological distress. *Journal of Family Issues, 18,* 403–428.

Barrera, M., Jr., Caples, H., & Tein, J-Y. (2001). The psychological sense of economic hardship: Measurement models, validity, and cross-ethnic equivalence for urban families. *American Journal of Community Psychology, 29,* 493–517.

Bass, B. L., Grzywacz, J. G., Butler, A. B., & Linney, K. D. (2004, November). *The impact of job demands on daily parent–child interactions.* Paper presented at the annual meetings of the National Council on Family Relations, Orlando, FL.

Batt, R. & Valcour, P. M. (2003). Human resource practices as predictors of work–family outcomes and employee turnover. *Industrial Relations, 42,* 189–200.

Beauregard, T. A. (2005, March). *Factors contributing to work–home interference: Opposite-domain effects and gender differences*. Paper presented at the Community, Work, and Family: Change and Transformation Conference, Manchester, UK.

Becker, P. E., & Moen, P. (1999). Scaling back: Dual-earner couples' work–family strategies. *Journal of Marriage and the Family, 61,* 995–1007.

Beers, T. M. (2000). Flexible schedules and shift work: Replacing the '9-to-5' workday? *Monthly Labor Review, 120/6,* 33–40.

Behson, S. J. (2002a). Coping with family-to-work conflict: The role of informal work accommodations to family. *Journal of Occupational Health Psychology, 7,* 324–341.

Behson, S. J. (2002b). Which dominates? The relative importance of work–family organizational support and general organizational context on employee outcomes. *Journal of Vocational Behavior, 61,* 53–72.

Bellavia, G. M., & Frone, M. R. (2005). Work–family conflict. In J. Barling, E. K. Kelloway, & M. R. Frone (Eds.), *Handbook of work stress* (pp. 113–147). Thousand Oaks, CA: Sage.

Bernstein, J., McNichol, E., & Lyons, K. (2006). *Pulling apart: A state-by-state analysis of income trends*. Washington, DC: Center on Budget and Policy Priorities.

Bianchi, S. M., & Raley, S. B. (2005). Time allocation in families. In S. M. Bianchi, L. M. Casper, & R. B. King (Eds.), *Work, family, health, and well-being* (pp. 21–42). Mahwah, NJ: Lawrence Erlbaum Associates.

Bliese, P. D., & Jex, S. M. (1999). Incorporating multiple levels of analysis into occupational stress literature. *Work & Stress, 13,* 1–6.

Bluestone, B., & Rose, S. (1997). Overworked and underemployed. *American Prospect, 31,* 58–69.

Bond, J. T., Galinsky, E., & Swanberg, J. E. (1998). *The 1997 National Study of the Changing Workforce*. New York: Families and Work Institute.

Bond, J. T., Thompson, C., Galinsky, E., & Prottas, D. (2003). *Highlights of the 2002 National Study of the Changing Workforce*. New York: Families and Work Institute.

Bookman, A. (2004). *Starting in our own backyards*. London: Routledge.

Boraas, S. (2003). Volunteerism in the United States. *Monthly Labor Review, 126,* 3–11.

Bowen, G. L. (1998). Effects of leader support in the work unit on the relationship between work spillover and family adaptation. *Journal of Family and Economic Issues, 19,* 25–52.

Bowen, N. K., & Bowen, G. L. (1999). Effects of crime and violence in neighborhoods and schools on the school behavior and performance of adolescents. *Journal of Adolescent Research, 14,* 319–342.

Boyar, S. L., Maertz, C. P., Jr., & Pearson, A. W. (2005). The effects of work–family conflict and family–work conflict on nonattendance behaviors. *Journal of Business Research, 58,* 919–925.

Brayfield, A. (1995). Juggling jobs and kids: The impact of employment schedules on fathers' caring for children. *Journal of Marriage and the Family, 57,* 321–332.

Broman, C. L., Hamilton, V. L., & Hoffman, W. S. (2002). *Stress and distress among the unemployed*. New York: Kluwer Academic/Plenum.

Bronfenbrenner, U. (1979). *The ecology of human development.* Cambridge, MA: Harvard University Press.

Bronfenbrenner, U. (1989). Ecological systems theory. *Annals of Child Development, 6,* 187–249.

Buchel, F., & Duncan, G. J. (1998). Do parents' social activities promote children's school attainments? Evidence from the German socioeconomic panel. *Journal of Marriage and the Family, 60,* 95–108.

Buffardi, L. C., Smith, J. L., O'Brien, A. S., & Erdwins, C. J. (1999). The impact of dependent care responsibility and gender on work attitudes. *Journal of Occupational Health Psychology, 4,* 356–367.

Burchell, B. (2002). The prevalence and redistribution of job insecurity and work intensification. In B. Burchell, D. Ladipo, & F. Wilkinson (Eds.), *Job insecurity and work intensification* (pp. 61–76). New York: Routledge.

Byron, K. (2005). A meta-analytic review of work–family conflict and its antecedents. *Journal of Vocational Behavior, 67,* 169–198.

Cardenas, R. A., Major, D. A., & Bernas, K. H. (2004). Exploring work and family distractions: Antecedents and outcomes. *International Journal of Stress Management, 11,* 346–365.

Carlson, D. S., Kacmar, K. M., Wayne, J. H., & Grzywacz, J. G. (2006). Measuring the positive side of the work–family interface: Development and validation of a work–family enrichment scale. *Journal of Vocational Behavior, 68,* 131–164.

Carlson, D. S., & Witt, L. A. (2004, April). *The work—family interface and job performance.* Paper presented at the Annual Meetings of the Society for Industrial and Organizational Psychology, Chicago.

Carnoy, M. (2000). *Sustaining the new economy.* Cambridge, MA: Harvard University Press.

Casper, L. M., & Bianchi, S. M. (2002). *Continuity and change in the American family.* Thousand Oaks, CA: Sage.

Casper, L. M., & O'Connell, M. (1998). Work, income, the economy, and married fathers as child-care providers. *Demography, 35,* 243–250.

Clark, S. C. (2000). Work/family border theory. *Human Relations, 53,* 747–770.

Clark, S. C. (2001). Work cultures and work/family balance. *Journal of Vocational Behavior, 58,* 348–365.

Clark, S. C. (2002, August). *Borders between work and home and work/family conflict.* Paper presented at the annual meeting of the Academy of Management, Denver, CO.

Clarke, M. C., Koch, L. C., & Hill, E. J. (2004). The work–family interface. *Family and Consumer Sciences Research Journal, 31,* 121–140.

Colton, C. L., Hammer, L. B., & Neal, M. B. (2002, April). *Informal organizational support and work and family outcomes.* Paper presented at the annual meetings of the Society of Industrial and Organizational Psychology, Toronto.

Coltrane, S. (2000). Research on household labor: Modeling and measuring the social embeddedness of routine family work. *Journal of Marriage and the Family, 62,* 1208–1233.

Conger, K. J., Rueter, M. A., & Conger, R. D. (2000). The role of economic pressure in the lives of parents and their adolescents: The family stress model. In L. Crockett & R. Silbereisen (Eds.), *Negotiating adolescence in times of social change* (pp. 201–233). Cambridge, UK: Cambridge University Press.

Conger, R. D., & Conger, K. J. (2002). Resilience in Midwestern families: Selected findings from the first decade of a prospective, longitudinal study. *Journal of Marriage and Family, 64*, 361–373.

Conger, R. D., & Elder, G. H., Jr. (1994). *Families in troubled times. Adapting to changes in rural America.* New York: Aldine de Gruyter.

Conger, R. D., Rueter, M.A., & Elder, G. H., Jr. (1999). Couple resilience to economic pressure. *Journal of Personality and Social Psychology, 76*, 54–71.

Conger, R. D., Wallace, L. E., Sun, Y., Simons, R. L., McLoyd, V. C., & Brody, G. H. (2002). Economic pressure in African American families: A replication and extension of the family stress model. *Developmental Psychology, 38*, 179–193.

Cotton, S. R., Burton, R. P. D., & Rushing, B. (2003). The mediating effects of attachment to social structure and psychosocial resources on the relationship between marital quality and psychological distress. *Journal of Family Issues, 24*, 547–577.

Crooker, K. J., Smith, F. L., & Tabak, R. (2002). Creating work–family balance. *Human Resource Development Review, 1*, 387–419.

Crouter, A. C. (1984). Participative work as an influence on human development. *Journal of Applied Developmental Psychology, 5*, 71–90.

Crouter, A. C., Bumpus, M. F., Head, M. R., & McHale, S. M. (2001). Implications of overwork and overload for the quality of men's family relationships. *Journal of Marriage and Family, 63*, 404–416.

Crouter, A. C., Bumpus, M. F., Maguire, M. C., & McHale, S. M. (1999). Linking parents' work pressure and adolescents' well-being: Insights into dynamics in dual-earner families. *Developmental Psychology, 35*, 1453–1461.

Crouter, A. C., McHale, S. M. (2005). Work, family, and children's time: Implications for youth. In S. M. Bianchi, L. M. Casper, & R. B. King (Eds.), *Work, family, health, and well-being* (pp. 49–66). Mahwah, NJ: Lawrence Erlbaum Associates.

Cutrona, C. E., Russell, D. W., Hessling, R. M., Brown, P. A., & Murry, V. (2000). Direct and moderating effects of community context on the psychological well-being of African American Women. *Journal of Personality and Social Psychology, 79*, 1088–1101.

Davis, R. D., Pirretti, A. E., Almeida, D. M., & Goodman, B. (2005, November). *Shift work: Relations with work–family spillover and marital quality.* Paper presented at the Annual Meetings of the National Council on Family Relations, Phoenix, AZ.

DeBord, K., Canu, R. G., & Kerpelman, J. (2000). Understanding work–family fit for single parents moving from welfare to work. *Social Work, 45*, 313–324.

de Lange, A. H., Taris, T. W., Kompier, M. A. J., & Houtman, I. L. D. (2003). "The *very* best of the millennium": Longitudinal research and the demand-control-support model. *Journal of Occupational Health Psychology, 8*, 283–305.

Demerouti, E. (2006). Human resource policies for work-personal life integration. In R. Burke & C. Cooper (Eds.), *The human resources revolution* (pp. 147–169). Oxford, UK: Elsevier.

Demerouti, E., Geurts, S. A. E., & Kompier, M. (2004). Positive and negative work–home interaction: Prevalence and correlates. *Equal Opportunities International, 23,*6–35.

Desrochers, S., & Sargent, L. D. (2005, August). *Within individual and cross-over effects of work and boundary stressors of dual-earner couples work and family outcomes.* Paper presented at the Annual Meetings of the Academy of Management, Honolulu, HI.

Dilworth, J. E. L. (2004). Predictors of negative spillover from family to work. *Journal of Family Issues, 25,* 241–261.

Dilworth, J. E. L., & Kingsbury, N. (2005). Home-to-job spillover for generation X, boomers, and matures: A comparison. *Journal of Family and Economic Issues, 26,* 267–281.

Dishion, T. J., Capaldi, D. M., & Yoerger, K. (1999). Middle childhood antecedents to progressions in male adolescent substance use: An ecological analyis of risk and protection. *Journal of Adolescent Research, 14,* 175–205.

Dooley, D. (2003). Unemployment, underemployment, and mental health: Conceptualizing employment status as a continuum. *American Journal of Community Psychology, 32,* 9–20.

Drago, R., & Hyatt, D. (2003). Symposium: The effect of work–family policies on employees and employers. *Industrial Relations, 42,* 139–144.

Eccles, J. S., Barber, B. L., Stone, M., & Hunt, J. (2003). Extracurricular activities and adolescent development. *Journal of Social Issues, 59,* 865–889.

Ecob, R., & Smith, G. D. (1999). Income and health: What is the nature of the relationship? *Social Science and Medicine, 48,* 693–705.

Edwards, J. R., Caplan, R. D., & Harrison, R. V. (1998). Person–environment fit theory. In C. L. Cooper (Eds.), *Theories of organizational stress* (pp. 29–47). New York: Oxford.

Edwards, J. R., & Rothbard, N. P. (1999). Work and family stress and well-being. *Organizational Behavior and Human Decision Processes, 77,* 85–129.

Edwards, J. R., & Rothbard, N. P. (2005). Work and family stress and well-being. In E. E. Kossek & S. J. Lambert (Eds.), *Work and life integration* (pp. 211–242). Mahwah, NJ: Lawrence Erlbaum Associates.

Elder, G. H., Jr., Eccles, J. S., Ardelt, M., & Lord, S. (1995). Inner-city parents under economic pressure: Perspectives on the strategies of parenting. *Journal of Marriage and the Family, 57,* 771–784.

Erickson, R. J., Nichols, L., & Ritter, C. (2000). Family influences on absenteeism: Testing an expanded process model. *Journal of Vocational Behavior, 57,* 246–272.

Estes, S. B. (2004). How are family-responsive workplace arrangements family friendly? Employer accommodations, parenting, and children's socioemotional well-being. *Sociological Quarterly, 45,* 637–661.

Estes, S. B. (2005). Work–family arrangements and parenting: Are "family-friendly" arrangements related to mothers' involvement in children's lives? *Sociological Perspectives, 48,* 293–317.

Estes, S. B., Maume, D. J., & Noonan, M. C. (2005). *Is work–family policy use related to the gendered division of housework?* Under review.

Ettner, S. L., & Grzywacz, J. G. (2001). Workers' perceptions of how jobs affect health: A social ecological perspective. *Journal of Occupational Health Psychology, 6,* 101–113.

Ezra, M., & Deckman, M. (1996). Balancing work and family responsibilities. *Public Administration Review, 56,* 174–179.

Fein, D. J. (2004). *Married and poor: Basic characteristics of economically disadvantaged married couples in the U.S.* Bethesda, MD: Abt Associates. Retrieved May 20, 2005, from http://www.mdrc.org/publications/393/workpaper.pdf.

Fenwick, R., & Tausig, M. (2004). The health and family social consequences of shift work and schedule control: 1977 and 1997. In C. F. Epstein & A. L. Kalleberg (Eds.), *Fighting for time* (pp. 77–110). New York: Russell Sage Foundation.

Fisher-McAuley, G., Stanton, J. M., Jolton, J. A., & Gavin, J. A. (2003, April). *Modeling the relationship between work/life balance and organizational outcomes.* Paper presented at the Annual Meeting of the Society for Industrial and Organizational Psychology, Orlando, FL.

Ford, M. T., Kitka, B., & Langkamer, K. L. (2005, April). *Work and family satisfaction and conflict: A meta-analysis of cross-domain relationships.* Paper presented at the Annual Meetings of the Society for Industrial and Organizational Psychology, Los Angeles.

Forthofer, M. S., Markman, H. J., Cox, M., Stanley, S., & Kessler, R. C. (1996). Associations between marital distress and work loss in a national sample. *Journal of Marriage and the Family,58,* 597–605.

Fox, G. L., Benson, M. L., DeMaris, A. A., & Van Wyk, J. (2002). Economic distress and intimate violence: Testing family stress and resource theories. *Journal of Marriage and Family, 64,* 793–807.

Friedland, D. S., & Price, R. H. (2003). Underemployment: Consequences for the health and well-being of workers. *American Journal of Community Psychology, 32,* 33–45.

Friedman, S. D., & Greenhaus, J. H. (2000). *Work and family—Allies or enemies?* New York: Oxford.

Frone, M. R. (2003). Work–family balance. In J. C. Quick & L. E. Tetrick (Eds.), *Handbook of occupational health psychology* (pp. 143–162). Washington, DC: American Psychological Association.

Frone, M. R., Yardley, J. K., & Markel, K. S. (1997). Developing and testing an integrative model of the work–family interface. *Journal of Vocational Behavior, 50,* 145–167.

Fu, C. K., & Shaffer, M.A. (2001). The tug of work and family: Direct and indirect domain-specific determinants of work–family conflict. *Personnel Review, 30,* 502–522.

Furstenberg, F. F., Jr., & Hughes, M. E. (1995). Social capital and successful development among at-risk youth. *Journal of Marriage and the Family, 57,* 580–592.

Galinsky, E., Bond, J. T., & Hill, E. J. (2004). *When work works: A status report on workplace flexibility.* New York: Families and Work Institute.

Ganster, D. C., & Bates, C. A. (2003, August). *Do long work hours decrease general well-being and increase work–family conflict?* Paper presented at the annual meetings of the Academy of Management, Seattle.

Gerard, J. M., & Buehler, C. (2004). Cumulative environmental risk and youth problem behavior. *Journal of Marriage and Family, 66,* 702–720.

Geurts, S. A. E., & Demerouti, E. (2003). Work/non-work interface: A review of theory and findings. In M. J. Schabracz, J. A. M. Winnubst, & C. L. Cooper (Eds.), *The handbook of work and health psychology* (pp. 279–312). London: John Wiley & Sons.

Geurts, S. A. E., Kompier, M. A. J., Roxburgh, S., & Houtman, I. L. D. (2003). Does work–home interference mediate the relationship between workload and well-being? *Journal of Vocational Behavior, 63,* 532–559.

Geurts, S., Rutte, C., & Peeters, M. (1999). Antecedents and consequences of work–home interference among medical residents. *Social Science and Medicine, 48,* 1135–1148.

Geurts, S. A. E., Toon, T. W., Kompier, M. A. J., Dikkers, J. S. E., Van Hooff, L. M., & Kinnunen, U. M. (2005). Work–home interaction from a work psychological perspective: Development and validation of a new questionnaire, the SWING. *Work & Stress, 19,* 319–329.

Glass, J., & Finley, A. (2002). Coverage and effectiveness of family-responsive workplace policies. *Human Resource Management Review, 12,* 313–337.

Glass, J., & Fujimoto, T. (1994). Housework, paid work, and depression among husbands and wives. *Journal of Health and Social Behavior, 35,* 179–191.

Gonzales, N. A., Cauce, A. M., Friedman, R. J. & Mason, C. A. (1996). Family, peer, and neighborhood influences on academic achievement among African-American adolescents. *American Journal of Community Psychology, 24,* 365–387.

Grandey, A. A., Cordeiro, B. L., & Crouter, A. C. (2005). A longitudinal and multi-source test of the work–family conflict and job satisfaction relationship. *Journal of Occupational and Organizational Psychology, 78,* 305–323.

Grant, K. E., Compas, B. E., Stuhlmacher, A. F., Thurm, A E., McMahon, S. D., & Halpert, J. A. (2003). Stressors and child and adolescent psychopathology: Moving from markers to mechanisms of risk. *Psychological Bulletin, 129,* 447–466.

Greenberger, E. & O'Neil, R. (1993). Spouse, parent, worker: Role commitments and role-related experiences in the construction of adults' well-being. *Developmental Psychology, 29,* 181–197.

Greenhaus, J. H., Allen, T. D., & Spector, P. E. (2006). Health consequences of work–family conflict: The dark side of the work–family interface. In P. L. Perrewe & D. C. Ganster (Eds.), *Employee health, coping and methodologies* (pp. 61–98). Greenwich, CT: JAI.

Greenhaus J. H., & Beutell, N. J. (1985). Sources of conflict between work and family roles. *Academy of Management Journal, 10,* 76–88.

Greenhaus, J. H., Collins, K. M., & Shaw, J. D. (2003) The relation between work–family balance and quality of life. *Journal of Vocational Behavior, 63,* 510–531.

Greenhaus, J. H., & Parasuraman, S. (1987). A work-nonwork interactive perspective of stress and its consequences. In J. M. Ivancevich and D. C. Ganster (Eds.), *Job stress: From theory to suggestion* (pp. 37–60). New York: Haworth Press.

Greenhaus, J. H., & Parasuraman, S. (1994). Work–family conflict, social support and well-being. In M. J. Davidson & R. J. Burke (Eds.), *Women in management: Current research issues* (pp. 213–229). London: Paul Chapman.

Greenhaus, J. H., Parasuraman, S. (1999). Research on work, family, and gender: Current status and future directions. In G. N. Powell (Ed.), *Handbook of gender and work* (pp. 391–412).

Greenhaus, J. H., & Powell, G. N. (2006). When work and family are allies. *Academy of Management Review.31*, 72–92.

Grover, S. L., & Crooker, K. J. (1995). Who appreciates family-responsive human resource policies. *Personnel Psychology, 48*, 271–288.

Grzywacz, J. G. (2000). Work–family spillover and health during midlife. *American Journal of Health Promotion, 14*, 236–243.

Grzywacz, J. G., & Bass, B. L. (2003). Work, family, and mental health: Testing different models of work–family fit. *Journal of Marriage and Family, 65*, 248–262.

Grzywacz, J. G., & Dooley, D. (2003). "Good jobs" to "bad jobs": Replicated evidence of an employment continuum from two large surveys. *Social Science and Medicine, 56*, 1749–1760.

Grzywacz, J. G., & Marks, N. F. (2000). Reconceptualizing the work–family interface. *Journal of Occupational Health Psychology, 5*, 111–126.

Grzywacz, J. G., & Marks, N. F. (2001). Social inequalities and exercise during adulthood: Toward an ecological perspective. *Journal of Health and Social Behavior, 42*, 202–220.

Grzywacz, J. G., Rao, P., Woods, C. R., Preisser, J. S., Gesler, W. M., & Arcury, T. A. (2005). Children's health and workers' productivity: An examination of family interference with work in rural America. *Journal of Occupational Health Psychology, 10*, 382–392.

Guelzow, M. G., Bird, G. W., & Koball, E. H. (1991). An exploratory path analysis of the stress process for dual-career men and women. *Journal of Marriage and the Family, 53*, 151–164.

Gutman, L. M., & Eccles, J. S. (1999). Financial strain, parenting behaviors, and adolescents' achievement: Testing model equivalence between African American and European American single- and two-parent families. *Child Development, 70*, 1464–1476.

Haas, L. (1999). Families and work. In S. K. Steinmetz & G. W. Peterson (Eds.), *Handbook of marriage and the family* (2nd ed., pp. 571–611). New York: Plenum.

Hammer, L. B., Bauer, T. N., & Grandey, A. A. (2003). Work–family conflict and work-related withdrawal behaviors. *Journal of Business and Psychology, 17*, 419–436.

Hammer, L. B., Neal, M.B., Newsom, J. T., Brockwood, K. J., & Colton, C. L. (2005). A longitudinal study of the effects of dual-earner couples' utilization of family-friendly workplace supports on work and family outcomes. *Journal of Applied Psychology, 90*, 799–810.

Han, S., & Moen, P. (1999). Work and family over time: A life course approach. *Annals of the American Academy of Political and Social Science, 562*, 98–110.

Han, W. (2005). Maternal nonstandard work schedules and child cognitive outcomes. *Child Development, 76*, 137–154.

Hanisch, K. A. (1999). Job loss and unemployment research from 1994 to 1998: A review and recommendations for research and intervention. *Journal of Vocational Behavior, 55*, 188–220.

Hanson, G. C., Hammer, L. B., & Colton, C. L. (in press). Development and validation of a multidimensional scale of perceived work–family positive spillover, *Journal of Occupational Health Psychology*.

Hanson, S., & Pratt, G. (1988). Reconceptualizing the links between home and work in urban geography. *Economic Geography, 64*, 299–321.

Hashima, P. Y., & Amato, P. R. (1994). Poverty, social support, and parental behavior. *Child Development, 65,* 394–403.

Hayghe, H. V. (1991). Volunteers in the U.S.: Who donates the time? *Monthly Labor Review, 114 (February),* 17–23.

Hecht, T. D., & Allen, N. J. (2004a, April). *Drawing the line: Validating a measure of work/nonwork boundary strength.* Paper presented at the Annual Meeting of the Society for Industrial and Organizational Psychology, Chicago.

Hecht, T. D., & Allen, N. J. (2004b, April). *Exploring the nomological network of work/nonwork boundary strength.* Paper presented at the Annual Meeting of the Society for Industrial and Organizational Psychology, Chicago.

Hepburn, C. G., & Barling, J. (1996). Eldercare responsibilities, interrole conflict, and employee absence. *Journal of Occupational Health Psychology, 1,* 311–318.

Hertel, B. L. (1995). Work, family, and faith: Recent trends. In N. T. Ammerman & W. C. Roof (Eds.), *Work, family, and religion in contemporary society* (pp. 81–121). New York: Routledge.

Higgins, C., Duxbury, L., & Johnson, K. L. (2000). Part-time work for women: Does it really help balance work and family? *Human Resource Management, 39,* 17–32.

Hill, E. J. (2005). Work–family facilitation and conflict, working fathers and mothers, work–family stressors and support. *Journal of Family Issues, 26,* 793–819.

Hill, E. J., Ferris, M., & Martinson, V. (2003). Does it matter where you work? *Journal of Vocational Behavior, 63,* 220–241.

Hill, E. J., Hawkins, A. J., Martinson, V., & Ferris, M. (2003). Studying "working fathers.": Comparing fathers' and mothers' work–family conflict, fit, and adaptive strategies in a global high-tech company. *Fathering, 1,* 239–261.

Hill, E. J., Hawkins, A. J., & Miller, B. C. (1996). Work and family in the virtual office: Perceived influences of mobile telework. *Family Relations, 45,* 293–301.

Hill, E. J., Martinson, V. K., Ferris, M., & Baker, R. Z. (2004). Beyond the mommy track. *Journal of Family and Economic Issues, 25,* 121–136.

Hill, M. S., & Yeung, W. J. (2003, August). *Helping elderly parents: Are baby-boomers different from their predecessors?* Paper presented at the Annual Meeting of the American Sociological Association, Atlanta.

Hill, T. D., Ross, C. E., & Angel, R. J. (2005). Neighborhood disorder, psychophysiological distress, and Health. *Journal of Health and Social Behavior, 46,* 170–186.

Hilton, J. M., & Devall, E. L. (1997). The family economic strain scale: Development and evaluation of the instrument with single- and two-parent families. *Journal of Family and Economic Issues, 18,* 247–271.

Hofferth, S. L., & Sandberg, J. F. (2001). How American children spend their time. *Journal of Marriage and Family, 63,* 295–308.

Hofmeister, H. (2003). Commuting clocks: Journey to work. In P. Moen (Ed.), *It's about time* (pp. 60–79). Ithaca, NY: Cornell University Press.

Holtzman, M., & Glass, J. (1999). Explaining changes in mothers' job satisfaction following childbirth. *Work and Occupations, 26,* 365–404.

Homel, R., Burns, A., & Goodnow, J. (1987). Parental social networks and child development. *Journal of Social and Personal Relationships, 4,* 159–177.

Hook, J. L. (2004). Reconsidering the division of household labor: Incorporating volunteer work and informal support. *Journal of Marriage and Family, 66,* 101–117.

Hook, J. L. (2006, August). *Care in context—Men's unpaid work in 20 countries, 1965–1998. American Sociological Review.*

Howe, G. W., Levy, M. L., & Caplan, R. D. (2004). Job loss and depressive symptoms in couples: Common stressors, stress transmission, or relationship disruption? *Journal of Family Psychology, 18,* 639–650.

Hrba, J., Lorenz, F. O., & Pechacova, Z. (2000). Family stress during the Czech transformation. *Journal of Marriage and the Family, 62,* 520–531.

Huffman, A. H., Payne, S. C., & Casper, W. J. (2004, April). *A comparative analysis of work–family balance on retention.* Paper presented at the Annual Meeting of the Society for Industrial and Organizational Psychology, Chicago.

Hughes, D., & Galinsky, E. (1994). Work experiences and marital interactions: Elaborating the complexity of work. *Journal of Organizational Behavior, 15,* 423–438.

Hughes, D., Galinsky, E., & Morris, A. (1992). The effects of job characteristics on marital quality: Specifying linking mechanisms. *Journal of Marriage and the Family, 54,* 31–42.

Humble, A. M., & Zvonkovic, A. M. (2005). On the road again: Job-related travel and work-to-family spillover. Under review.

Hyman, J., Baldry, C., Scholarios, D., & Bunzel, D. (2003). Work-life imbalance in call centres and software development. *British Journal of Industrial Relations, 41,* 215–239.

Hynes, K. (2003). *The influence of parents' work–family strategies on children's development: A review.* BLCC Working Paper #03–04, Cornell University, Ithaca, NY.

Ishii-Kuntz, M. (1994). Work and family life: Findings from international research and suggestions for future study. *Journal of Family Issues, 15,* 490–506.

Jacobs, J. A., & Gerson, K. (2004). *The time divide: Work, family, and gender inequality.* Cambridge, MA: Harvard University Press.

Jahn, E. W., Thompson, C. A., Kopelman, R. E., & Prottas, D. (2001, April). *The impact of perceived organizational and supervisory family support on organizational commitment, work–family conflict and job search behavior.* Paper presented at the annual meeting of the Society for Industrial and Organizational Psychology, San Diego, CA.

John, D., & Shelton, B. A. (1997). The production of gender among Black and White women and men: The case of household labor. *Sex Roles, 36,* 171–193.

Joplin, J. R. W., Shaffer, M. A., Lau, T., & Francesco, A. M. (2003, August). *Life balance: Developing and validating a cross-cultural model.* Paper presented at the Annual Meeting of the Academy of Management, Seattle, WA.

Judge, T. A., Boudreau, J. W., & Bretz, R. D. Jr. (1994). Job and life attitudes of male executives. *Journal of Applied Psychology, 79,* 767–782.

Kahil, A., & Ziol-Guest, K. M. (2005). Single mothers' employment dynamics and adolescent well-being. *Child Development, 76,* 196–211.

Kanter, R. M. (1977). *Work and family in the United States: A critical review and agenda for research and policy.* New York: Russell Sage Foundation.

Keene, J. R., & Quadagno, J. (2004). Predictors of perceived work–family balance. *Sociological Perspectives, 47,* 1–23.

Kelloway, E. K., & Gottlieb, B. H. (1998). The effects of alternative work arrangements on women's well-being: A demand-control model. *Women's Health: Research on Gender, Behavior, and Policy, 4,* 1–18.

Kiecolt-Glaser, J. K., & Newton, T. L. (2001). Marriage and health: His and hers. *Psychological Bulletin, 127,* 472–503.

Kinnunen, U., & Feldt, T. (2004). Economic stress and marital adjustment aamong couples: Analyses at the dyadic level. *European Journal of Social Psychology, 34,* 519–532.

Kinnunen, U., & Mauno, S. (1998). Antecedents and outcomes of work–family conflict among employed women and men in Finland. *Human Relations, 51,* 157–177.

Kinnunen, U., & Pulkkinen, L. (2001). Linking job characteristics of parenting behavior via job-related affect. In J. R. M. Gereris (Ed.), *Dynamics of parenting* (pp. 233–249).

Kirchmeyer, C. (1992). Nonwork participation and work attitudes: A test of scarcity vs. expansion models of personal resources. *Human Relations, 45,* 775–795.

Kofodimos, J. R. (1990). Why executives lose their balance. *Organizational Dynamics, 19,* 58–73.

Kossek, E. E., Lautsch, B. A., & Eaton, S. C. (2006). Telecommuting, control, and boundary management: Correlates of policy use and practice, job control, and work–family effectiveness. *Journal of Vocational Behavior, 68,* 347–367.

Kossek, E. E., Noe, R. A., & DeMarr, B. J. (1999). Work–family role synthesis: Individual and organizational determinants. *International Journal of Conflict Resolution, 10,* 102–129.

Ladd, E. C. (1999). *The Ladd report.* New York: Free Press.

Lambert, S. J. (1993). Workplace policies as social policies. *Social Service Review, 67,* 237–260.

Lapierre, L. M., & Allen, T. D. (2006). Work-supportive family, family-supportive supervision, use of organizational benefits, and problem-focused coping: Implications for work–family conflict and employee well-being. *Journal of Occupational Health Psychology, 11,* 169–181.

Lareau, A. (2000). Social class and the daily lives of children: A study from the United States. *Childhood, 7,* 155–171.

Lazarus, R. S., & Folkman, S. (1984). *Stress, appraisal, and coping.* New York: Springer.

Leana, C. R., & Feldman, D. C. (1992). Individual responses to job loss: Empirical findings from two field studies. *Human Relations, 43,* 1155–1181.

Lee, M. D., MacDermid, S. M., Williams, M. L., Buck, M. L., & Leiba-O'Sullivan, S. (2002). Contextual factors in the success of reduced-load work arrangements among managers and professionals. *Human Resource Management, 41,* 209–223.

Levanthal, T., & Brooks-Gunn, J. (2000). The neighborhoods they live in: The effects of neighborhood residence on child and adolescent outcomes. *Psychological Bulletin, 126*, 309–337.

Levy, F. (1998). *The new dollars and dreams: American incomes and economic change.* New York: Russell Sage Foundation.

Lewis, S. (1997). An international perspective on work–family issues. In S. Parasuraman & J. H. Greenhaus (Eds.), *Integrating work and family: Challenges and choices for a changing world* (pp. 91–103). Westport, CT: Quorum Books.

Lewis, S., & Cooper, C. L. (1999). The work–family research agenda in changing contexts. *Journal of Occupational Health Psychology, 4*, 382–392.

Lyness, K. S., & Kropf, M. B. (2005). The relationships of national gender equality and organizational support with work–family balance: A study of European managers. *Human Relations, 58*, 33–60.

MacEwen, K. E., & Barling, J. (1994). Daily consequences of work interference with family and family interference with work. *Work & Stress, 8*, 244–254.

Major, D. A., & Germano, L. M. (2005). The changing nature of work and its impact on the work–home interface. In F. Jones, R. J. Burke, & M. Westman (Eds.), *Work–life balance: A psychological perspective* (pp. 13–38). Hove, UK: Psychology Press.

Major, V. S., Klein, K. J., & Ehrhart, M. G. (2002). Work time, work interference with family, and psychological distress. *Journal of Applied Psychology, 87*, 427–436.

Mancini, J. A., Martin, J. A., & Bowen, G. L. (2003). Community capacity. In T. P. Gullotta & M. Bloom (Eds.), *Encyclopedia of primary prevention and health promotion* (pp. 319–330). New York: Kluwer Academic/Plenum.

Mangan, J. (2000). *Workers without traditional employment: An international study of non-standard work.* Cheltenham, UK: Edward Elger.

Marchand, A., Demers, A., & Durand, P. (2005a). Does work really cause distress? The contribution of occupational structure and work organization to the experience of psychological distress. *Social Science and Medicine, 61*, 1–14.

Marchand, A., Demers, A., & Durand, P. (2005b). Do occupation and work conditions really matter? A longitudinal analysis of psychological distress experiences among Canadian workers. *Sociology of Health & Illness, 27*, 602–627.

Markel, K. S. (2000, August). *Does the presence of family-friendly and flexible human resource practices alleviate work–family conflict?* Paper presented at the annual meetings of the Academy of Management, Toronto.

Marks, S. R. (1977). Multiples roles and role strain. *American Sociological Review, 42*, 921–936.

Marks, S. R. (2006). Understanding diversity of families in the 21st century and its impact on the work–family area of study. In M. Pitt-Catsouphes, E. E. Kossek, & S. Sweet (Eds.), *The work and family handbook* (pp. 41–65). Mahwah, NJ: Lawrence Erlbaum Associates.

Marks, S. R., & Leslie, L. A. (2000). Family diversity and intersecting categories. In D. Demo, K. Allen, & M. A. Fine (Eds.), *Handbook of family diversity* (pp. 402–423). New York: Oxford.

Marks, S. R., & MacDermid, S. M. (1996). Multiple roles and the self. *Journal of Marriage and the Family, 58,* 417–432.

Marshall, N. L., Noonan, A. E., McCartney, K., Marx, F., & Keefe, N. (2001). It takes an urban village: Parenting networks of urban families. *Journal of Family Issues, 22,* 163–182.

Martin, G., & Kats, V. (2003). Families and work in transition in 12 countries, 1980–2001. *Monthly Labor Review, 126,* September, 3–31.

Martire, L. M., Stephens, M. A. P., & Atienza, A. A. (1997). The interplay of work and caregiving: Relationships between role satisfaction, role involvement, and caregivers' well-being. *Journal of Gerontology: Social Sciences, 52B,* S279–S289.

Massey, D. (2001). The prodigal paradigm returns: Ecology comes back to sociology. In A. Booth & A. C. Crouter (Eds.), *Does it take a village? Community effects on children, adolescents, and families* (pp. 41–47). Mahwah, NJ: Lawrence Erlbaum Associates.

Matthews, L. S., Conger, R. D., & Wickrama, K. A. S. (1996). Work–family conflict and marital quality: Mediating processes. *Social Psychology Quarterly, 59,* 62–79.

Mauno, S., & Kinnunen, U. (1999). The effects of job stressors on marital satisfaction in Finnish dual-earner couples. *Journal of Organizational Behavior, 20,* 879–895.

McKee-Ryan, F. M., Song, Z., Wanberg, C. R., & Kinicki, A. J. (2005). Psychological and physical well-being during unemployment: A meta-analytic study. *Journal of Applied Psychology, 90,* 53–76.

Milardo, R. M., & Allan, G. (2000). Social networks and marital relationships. In R. M. Milardo & S. Duck (Eds.), *Families as relationships* (pp. 117–133). New York: Wiley & Sons.

Milkie, M. A., & Peltola, P. (1999). Playing all the roles. *Journal of Marriage and the Family, 61,* 476–490.

Mirowsky, J. (1985). Depression and marital power: An equity model. *American Journal of Sociology, 91,* 557–592.

Mishel, L., Bernstein, J., & Allegretto, S. (2005). *The state of working America 2004/2005.* Ithaca, NY: Cornell University Press.

Mistry, R. S., Vandewater, E. A., Huston, A. C., & McLoyd, V. C. (2002). Economic well-being and children's social adjustment: The role of family process in an ethnically diverse low-income sample. *Child Development, 73,* 935–951.

Moen, P., & Sweet S. (2003). Time clocks: Work-hour strategies. In P. Moen (Ed.), *It's about time: Couples and careers* (pp. 17–34). Ithaca, NY: Cornell University Press.

Moen, P., Sweet, S., & Townsend, B. (2001). *How family friendly is upstate New York?* Ithaca, NY: Cornell Employment and Family Careers Institute.

Moen, P., Waismel-Manor, R., & Sweet, S. (2003). Success. In P. Moen (Ed.) *It's about time* (pp. 133–152). Ithaca, NY: Cornell University Press.

Moen, P., & Wethington, E. (1992). The concept of family adaptive strategies. *Annual Review of Sociology, 18,* 233–251.

Moen, P., & Yu, Y. (2000). Effective work/life strategies: Working couples, work conditions, gender, and life quality. *Social Problems, 47,* 291–326.

Morisi, T. L. (2005). Household survey indicators show some improvement in 2004. *Monthly Labor Review, 128,* 3–17.

Morris, A., Shinn, M., & DuMont, K. (1999). *American Journal of Community Psychology, 27*, 75–105.

Newman, K. S. (1988). *Falling from grace: The experience of downward mobility in the American middle class.* New York: Free Press.

Nippert-Eng, C. E. (1996). *Home and work: Negotiating boundaries through everyday life.* Chicago: University of Chicago Press.

Nomaguchi, K. M., Milkie, M., & Bianchi, S. M. (2005). Time strains and psychological well-being. *Journal of Family Issues, 26*, 756–792.

Noonan, M. C. (2001). The impact of domestic work on men's and women's wages. *Journal of Marriage and Family, 63*, 1134–1145.

Noonan, M. C., Estes, S. B., & Glass, J. L. (in press). Does the use of work–family policies influence time spent in domestic labor? *Journal of Family Issues.*

O'Driscoll, M. P., Poelmans, S., Spector, P. E., Kalliath, T., Allen, T. D., Cooper, C. L., & Sanchez, J. I. (2003). Family-responsive interventions, perceived organizational and supervisor support, work–family conflict, and psychological strain. *International Journal of Stress Management, 10*, 326–344.

Olson, D. H., McCubbin, H. I., & Associates. (1983). *Families: What makes them work.* Beverly Hills, CA: Sage.

Parasuraman, S., & Greenhaus, J. H. (2002). Toward reducing some critical gaps in work–family research. *Human Resource Management Review, 12*, 299–312.

Parasuraman, S., Purohit, Y. S., Godshalk, V. M., & Beutell, N. J. (1996). Work and family variables, entrepreneurial career success, and psychological well-being. *Journal of Vocational Behavior, 48*, 275–300.

Patterson, J. M. (1988). Families experiencing stress. *Family Systems Medicine, 5*, 202–237.

Patterson, J. M. (2002). Integrating family resilience and family stress theory. *Journal of Marriage and Family, 64*, 349–360.

Pearlin, L. I., Aneshensel, C. S., Mullan, J. T., & Whitlatch, C. J. (1996). Caregiving and its social support. In R. H. Binstock, & L. K. George (Eds.), *Handbook of aging and the social sciences* (4th ed., pp. 283–302). Orlando, FL: Academic Press.

Peeters, M. C. W., de Jonge, J., Janssen, P. P. M., & van der Linden, S. (2004). Work–home interference, job stressors, and employee health in a longitudinal perspective. *International Journal of Stress Management, 11*, 305–322.

Perrin, A. J. (1998). Economic transition in a company town: The politics of work and possibility in postindustrial Rochester. In D. Vannoy & P. J. Dubeck (Eds.), *Challenges for work and family in the twenty-first century* (pp. 93–110). New York: Aldine de Gruyter.

Perry-Jenkins, M., Repetti, R. L., & Crouter, A. C. (2000). Work and family in the 1990s. *Journal of Marriage and the Family, 62*, 981–998.

Pierce, R. S., Frone, M. R., Russell, M., & Cooper, M. L. (1994). Relationship of financial strain and psychosocial resources to alcohol use and abuse: The mediating role of negative affect and drinking motives. *Journal of Health and Social Behavior, 35*, 291–308.

Pinderhughes, E E., Nix, R., Foster, E. M., Jones, D., & The Conduct problems Prevention Research Group. (2001). Parenting in context: Impact of neighborhood poverty, residential stability, public services, social networks, and danger on parental behaviors. *Journal of Marriage and Family, 63,* 941–953.

Piotrkowski, C. (1979). *Work and the family system.* New York: Free Press.

Piotrkowski, C. S., Rapoport, R. N., & Rapoport, R. (1987). Families and work. In M. B. Sussman & S. K. Steinmetz (Eds.), *Handbook of marriage and family* (pp. 251–283). New York: Plenum Press.

Pittman, J. F. (1994). Work/family fit as a mediator of work factors on marital tension. *Human Relations, 47,* 183–209.

Poarch, M. T. (1998). Ties that bind: US suburban residents on the social and civic dimensions of work. *Community, Work & Family, 1,* 125–147.

Poelmans, S. (Ed.). (2005). *Work and family: An international research perspective.* Mahwah, NJ: Lawrence Erlbaum Associates.

Poelmans, S., O'Driscoll, M., & Beham, B. (2005). An overview of international research on the work–family interface. In S. A. Y. Poelmans (Ed.), *Work and family: An international research perspective* (pp. 3–46). Mahwah, NJ: Lawrence Erlbaum Associates.

Presser, H. B. (2003). *Working in a 24/7 economy: Challenges for American families.* New York: Russell Sage Foundation.

Presser, H. B., & Hermsen, J. M. (1996). Gender differences in the determinants of work-related overnight travel among employed Americans. *Work and Occupations, 23,* 87–115.

Price, R. H., Choi, J. N., & Vinokur, A. (2002). Links in the chain of adversity following job loss: How financial strain and loss of personal control lead to depression, impaired functioning and poor health. *Journal of Occupational Health Psychology, 7,* 302–312.

Probst, T. M. (2005). Economic stressors. In J. Barling, E. K. Kelloway, & M. R. Frone (Eds.), *Handbook of work stress* (pp. 267–297). Thousand Oaks, CA: Sage.

Putnam, R. D. (2000). *Bowling alone: The collapse and revival of American community.* New York: Simon & Schuster.

Radcliffe Public Policy Institute. (2000). *Life's work: Generational attitudes toward work and life integration.* Cambridge, MA: Harvard University.

Rapoport, R., Bailyn, L., Fletcher, J. K., & Pruitt, B. H. (2002). *Beyond work–family balance.* San Francisco: Jossey-Bass.

Rau, B., & Hyland, M. M. (2002). Role conflict and flexible work arrangement. *Personnel Psychology, 55,* 111–136.

Repetti, R. (2005). A psychological perspective on the health and well-being consequences of employment experiences for children and families. In S. M. Bianchi, L. M. Casper, & R. King (Eds.), *Work, family, health and well-being* (pp. 245–258). Mahwah, NJ: Lawrence Erlbaum Associates.

Robinson, J. P., & Godbey, G. (1997). *Time for life: The surprising ways American use their time.* University Park: Pennsylvania State University Press.

Rodgers, K. G., & Rose, H. A. (2002). Risk and resiliency factors among adolescents who experience marital transitions. *Journal of Marriage and Family, 64,* 1024–1037.

Roehling, P. V., & Bultman, M. (2002). Does absence make the heart grow fonder? Work-related travel and marital satisfaction. *Sex Roles, 46,* 279–293.

Roehling, P. V., Moen, P., & Batt, R. (2003). Spillover. In P. Moen (Ed.), *It's about time: Couples and careers* (pp. 101–121). Ithaca, NY: Cornell University Press.

Roehling, P., Moen, P., & Wilson, E. A. (2004, February). *The effect of "family-friendly" policy use on family well-being.* Paper presented at the Annual Meetings of the Eastern Sociological Society, New York.

Rogers, S. J. (1999). Wives' income and marital quality: Are there reciprocal effects? *Journal of Marriage and the Family, 61,* 123–132.

Rogers, S. J., & May, D. C. (2003). Spillover between marital quality and job satisfaction: Long-term patterns and gender differences. *Journal of Marriage and Family, 65,* 482–495.

Roosa, M. W., Deng, S., Ryu, E., Burrell, G. L., Tein, J., Jones, S., Lopez, V., & Crowder, S. (2005). Family and child characteristics linking neighborhood context and child externalizing behavior. *Journal of Marriage and Family, 67,* 515–529.

Ross, C. E. (2000). Neighborhood disadvantage and adult depression. *Journal of Health and Social Behavior, 41,* 177–187.

Ross, C. E., Reynolds, J. R., Geis, K. J. (2000). The contingent meaning of neighborhood stability for residents' psychological well-being. *American Sociological Review, 65,* 581–597.

Rothausen, T. J. (1999). "Family" in organizational research: A review and comparison of definitions and measures. *Journal of Organizational Behavior, 20,* 817–836.

Rothbard, N. P. (2001). Enriching or depleting? The Dynamics of engagement in work and family roles. *Administrative Science Quarterly, 46,* 655–684.

Rotondo, D. M., & Kincaid, J. F. (2005, April). *Work–family conflict, work–family facilitation, and individual coping style.* Paper presented at the Annual Meetings of the Society for Industrial and Organizational Psychology, Los Angeles.

Roxburgh, S. (1997). The effect of children on the mental health of women in the paid labor force. *Journal of Family Issues, 18,* 270–289.

Roxburgh, S. (1999). Exploring the work and family relationship. *Journal of Family Issues, 20,* 771–788.

Roxburgh, S. (2005). Parenting strains, distress, and family paid labor. *Journal of Family Issues, 26,* 1062–1081.

Roy, K. M., Tubbs, C. Y., & Burton, L. M. (2004). Don't have no time: Rhythms and the organization of time for low-income families. *Family Relations, 53,* 168–178.

Saltzstein, A. L., Ting, Y., & Saltzstein, G. H. (2001). Work–family balance and job satisfaction. *Public Administration Review, 61,* 452–466.

Sampson, R. J. (1991). Linking the micro- and macrolevel dimensions of community social organization. *Social Forces, 70,* 54–64.

Sampson, R. J. (1999). R. J. (1999). What "community" supplies. In R. F. Ferguson & W. T. Dickens (Eds.), *Urban problems and community development* (pp. 241–292). Washington: Brookings Institution.

Sampson, R. J. (2001). How do communities undergird or undermine human development? Relevant contexts and social mechanisms. In A. Booth & A. C. Crouter (Eds.), *Does it take a village? Community effects on children, adolescents, and families* (pp. 3–30). Mahwah, NJ: Lawrence Erlbaum Associates.

Sarkisian, N., & Gerstel, N. (2004). Explaining the gender gap in help to parents: The importance of employment. *Journal of Marriage and Family, 66,* 431–451.

Sayer, L. C., Bianchi, S. M., & Robinson, J. P. (2004). Are parents investing less in children? Trends in mothers' and fathers' time with children. *American Journal of Sociology,110,* 1–43.

Sayer, L. C., Cohen, P. N., & Casper, L. M. (2004). *Women, men, and work.* Washington, DC: Population Reference Bureau.

Sayer, L. C., Gauthier, A. H., & Furstenberg, F. F., Jr. (2004). Educational differences in parents' time with children: Cross-national variations. *Journal of Marriage and Family, 66,* 1152–1169.

Schuster, T. L., Kessler, R. C., & Aseltine, R. H., Jr. (1990). Supportive interactions, negative interactions, and depressed mood. *American Journal of Community Psychology, 18,* 423–438.

Seccombe, K. (2000). Families in poverty in the 1990s: Trends, causes, consequences and lessons learned. *Journal of Marriage and the Family, 62,* 1094–1113.

Siddique, C. M. (1981). Orderly careers and social integration. *Industrial Relations, 20,* 297–305.

Sieber, S. D. (1974). Toward a theory of role accumulation. *American Sociological Review, 39,* 567–578.

Siegrist, J. (1998). Adverse health effects of effort–reward imbalance at work. In C. L. Cooper (Ed.), *Theories of organizational stress* (pp. 190–204). New York: Oxford University Press.

Silver, H., & Goldscheider, F. (1994). Flexible work and housework: Work and family constraints on women's domestic labor. *Social Forces, 72,* 1103–1119.

Simon, R. W. (1998). Assessing sex differences in vulnerability among employed parents: The importance of marital status. *Journal of Health and Social Behavior, 39,* 38–54.

Simons, R. L., Johnson, C., Beaman, J., Conger, R. D., & Whitbeck, L. B. (1996). Parent and peer group as mediators of the effect of community structure on adolescent problem behavior. *American Journal of Community Psychology, 24,* 145–171.

Simons, R. L., Lin, K.-H., Gordon, L. C., Brody, G. H., Murry, V., & Conger, R. D. (2002). Community differences in the association between parenting practices and child conduct problems. *Journal of Marriage and Family, 64,* 331–345.

Simons, R. L., Lorenz, F. O., Conger, R. D., & Wu, C. (1992). Support from spouse as mediator and moderator of the disruptive influence of economic strain on parenting. *Child Development, 63,* 1282–1301.

Simons, R. L., Lorenz, F. O., Wu, C., & Conger, R. D. (1993). Social network and marital support as mediators and moderators of the impact of stress and depression on parental behavior. *Developmental Psychology, 29,* 368–381.

Skocpol, T. (2003). *Diminished democracy: From membership to management in American civic life.* Norman: University of Oklahoma Press.

Skolnick, A. (2001). *A time of transition. Work, family and community in the information age.* New York: Families and Work Institute.

Smith, R. E. (2004). *Family income of unemployment insurance recipients.* Washington, DC: Congressional Budget Office. Retrieved May 18, 2005, from http://www.cbo.gov/showdoc.cfm?index=5144&sequence=0.

Sonnentag, S., & Bayer, U.-V. (2005). Switching off mentally: Predictors and consequences of psychological detachment from work during off-job time. *Journal of Occupational Health Psychology, 10,* 393–414.

Sparks, K., Cooper, C., Fried, Y., & Shirom, A. (1997). The effects of work hours on health. *Journal of Occupational and Organizational Psychology, 70,* 391–408.

Stephens, M. A. P., & Townsend, A. L. (1997). Stress of parent care: Positive and negative effects of women's other roles. *Psychology and Aging, 12,* 376–386.

Steptoe, A., & Feldman, P. J. (2001). Neighborhood problems as sources of chronic stress. *Annals of Behavior Medicine, 23,* 177–185.

Stevens, D. P., Minnotte, K. L., & Kiger, G. (2005). *Domestic labor and marital quality: Testing an expanded definition of household work.* Under review.

Stewart, W., & Barling, J. (1996). Fathers' work experiences effect children's behaviors via job-related affect and parenting behaviors. *Journal of Organizational Behavior, 17,* 221–232.

Strazdins, L., Korda, R. J., Lim, L. L., Broom, D. H., and D'Souza, R. M. (2004). Around the clock: Parent work schedules and children's well-being in a 24-h economy. *Social Science and Medicine, 59,* 1517–1527.

Strom, S. (2003). Unemployment and families: A review of research. *Social Service Review, 77,* 399–430.

Sturm, R., & Gresenz, C. R. (2002). Relations of income inequality and family income to chronic medical conditions and mental health disorders; National survey in USA. *British Medical Journal, 324,* 20–23.

Sullivan, C., & Hoole, G. (2005, March). *A longitudinal study of work–family conflict and enhancement in the UK banking industry.* Paper presented at the Community, Work and Family Conference, Manchester, England.

Sverke, M., Hellgren, J., & Naswall, K. (2002). No security: A meta-analysis and review of job insecurity and its consequences. *Journal of Occupational Health Psychology, 7,* 242–264.

Swanberg, J. E., Pitt-Catsouphes, M., & Drescher-Burke, K. (2005). A question of justice: Disparities in employees' access to flexible schedule arrangements. *Journal of Family Issues, 26,* 866–895.

Swisher, R., Sweet, S., & Moen, P. (2004). The family-friendly community and its life course fit for dual-earner couples. *Journal of Marriage and Family, 66,* 281–292.

Tang, C-Y., & MacDermid, S. M. (2005, November). *Asking "How much control do you really have?"* Paper presented at the Annual Meetings of the National Council on Family Relations, Phoenix, AZ.

Tausig, M., & Fenwick, R. (2001). Unbinding time. *Journal of Family and Economic Issues, 22,* 101–119.

Tenbrunsel, A. E., Brett, J. M., Maoz, E., Stroh, L. K., & Reilly, A. H. (1995) Dynamic and static work–family relationships. *Organizational Behavior and Human Decision Processes, 63,* 223–246.

Teng, W. (1999). *Assessing the work–family interface.* Dissertation, Auburn University.

Tetrick, L. E., & Buffardi, L. C. (2005). Measurement issues in research on the work–home interface. In F. Jones, R. J. Burke, & M. Westman (Eds.), *Work–life balance: A psychological perspective* (pp. 90–114). Hove, UK: Psychology Press.

Theorell, T. (1998). Job characteristics in a theoretical and practical health context. In C. L. Cooper (Ed.), *Theories of organizational stress* (pp. 205–219). New York: Oxford University Press.

Thoits, P. A. (1995). Stress, coping, and social support processes. *Journal of Health and Social Behavior, 36,* 53–79.

Thoits, P. A., & Hewitt, L. N. (2001). Volunteer work and well-being. *Journal of Health and Social Behavior, 42,* 115–131.

Thomas, L. T., & Ganster, D. C. (1995). Impact of family-supportive work variables on work–family conflict and strain. *Journal of Applied Psychology, 80,* 6–15.

Thompson, C. A., Beauvais, L. L., & Lyness, K. S. (1999). When work–family benefits are not enough. *Journal of Vocational Behavior, 54,* 392–415.

Thompson, C. A., & Prottas, D. J. (2006). The mediating role of perceived control on the relationship between organizational family support, job autonomy, and employee well-being. *Journal of Occupational Health Psychology, 10,* 100–118.

Thorne, B. (2001). Pick-up time at Oakdale elementary school. In R. Hertz & N. L. Marshall (Eds.), *Working families: The transformation of the American home* (pp. 354–376). Berkeley: University of California Press.

Thornton, A., & Young-DeMarco, L. (2001). Four decades of trends in attitudes toward family issues in the United States: The 1960s through the 1990s. *Journal of Marriage and Family, 63,* 1009–1037.

Totterdell, P. (2005). Work schedules. In J. Barling, E. K. Kelloway, & M. R. Frone (Eds.), *Handbook of work stress* (pp. 35–62). Thousand Oaks, CA: Sage.

Tucker, P., & Rutherford, C. (2005). Moderators of the relationship between long work hours and health. *Journal of Occupational Health Psychology, 10,* 465–476.

Turner, R. J., & Marino, F. (1994). Social support and social structure: A descriptive epidemiology. *Journal of Health and Social Behavior, 35,* 193–212.

Ueno, K. (2005). The effects of friendship networks on adolescent depressive symptoms. *Social Science Research, 34,* 484–510.

Umberson, D., Chen, M. D., House, J. S., Hopkins, K., & Slaten, E. (1996). The effect of social relationships on psychological well-being: Are men and women really so different? *American Sociological Review, 61,* 837–859.

U.S. Census Bureau. (2004). *Journey to work: 2000.* Washington, DC: U.S. Government Printing Office.

U.S. Census Bureau. (2005). *Who's minding the kids? Child care arrangements.* Washington, DC: U.S. Government Printing Office.

U.S. Department of Education (2004). *Before- and after-school care, programs, and activities of children in kindergarten through eighth grade: 2001.* nces.ed.gov/pubs2004/2004008.pdf, accessed October 25, 2005.

U.S. Department of Labor. (2004). *Women in the labor force: A databook.* Washington, DC: U.S. Government Printing Office.

Valcour, P. M., & Batt, R. (2003, February). *Work exhaustion, organizational commitment and work–life integration*. Paper presented at the Business and Professional Women's Foundation Conference, Orlando, FL.

van der Doef, M., & Maes, S. (1999). The job demand-control (-support) model and psychological well-being: A review of 20 years of empirical research. *Work & Stress, 13*, 87–114.

van Rijswijk, K., Bekker, M. H. J., Rutte, C. G., & Croon, M. A. (2004). The relationships among part-time work, work–family interference, and well-being. *Journal of Occupational Health Psychology, 9*, 286–295.

van Vegchel, N., de Jonge, J., Bosma, H., & Schaufeli, W. (2005). Reviewing the effort–reward imbalance model: Drawing up the balance of 45 empirical studies. *Social Science and Medicine, 60*, 1117–1131.

Ventura, S. J., & Bachrach, C. A. (2000). *Nonmarital childbearing in the United States, 1940–49*. Washington, DC: National Center for Health Statistics.

Voydanoff, P. (1987). *Work and family life*. Thousand Oaks, CA: Sage.

Voydanoff, P. (1988). Work role characteristics, family structure demands, and work/family conflict. *Journal of Marriage and the Family, 50*, 749–761.

Voydanoff, P. (1990). Economic distress and family relations: A review of the eighties. *Journal of Marriage and Family, 52*, 1099–1115.

Voydanoff, P. (2001a). Conceptualizing community in the context of work and family. *Community, Work & Family, 4*, 133–156. Retrieved from http://www.tandf.co.uk.

Voydanoff, P. (2001b). Incorporating community into work and family research: A review of basic relationships. *Human Relations, 54*, 1609–1637.

Voydanoff, P. (2002). Linkages between the work–family interface and work, family, and individual outcomes. *Journal of Family Issues, 23*, 138–164.

Voydanoff, P. (2004a). The effects of work, community, and parenting resources and demands on family integration. *Journal of Family and Economic Issues, 25*, 7–23.

Voydanoff, P. (2004b). The effects of work demands and resources on work-to-family conflict and facilitation. *Journal of Marriage and Family, 66*, 398–412.

Voydanoff, P. (2004c). Implications of work and community demands and resources for work-to-family conflict and facilitation. *Journal of Occupational Health Psychology, 9*, 275–285.

Voydanoff, P. (2004d). Implications of work and community resources and demands for marital quality. *Community, Work & Family, 7*, 311–325.

Voydanoff, P. (2004e). Work community, and parenting resources and demands as predictors of adolescent problems and grades. *Journal of Adolescent Research, 19*, 155–173.

Voydanoff, P. (2005a). Consequences of boundary-spanning demands and resources for work–family conflict and perceived stress. *Journal of Occupational Health Psychology, 10*, 491–503.

Voydanoff, P. (2005b). The differential salience of family and community demands and resources for family-to-work conflict and facilitation. *Journal of Family and Economic Issues, 26*, 395–417.

Voydanoff, P. (2005c). The effects of community demands, resources, and strategies on the nature and consequences of the work–family interface: An agenda for future research. *Family Relations, 54,* 583–595.

Voydanoff, P. (2005d). Social integration, work–family conflict and facilitation, and job and marital quality. *Journal of Marriage and Family, 67,* 666–679.

Voydanoff, P. (2005e). Toward a conceptualization of work–family fit and balance: A demands and resources approach. *Journal of Marriage and Family, 67,* 822–836.

Voydanoff, P. (2005f). Work demands and work-to-family and family-to-work conflict. *Journal of Family Issues, 26,* 707–726.

Voydanoff, P., & Donnelly, B. W. (1988). Economic distress, family coping, and quality of family life. In P. Voydanoff & L. C. Majka (Eds.), *Families and economic distress* (pp. 97–115). Newbury Park, CA: Sage.

Voydanoff, P., & Donnelly, B. W. (1989). Economic distress and mental health: The role of family coping resources and behaviors. *Lifestyles: Family and Economic Issues, 10,* 139–162.

Voydanoff, P., & Donnelly, B. W. (1998). Parents' risk and protective factors as predictors of parental well-being and behavior. *Journal of Marriage and the Family, 60,* 344–355.

Voydanoff, P., & Donnelly, B. W. (1999a). The intersection of time in activities and perceived unfairness in relation to psychological distress and marital quality. *Journal of Marriage and the Family, 61,* 739–751.

Voydanoff, P., & Donnelly, B. W. (1999b). Multiple roles and psychological distress: The intersection of the paid worker, spouse, and parent roles with the role of the adult child. *Journal of Marriage and the Family, 61,* 725–738.

Voydanoff, P., & Donnelly, B. W. (1999c). Risk and protective factors for psychological adjustment and grades among adolescents. *Journal of Family Issues, 20,* 328–349.

Voydanoff, P., Donnelly, B. W., & Fine, M. A. (1988). Economic distress, social integration, and family satisfaction. *Journal of Family Issues, 9,* 545–564.

Walen, H. R., & Lachman, M. E. (2000). Social support and strain from partner, family, and friends: Costs and benefits for men and women in adulthood. *Journal of Social and Personal Relationships, 17,* 5–30.

Wallen, J. (2002). *Balancing work and family. The role of the workplace.* Boston: Allyn and Bacon.

Wayne, J. H., Musica, N., & Fleeson, W. (2004). Considering the role of personality in the work–family experience: Relationships of the big five to work–family conflict and facilitation. *Journal of Vocational Behavior, 64,* 108–130.

Weininger, E., & Lareau, A. (2002, August). *Children's participation in organized activities and the gender dynamics of the "time bind."* Paper presented at the Annual Meetings of the American Sociological Association, Chicago.

Westman, M. (2001). Stress and strain crossover. *Human Relations, 54,* 717–751)

Westman, M., Etzion, D., & Horovitz, S. (2004). The toll of unemployment does not stop with the unemployed. *Human Relations, 57,* 823–844.

Westman, M., Vinokur, A. D., Hamilton, V. L., & Roziner, I. (2004). Crossover of marital dissatisfaction during military downsizing among Russian army officers and their spouses. *Journal of Applied Psychology, 89,* 769–779.

Wharton, A. S. (2006). Understanding diversity of work in the 21st century and its impact on the work–family area of study. In M. Pitt-Catsouphes, E. E. Kossek, & S. Sweet (Eds.), *The work and family handbook* (pp. 17–29). Mahwah, NJ: Lawrence Erlbaum Associates.

Wharton, A. S., Rotolo, T., & Bird, S. R. (2000). Social context at work: A multilevel analysis of job satisfaction. *Sociological Forum, 15,* 65–90.

Whitbeck, L. B., Simons, R. L., Conger, R. D., Lorenz, F. O., Huck, S., & Elder, G. H., Jr. (1991). Family economic hardship, parental support, and adolescent self-esteem. *Social Psychology Quarterly, 54,* 353–363.

Whitbeck, L. B., Simons, R. L., Conger, R. D., Wickrama, K. A. S., Ackley, K. A., & Elder, G. H., Jr. (1997). The effects of parents' working conditions and family economic hardship on parenting behaviors of and children's self-efficacy. *Social Psychology Quarterly, 60,* 291–303.

White, L., & Rogers, S. J. (2000). Economic circumstances and family outcomes: A review of the 1990s. *Journal of Marriage and the Family, 62,* 1035–1051.

Wichert, I. (2002). Job insecurity and work intensification: The effects on health and well-being. In B. Burchell, D. Ladipo, & F. Wilkinson (Eds.), *Job insecurity and work intensification* (pp. 92–111). New York: Routledge.

Wickrama, K. A. S., & Bryant, C. M. (2003). Community context of social resources and adolescent mental health. *Journal of Marriage and Family, 65,* 850–866.

Wickrama, K. A. S., Lorenz, F. O., Conger, R. D., Matthews, L., & Elder, G. H., Jr. (1997). Linking occupational conditions to physical health through marital, social, and intrapersonal processes. *Journal of Health and Social Behavior, 38,* 363–375.

Wildman, J. (2003). Income related inequalities in mental health in Great Britain: Analysing the causes of health inequality over time. *Journal of Health Economics, 22,* 295–313.

Wilson, J. (2000). Volunteering. *Annual Review of Sociology, 26,* 215–240.

Wilson, J., & Musick, M. (1997a). Who cares? Toward an integrated theory of volunteer work. *American Sociological Review, 62,* 6949–713.

Wilson, J. & Musick, M. (1997b). Work and volunteering: The long arm of the job. *Social Forces, 76,* 251–272.

Wilson, J., & Musick, M. (2003). Doing well by doing good: Volunteering and occupational achievement among American women. *The Sociological Quarterly, 44,* 433–450.

Woolf, J., & Adams, G. A. (2005, April). *Flexible scheduling options moderate job demands and work–family conflict.* Paper presented at the Annual Meetings of the Society for Industrial and Organizational Psychology, Los Angeles, CA.

Wuthnow, R. (1998). *Loose connections.* Cambridge, MA: Harvard University Press.

Zedeck, S. (1992). Introduction: Exploring the domain of work and family concerns. In S. Zedeck (Ed.), *Work, families, and organizations* (pp. 1–32). San Francisco: Jossey-Bass.

Zvonkovic, A. M., & Peters, C. L. (2003, November). *Facilitating worker identity and involvement: A qualitative study of women who travel for work.* Paper presented at the Annual Meeting of the National Council on Family Relations.

Author Index

Subject Index

A

Additive relationships, 144–145
After-school programs, xiii, 109–110,
  120–121, 123, 136, 147
Appraisal, 8, 24, 45, 49, 89, 128–129,
  131, 150
  cognitive, 24, 34, 43, 73, 131

B

Benefits, 111–112, 113
Boundary-spanning demands, xii, xv,
  11–12, 20–21, 41–42, 92–94,
  96, 101, 103, 105–107, 109,
  125–126, 129, 132–134,
  139–142, 144, 145, 147–151,
  155–156
  role blurring, xv, 94–96, 98–99,
    101–107, 134, 144
  transition problems, xv

Boundary-spanning resources, xv,
  93, 108–109, 111, 117–118,
  120–124, 134–138,
  146–147, 152, 155–156
  family support programs, 115
Boundary-spanning strategies, xii,
  xvi, 12, 21, 125–130,
  136–141, 143, 151–153,
  156
  feedback loops, 139

C

Caregiver strain, 43–44, 55, 58–60,
  71, 88
Child care services, xiii, 112,
  120–121
Children, 1–2, 6, 8, 13, 28–29,
  31–32, 35–36, 38, 49–50,
  52–53, 55–59, 65, 76, 82,
  87, 97, 104–105, 115–116,
  120, 131, 134, 146–147,
  155